ORAL LIT... ...D MBEERE

Oral literature titles from E.A.E.P.

Encounter with Oral Literature — Okumba Miruka

Gikuyu Oral Literature — Wanjiku M. Kabira & Karega Mutahi

Oral Literature: A School Certificate Course — S. Kichamu Akivaga & A. Bole Odaga

Oral Literature of the Embu and Mbeere — Ciarunji Chesaina

Oral Literature of the Kalenjin — Ciarunji Chesaina

Oral Literature of the Luo — Okumba Miruka

Oral Literature of the Maasai — Naomi Kipury

Oral Literature of the
Embu and Mbeere

Ciarunji Chesaina

EAST AFRICAN EDUCATIONAL PUBLISHERS
Nairobi • Kampala

Published by
East African Educational Publishers Ltd.
Brick Court, Mpaka Road/Woodvale Grove
Westlands
P.O. Box 45314
Nairobi

East African Educational Publishers Ltd.
Pioneer House, Jinja Road
P.O. Box 11542
Kampala

First published 1997

ISBN 9966 46 407 7

Electronic typeset by Belbran Enterprises
P.O. Box 67467, Nairobi

Printed by Kenya Litho Ltd.
Changamwe Road, P.O. Box 40775, Nairobi

CONTENTS

CONTENTS

FOREWORD

Most Kenyans, with their complexity of over forty tribes hardly think of Nairobi, Eldoret or Mombasa as home, but rather think of home in terms of their original parental or tribal home. This classification by tribe has identified us for years. Nonetheless, the contemporary lives of most Kenyans are slowly drifting away from these original roots and the Nairobian, or Mombasan, is finding himself more and more hesitant in proclaiming these roots.

The question of cultural identity continues to humbug many and will do so as we march further and further from our "roots" to modern, Westernised and higher economic lives. Professor Ciarunji Chesaina like most of us, must be a victim of these erosional forces in our cultures and traditions. However, in her other book, *Oral Literature of the Kalenjin* (1991), she offers cushions from the effects of these forces not only for herself, but also for many other Kenyans through the web of traditions, lifestyles, and the socio-economic and political settings displayed in this rich literary work.

Oral Literature of the Embu and Mbeere has been written with an equally forceful style. The beauty of this book, and of those before it, is in making those of us that Mugo wa Gatheru calls "children of two worlds" to enjoy the worlds we belong to. It is with nolstagia for those times — the riddles, circumcision ceremonies and weddings, and the tranquility of ancestral lives, that one goes through this book. Fortunately, one need not be an Embu, Mbeere, or Kalenjin to enjoy Chesaina's books. One very clear message is that Kenyan cultures, though varied as the tribes that originate them, are extremely similar. This similarity stems from common norms only made slightly different by the geographical and socio-economic settings that we are in.

The value of oral literature, be it that of Miji Kenda, the Kamba or the Pokomo lies in the archiving and storage of material with the possibility of retrieval and being blended with modern elements for various socio-economic settings. Furthermore, oral literature rekindles that pride in our culture and traditions and enables us to compare our social systems with those from other parts of the world.

This book, as Prof. Chesaina's other works, provides students at all levels and readers at large with enjoyable creative oral literature. It strongly exemplifies how different groups of people living in different parts of the world can have similar moral values. The Embu riddle of the father who wants an explanation for a son intending to marry grandma parallels a contemporary joke about a Texan father who wants to shoot a son for making love to Grandma. This work is indeed a great contribution to our heritage and socio-economic development.

Wamugunda Geteria
Author of *Nice People* and *Black Gold of Chepkube*
March 1997

ACKNOWLEDGEMENTS

I wish to express my gratitude to everyone who contributed in any way to the writing of this book.

Many thanks go to the oral artists and other informants through whose co-operation the oral texts and background information were collected. Thanks and best wishes to Bancy Muthoni Nthiga of the University of Nairobi who acted as my research assistant during her first year of undergraduate studies.

My gratitude to Jimmi Makotsi of East African Educational Publishers for his constructive criticism and encouragement, and my appreciation to Prof. H.S.K. Mwaniki of Egerton University whose historical records on the Embu and the Mbeere I found most useful as background material.

Special thanks go to Benjamin Wamugunda Geteria of Coast ASAL Development Project for showing a keen interest in the book and agreeing to write the foreword.

Thanks to Hi-Tech Typesetters and to Joyce Oneko of Archer and Wilcock for typing the final draft of the manuscript.

It is impossible for me to fully express my gratitude to my father, Rowland Njeru Geteria and to my mother, Sarah Njeri Geteria who introduced me to oral art and assisted me tremendously in creating rapport with my informants during the fieldwork.

My heartfelt gratitude to my children, Rottok, Chebet, Kaptuiya and Kimulwon for their support, especially in boosting story-telling audiences.

Ciarunji Chesaina
Department of Literature,
University of Nairobi
April 1997

INTRODUCTION

Oral literature is one of the most vibrant aspects of the African's cultural heritage. Indeed, if culture is a dynamic process, then it is inevitable that oral literature should be equally dynamic.

Oral literature is both a reservoir and a creative expression of cultural values, hence, it is a vehicle for propelling a society along its moral path. It is an art based on the cultural aesthetics of a people so that, besides giving a society a sense of direction, it also responds to the human need to appreciate beauty, and in this way contributes towards making the world a better place to live in.

The contention that oral literature has been handed down from generation to generation has become a cliché in oral literature scholarship. This contention needs a re-examination as it gives the impression that this art is static. Unlike written literature, which even when reprinted is handed down to the next generation of readers with very little modification besides the cover and the size of the print, oral literature has not been handed down from generation to generation *verbatim*. It is always being recreated.

The performance of the oral narrative, for example, illustrates this process of creation. Every oral artist has his own unique way of telling a story. As a committed custodian of culture, the oral artist needs to be sensitive to the audience at hand. The artist has to identify his audience's needs and level of comprehension. Therefore the story has to undergo certain modifications to suit the audience. If it is an audience of very young children, dramatisation is mandatory, while the use of ideophones and other characteristics of the language of animal characters adds life to the narrative and enhances comprehension. As there is no formula or recipe for narration, a story inevitably gains new literary elements every time it is told, while retaining its basic thematic motif.

Besides modification in the course of performance, oral literature's vibrancy is maintained by cultural development. No culture is static (a culture is given dynamism by its openness and willingness to respond to and adapt to changing social and historical circumstances).

Interaction between a people and external cultures introduces new elements. As an expression of culture, oral literature has had to respond to cultural changes. New songs are created and old ones acquire new overtones.

One of the challenges facing the researcher of oral literature is the need to maintain the dynamism of the art. How does a researcher record oral literature material for posterity without condemning it to freeze on cold inert pages?

The process involved in preparing oral literature texts for publication is a kind of grinding-stone to which this art was not exposed in its authentic form. A significant amount of its original flavour is lost as it goes through the various stages that are involved.

The intention of this book is three-fold: One is an attempt on the author's part to give something back for having benefitted from a childhood and an education which appreciated both the traditional and the modern cultures of Africa. Secondly, it is an attempt to record, and therefore preserve, a collection of Embu and Mbeere oral literature for present and future generations of audiences of oral literature. Finally, but not least in importance, it is hoped that this book will contribute towards the study of oral literature as an academic discipline.

Organisation of the book

The book is divided into two parts each comprising four chapters: Part One examines the historical and cultural background of the Embu and Mbeere, genres of oral literature and their performance, form and style and functions. In Part Two, collections of the literary texts from the two sub-ethnic groups are recorded in chapters according to genre: oral narratives, oral poetry (songs), proverbs, and riddles and puzzles.

Except for the introduction to Embu and Mbeere oral literature, the whole of Part One has information relevant to the general study of oral literature. This is a deliberate effort to contribute to this end. In Part Two, the literary texts in the original language and the respective translations attempt to retain as much of the original flavour as possible. At the transcription stage, some elements such as ideophones, detailed dialogue and relevant comments from the informants were retained. Translation was kept as faithful to the original as possible while at the same time trying not to hinder intelligibility. Key words or names with symbolic meanings which have no equivalents in English are retained in the original language and are subsequently explained in footnotes. However, lengthy explanations to the texts have been avoided in order not to interfere with the flexibility of the reader's interpretation.

Data collection

During fieldwork, the very presence of a researcher affects the type of performance from which the material is collected. More often than not, the tools the researcher uses as technical aids – tape recorders, cameras and even pen and paper – add to the self-consciousness of the performers hence detracting from the spontaneity of performances. At the transcription stage, the dramatisation, especially the gestures and facial expressions in performance, is completely lost.

The sharpest point of the grinding stone is the process of translating the material from the original language into the language of the reader; in our case, English. A great deal of the vocabulary, particularly the imagery and symbolic language, does not have English equivalents. Although the material reaches the publishers substantially affected, the editor has to have an input, particularly with regard to protecting the interests of the publisher, and therefore shape the material into a format that can reach as many readers as possible. With these problems in mind, how can we reconcile the ideal of preserving oral literature in its authentic form with that of contributing towards the objective of reaching the present and future generations of oral literature audiences?

It is important for the researcher to be not only clear about the objectives of the final product of the research, but also to be sensitive to the readers to whose appreciation of oral literature the work is directed. There are no prescribed guidelines in this; each researcher has to come up with the most appropriate methodology for her purposes. It is in this context that the comments on the methodology used for the preparation of this book should be seen.

In the collection of data, participatory and interview methodologies were used. Whenever possible, the researcher and the assistants attended actual functions where oral literature was being performed where the recording had to be done through the use of tape recorders. This had its own challenges as one had to be sure of the perfect working condition of the tape recorder and to be alert enough to make observations on aspects of the performance which are not usually captured through taping. In the final analysis, the participatory methodology enabled the researcher to retain some of the authenticity of oral literature which comes through spontaneous performances.

While interviewing informants, group interviews were found to create a better atmosphere than individual interviews. Two things were achieved through group interviews: first the informants were more relaxed in group interaction with people they knew than in individual interaction with the researcher or the research assistant. Secondly, the data collected from a group of informants were more reliable as a greater variety of view was allowed for, and the informants could also depend on each other to verify points on which they were not clear.

Sources of Material

The data for this book were collected between 1973 and 1993. There were lapses during this twenty-year period when teaching and other responsibilities kept the author tethered and hence made research on the book impossible. Some of the key informants have since joined the ancestors, but their inspiration has contributed tremendously to the completion of the book. The words of Rowland Njeru Geteria, the author's late father whose determination to succeed were a challenge to write the book, continued to kindle the enthusiasm to go on even after his death in 1977. These words still ring in the mind, "Try, try, try again!"

The materials from Mbeere were collected mainly from Kiritiri, Ivurori, Ishiara and Siakago, while those from Embu were mainly from Gitituri, Gakwegori, Kirigi, Kigari and Thau. Except for the riddles and puzzles which were collected from children, the informants were men and women aged between 40 and 90 years.

Background information was collected through interviews in group as well as individual situations. Most of the songs and oral narratives were collected through participatory methodology whereby the researcher or the assistant attended actual performances and narrative sessions. Proverbs, riddles and puzzles were recorded during group interview sessions.

Preliminary library research contributed to the data for the cultural and historical background of the Embu and the Mbeere; the works of Professor H.S.K. Mwaniki on the two ethnic groups were found to be very useful, especially *The Living History of the Embu and the Mbeere.**

The original language used in the texts

Vocabulary and meaning

Kiembu and Kimbeere are dialects of the same language, which in turn has been erroneously regarded as a primitive form of the Gikuyu language. It is a unique and independent language which borrows from Meru, Kamba and Gikuyu languages.

The Embu and the Mbeere have co-existed as neighbours for centuries. They have always regarded each other as brothers, albeit as rival brothers. Apart from the fact that they previously inhabitted the same district, they co-operate and mutually assist each other. In times of food shortage for example, the Embu offer the Mbeere maize and beans in exchange for sorghum and pigeon peas. Owing to this need for co-existence, the two ethnic groups have had to use a language that is mutually intelligible.

The main differences between the Embu and Mbeere dialects are in the intonation, pronunciation and usage of certain vocabulary. Owing to a long history of interaction between the two ethnic groups, however, these differences have become less pronounced in terms of communicability.

The literary texts in this book, therefore, have been recorded using both dialects; for instance an oral narrative collected from Mbeere appears in Kimbeere, while that from Embu appears in Kiembu. The vocabulary variation in these texts is insignificant and does not in any way hamper comprehension. Where a Mbeere text uses *Irimurimu* for *ogre*, the Embu text uses *irimarimu*. Even in cases where words are used differently in either dialect, the meaning is quite obvious from the context in which the word appears. An example of this is where the word *mwongia* is used to denote wife in Mbeere texts, whereas in Embu the word stands for old woman.

---

*H.S.K. Mwaniki, *The Living History of the Embu and the Mbeere to 1906* (Nairobi: East African Literature Bureau, 1973). See also by the same author, *Embu Historical Texts* (Nairobi: East Afrcan Literature Bureau, 1974).

Phonology and orthography

Embu and Mbeere dialects are distinguished by a prevalence of the "v" sound in the vocabulary, as in *avai* (my age-mate) and *vuva* (behind or below). The "m" or "n" is added to capture a stronger "v" sound in certain words. In this book the "n" in syllable has been added in words such as sound *nviti* (hyena) and *nvuko* (mole) which appear in some texts. It must be mentioned here that this orthography does not capture the sound exactly as it appears in the spoken language, but it is the closest the art of writing can get.

Another sound that deserves mention is the "u" sound pronounced as "o" such as in the English word "old". The sound occurs in Embu and Mbeere words — in such words as *muno* (very) and *mundu* (person). An attempt to capture the sound is usually made by writing the "u" as "û".

A close scrutiny of the texts both in the original language and in the translation will reveal that ideophones are significant on the aesthetic and semantic levels of many texts across the various genres of Embu and Mbeere oral literature. As is perhaps the case with most African languages, ideophones are difficult to represent through writing. A sound such as in the riddle, *Whoooo*! (pregnant woman) is difficult to record. Similarly, the ideophones *iyia*! and "ii", which are prevalent in songs, are difficult to represent in written language. Our recording therefore has many limitations, but in every case we have tried to get as close to the sound as possible.

It must be mentioned that almost all the ideophones have no equivalents in English. This explains why most of them have been recorded in the translated texts in the same way as they appear in the original texts.

PART ONE: THEORETICAL BACKGROUND

Chapter One

HISTORICAL AND CULTURAL BACKGROUND

The Embu and the Mbeere inhabit the Embu and Mbeere Districts of Eastern Province of Kenya respectively. The districts are situated in the south-eastern slopes of Mt. Kenya, spreading over 800 square miles of land demarcated by natural geographical features. To the north is Mt. Kenya, to the east is River Thuci, to the south is Thagana (Tana) River while to the west is River Ruvingaci.

The Embu and the Mbeere are neighbours to three ethnic groups: the Chuka of Tharaka Nithi to the north, the Gikuyu of Kirinyaga to the west, and the Kamba of Machakos to the south and east respectively.

The Embu occupy the land close to Mt. Kenya which is arable and has constant rainfall; annual rainfall ranges between 700 and 1300. Most of this area has fertile volcanic soil. The Mbeere, on their part, live on relatively poor land with scanty rainfall where annual rainfall averages 700 mm with some areas experiencing as low as 400 mm. The land is rocky in some parts and has poor sandy soils.

Historical and cultural background

The Embu and the Mbeere have often been erroneously regarded as a splinter group of the Kikuyu ethnic group. Even their language has been dismissed as a "primitive" dialect of the Gikuyu language. However, as oral history testifies, the Embu and the Mbeere are a community with a definite history as well as a culture that qualifies them to be recognised as an ethnic group with a definite cultural identity.

Prof. H.S.K. Mwaniki is perhaps the most rigorous researcher on the origins of the Embu and the Mbeere, his research makes use of information from oral tradition experts from the area.[1] Findings from the interviews carried out for background information correspond with Mwaniki's.

There are many oral versions of the historical origins of the Embu and the Mbeere, the most popular of which traces the origins to a common ancestor. The record holds that the Embu and the Mbeere settled in the modern Embu and Mbeere Districts between

3

the 16th and 17th centuries, having trekked as a unified group from a country in the north of the present Meru District. This country has been speculated to be modern Ethiopia, referred to as *Tuku* or *Uru* in oral history.

They trekked through Meru and initially settled at Ithanga in Mwea from where they were forced to move due to a great famine which struck the land.

After crossing the river Thuci at a place known as *Igamba Ng'ombe* (literally, where the noise of cattle is heard), they are said to have separated into two major groups. The Embu settled in the forested slopes of Mt. Kenya, while the Mbeere moved further south eventually settling near Kiambere Hill. Oral literature explains the separation as resulting from a conflict between the two groups whereby an Embu man eloped with a daughter of a Mbeere man, a girl named Cianthiga, and had to flee from the wrath of the girl's father. This man and Cianthiga eventually settled at Gitituri kia Mwene Ndega (Ndega's Grove) near the present day Runyenjes Town. Here they had many children who later multiplied to form the Embu community. The name of this ancestor of the Embu is given as Ndega and the grove is named after him.

It is not clear who inhabited Kiambere before the Mbeere settled there. Some Mbeere informants claim that the land was a desert with no inhabitants. The Embu, on the other hand, are said to have found a people known as the Dorobo or Gumba who were hunter-gatherers on the southern slopes of Mt. Kenya. One version has it that the Embu assumed a position of superiority over these inhabitants forcing them to flee and abandon their land. Another version claims that the hunter-gatherers left of their own accord having found it difficult to cope with the ecological changes and the new culture introduced by the Embu.

In the course of their migration, the Embu and the Mbeere encountered other ethnic groups. The most significant of these were the Ukavi (the Maasai) with whom they had inter-ethnic conflicts and raided cattle from each other. Although such warfare was detrimental to their numerical force, the Embu and the Mbeere nonetheless utilised the interaction with the Maasai to strengthen their culture. They learnt new pastoral methods and adopted the circumcision tradition which had not hitherto been part of their culture.

Besides inter-ethnic conflicts, the Embu and the Mbeere experienced depopulation from natural catastrophes, especially famines. One of the worst famines according to oral history is the one known as *Nvaraganu* (literally, the annihilator) which wiped out many livestock and human beings.

To counter depopulation, the people developed a new culture. The communities began to adopt people from neighbouring ethnic groups. This practice was more common among the Embu than among the Mbeere. The people who offered themselves for adoption were usually individuals who were dissatisfied in their own communities or had been mistreated by their own people. The people so adopted, most of whom came from Ukambani and Chuka, intermarried with the Embu and increased the population. Perhaps this would explain why the Embu language has elements of Meru and Kamba languages. The female names like Cuka and Ikamba, found in Embu, can be traced to girls named after women whose home of origin was Chuka or Ukambani respectively.

4

Economic activities

Originally, the Embu and the Mbeere were hunter-gatherers, thereby dependent on meat from wild animals, wild fruits and edible tubers. Later, they developed a pastoral culture, probably influenced by the Maasai encountered on their historical treks.

Gradually, they adopted agriculture as an additional economic activity, and they started growing tubers such as yams, sweet potatoes and cassava. They also grew grains such as millet, sorghum and pigeon peas. Though the Mbeere practised some farming, scanty rainfall and the infertility of the soil made them concentrate more on rearing livestock, especially goats.

With time, the Embu adopted other means of subsistence. They started trading with the Kamba and the Waswahili, whereby they exchanged grain and animal skins for honey, arrows and poison with the Kamba, and gave the Waswahili idiots and other social misfits as slaves in return for spices and ornaments.

Today, the Embu and the Mbeere depend on mixed farming as their chief means of livelihood. Traditional crops such as pigeon peas, millet, yams and sweet potatoes are still grown. However, maize and beans, which were introduced much later, have gained importance as major foodstuffs and are therefore given preference in cultivation. Traditional breeds of cattle are still found in many areas, but hybrid cattle are reared where money and land allow. Cash crops such as tea, coffee, pyrethrum and cotton have also become part of the economic culture. In large areas of Mbeere where the soil is poor and the rainfall scanty, pastoralism takes precedence over farming with goats constituting larger herds than cattle and sheep. Bee-keeping and honey-harvesting is practised in both Embu and Mbeere, but more so in the latter area.

Social organisation

The Embu and the Mbeere did not have a stratified society. People lived in communities where there was mutual inter-dependence between social units, families and individuals. As will be seen from the oral literature texts in this book, communalism was encouraged and people went to great lengths to foster good relations with each other. In order to ensure survival in a harsh untamed environment that had many geographical challenges, they established mechanisms which facilitated their day-to-day existence. Below are some of the major social institutions and practices common to both communities with the only difference being in the names used to identify them.

Government

The main generation age-sets or *nthuke* made laws and handled religious matters such as community-wide rituals and sacrifices. There were two age-sets from which others descended. The first was *Kimanthi* in Embu or *Thathi* in Mbeere. The second was called *Nyangi* in both Embu and Mbeere.

Kiama kia ngome or (*athuri a ngome*) in Embu and *athamaki* in Mbeere interpreted the law and judged cases. This was the highest council of elders who were respected for their authority and sense of justice. In Embu, these elders were known by the rings they wore (*ngome*) as their mark of identity. In Mbeere, however, their name (*athamaki*) connotes the absolute authority they had. It is said that these elders were so respected that a mere rumour of their presence in the vicinity was enough to fill the people with fear and force them to check on any corners that needed moral tidiness. *Kiama kia ngome* or *athamaki* adjudicated serious cases such as murder or those touching on the use of witchcraft. Ordinary cases and disputes were settled at a lower level by the council of elders known as *njama*. An institution known as *njama ya ita* or war council, was responsible for matters concerning warfare and security.

The clan

The clan institution was very important in providing a support system and facilitating people's inter-dependence among both the Embu and the Mbeere. A clan consisted of people who could trace their lineage to a common ancestor. Members of the same clan regarded each other as brothers and sisters.

The Embu and the Mbeere have numerous clans but it is difficult to ascertain the exact number of these clans. All the clans originate from either of two root clans. The first one, regarded as the senior, is called *Thagana* or *Nguua Migogo* in Embu, and *Mururi* in Mbeere. The Embu name for the senior clan, *Thagana*, is derived from the name used for River Tana which is held in great reverence by both communities. It is known to be so powerful that it can carry everything in its way including the traditional bridges known as *migogo* used by the people to cross the great rivers; hence the name *Nguua Migogo* (the one who carries away bridges). The second or junior root clan is known as *Irumbi* or *Gatavi* in Embu and *Ndamata* in Mbeere.

The clan system ensured social cohesion and provided the people with a sense of belonging. It was a pillar against which a person could lean in time of problems. When a person was confronted with a difficult decision, the first people to consult were the members of the respective clan. During times of extreme deprivation, such as famines, an individual or family was entitled to assistance from fellow clan members. Even in ordinary circumstances, if a person encountered danger, one would scream the name of his clan and any member of his clan within hearing distance would rush to the aid.

Initiation

The initiation ritual was very important among the Embu and the Mbeere. Over the years, the ceremony had become so deep-rooted within the culture of the people that it had gained the stature of a cultural pillar. The females underwent initiation at adolescence while the males had theirs slightly after puberty.

The importance of initiation was not in the operation *per se,* but in the education which the initiates received in preparation for adulthood as members of their culture. John Mbiti has summarised the didactic function of initiation thus:

> Initiation rites have a great educational purpose. The occasion often marks the beginning of acquiring knowledge which is otherwise not accessible to those who have not been initiated. It is a period of awakening to many things, a period of dawn for the young. They learn to endure hardships. They learn to live with one another, they learn to obey, they learn the secrets and mysteries of the man-woman relationships.*

Among the Embu and the Mbeere, initiation was the period when young people were prepared for the realities and responsibilities of adult life. It was also an initiation into the culture of one's people. The young people learnt about the cultural values that made one accepted and respected within the community. The rite was one of the support systems of communal life.

While undergoing the operation, initiates were expected to persevere and not show any sign of fear, regardless of the pain they felt. The period preceding the initiation was used to prepare them for this test of endurance. The males underwent rigorous exercises and ordeals as extra training. This was important because after initiation, the young men were expected to act as the defence corps of their families and of the community at large, i.e. as future warriors.

Initiation acted as a link to bind together those initiated at the same time. The women initiated together regarded each other as sisters and came to each other's aid in times of need. This solidarity is expressed in the worksong, 'Let Women be Supported' in Chapter Six. A similar expression of solidarity among males initiated together is evident in the song entitled 'I Thought it had Been Postponed'. The men on the other hand refer to each other as "warriors linked by the same secret". As earlier mentioned, these were the future warriors; a sense of brotherhood among them therefore greatly strengthened the security and defence of the community.

On a broad societal level, initiation acted as a binding force for people living in the same community. This ritual called for the participation of the entire community, not just those who had relatives among the initiates. The old and the young alike had a part to play in the preparations for the ceremony — especially the initiation dances. Dancing together has the effect of bringing people close to each other. These dances boosted the feeling of belonging to the same community while at the same time acting as physical and psychological therapy for everyone. In the final analysis, therefore, initiation was a

---

*J. Mbiti, *African Religions and Philosophy* (London: Heinemann Educational Books, 1969), p. 122.

ritual which fostered good relations and greatly enhanced social cohesion among the Embu and the Mbeere.

Religion

Belief in the supernatural and in superhuman beings is a universal phenomenon. This belief is perhaps as old as the human race itself.

Before contact with the West and the introduction of Christianity, the Embu and the Mbeere had a traditional form of religion which contributed greatly towards their social welfare. They believed in a superior god whom they referred to as *Mwene Njeru* or *Mwene Nyaga,* which literally means the owner of whiteness or the owner of brightness. He was believed to be omnipotent and omnipresent. His favourite place of abode was on top of Mt. Kenya. The association of the supreme deity with Mt. Kenya is implied by the name used by the Embu and the Mbeere to refer to the big mountain. They call it "Kirinyaga", which means the mountain which has brightness.

Events taking place in the world were believed to depend on the will of Mwene Nyaga or Mwene Njeru. If a natural catastrophe struck an individual, or a whole community, it was seen to be resulting from some bad behaviour or from some evil act by the victim which had displeased the supreme deity. A fatal disease for which no explanation could be found was seen as a curse or as a punishment from this god.

Besides the supreme deity, there were smaller gods (*ngai*) and devils (*ngoma*) which affected people's lives. The smaller gods were believed to come to people's assistance in day-to-day affairs. Devils were believed to live in such places as groves, caves and deserted places. It is for fear of catastrophic encounters with devils that people avoided visiting such places, especially at night. The manifestation of devils was seen in unnatural happenings such as mysterious uprooting of huge trees or destruction of property by natural phenomena like earthquakes and strong winds. Female devils were said to be very emotional and more malevolent than male ones. The whirlwind, for example, is known as *ngoma cia aka* (women's devils).

Ancestors occupy a very important place in the lives of the Embu and the Mbeere. While in spirit form, they are believed to interact with the living and have a great influence on the turn of events in the lives of the people. They are revered as they are feared, and it is this reverence that perhaps explains the respect extended to very old people who are about to die and join the ancestors. For example, it is believed that if a very old person blesses an individual, he will have a very prosperous life, but if the elder instead curses, everything possible has to be done to plead with thim to "unsay" the curse before dying is believed that the curse can have disastrous effects on the victim.

Sacrifices were an important religious ritual and they were offered to thank Mwene Nyaga or Mwene Njeru for his blessings, especially in such occurrences as abundant rainfall and bumper harvests. Sacrifices were also offered to ward off evil such as epidemics and droughts. Normally, a sheep without blemish was the accepted sacrificial

8

animal as it was seen to have the purity and cleanliness befitting the supreme deity. Part of the sacrifice (usually the bad parts and left-overs) were given to the devils so as to placate them and prevent them from turning blessings into curses. Ancestors were always given a share of food or drink even in ordinary circumstances. Before drinking beer or water, for example, a person would pour libations on the ground as the ancestors' share.

Gender roles

The Embu and the Mbeere were and still are patriarchal communities. The man is the head of the family and owner of property; he owns the land and the property it yields. Succession and inheritance is along the male lineage.

Except for very rare cases, the social institutions which maintain law and order are presided over and dominated by men. Women on the other hand have very low social status. Daughters are brought up to be docile to their husbands when they marry; the socialisation process which climaxes in the initiation ritual at adolescence, devotes significant time to teaching girls how to relate to their husbands as subordinates.

A woman is expected to be totally and unconditionally loyal to her husband and respectful to men in general. She is forbidden to argue with men whatever the circumstances. If a woman is wronged by her husband, social etiquette forbids her from seeking redress directly. She may, however, send him an emissary — either the man's mother or his male age-mate (man's age-mates have a lot of influence) who have the right to discipline his wife for him if they feel that she is not respectful. Such discipline often involves a severe beating of the woman from which the husband cannot save her.

Even if a woman has certain qualities which should make her feel self-confident, she must not show any signs to indicate that she is aware of her strength of character. She is expected to let others praise her if they find it necessary to do so. The traits which characterise a good woman among the Embu and the Mbeere include humility, patience, tolerance and obedience to men. Pride in a woman is frowned upon.

At marriage, a woman implicitly becomes the property of her husband. The payment of dowry by the bridegroom to the father of his bride ensures that a woman once married cannot go back to her parents, however badly she may be treated. Even in speeches made at modern-day weddings, a bride is told by her relatives that her maiden bed is set on fire the moment she marries; she is informed categorically that as a married woman, she no longer has a place in her parents' home.

Among the Embu and the Mbeere, a married woman's first duty is to procreate. She has to give birth to children, particularly boys, to continue the man's lineage. A woman who, for any reason, cannot give birth is viewed with contempt and is referred to as *nthata*. This term is derived from the word *kuthata* which is used to refer to foodstuffs such as beans or potatoes that fail to cook due to interruption in the course of cooking. Needless to say, it is derogatory. If a woman is unable to give birth, her husband is allowed to marry another wife to play this role. The childless wife, though conjugally neglected, is not free to return to her parents or marry someone else. She must remain in her marital home and be patient. Quite often, such a woman is no better than a servant or a beast of burden in the home.

In the two communities, women form the majority of the workforce, whereby the traditional division of labour assigns more work to women. Whereas the men attend to non-recurrent jobs such as breaking virgin land, the women's share of work needs to be done from sun up to sun down every single day.

Women plant, weed, chase away birds and animals from the crops, harvest and store the produce. And although they are traditionally not supposed to take livestock to the pasture, it is their duty to ascertain that the herdsboys have fed and watered the animals. If for some reason there are animals which have to be fed close to home, it is the women's responsibility to provide the feed and water. Milking is done by the women and herdsboys. Since the introduction of cash crops, the women now plant the crops, weed, harvest and take the produce to the co-operative centre. The women's role in the production process notwithstanding, it is the man's prerogative to collect the money accrued from the produce.

Chapter Two

THE GENRES OF ORAL LITERATURE AND THEIR PERFORMANCE

Classification of oral literature

Genre as a term may be new to the Embu and the Mbeere in relation to their own oral literature, but the concept is as old as the art itself. The absence of the term may be explained by the *raison d'être* of this art within the social context of the two sub-ethnic groups. As will be seen in greater detail in Chapter Three, the oral literature of the Embu and the Mbeere was functional. It served a specific social function, expressing the cultural values of the societies and thus provided them with a sense of moral direction.

The Embu and the Mbeere conceptualised their oral literature in terms of function. When addressing a certain given audience or occasion, the oral artist or ordinary user of oral literature did not choose a genre or text at random. A person versed in the culture of the people had indicators which the person used to choose one genre from among all the others or one text from a particular genre.

There are four major genres of Embu and Mbeere oral literature as conceptualised by these societies: *ng'ano* (oral narratives), *nyimbo* (songs or oral poetry), *nthimo* (proverbs) and *ndai* (riddles or puzzles).

The classification of texts in their appropriate types, gives each type recognition of its own peculiar artistic characteristics which acts as justification for its inclusion in the realm of oral art. It follows then that each category or sub-category, and each text within it, has literary characteristics which give it a unique identity as a text or a literary category. Generic classification facilitates research and scholarship of oral literature as it enables the scholar to give attention to the artistic components of the genres and selected types within the genres. In an oral narrative for example, the scholar is able to notice and scrutinise the vocabulary, the characterisation, the symbolism and the relation of the text to the social reality better than when dealing with the whole corpus of a given society's oral literature as an entity. Furthermore, in the case of oral literature (such as that of the Embu and the Mbeere) which emphasises the social function, generic classification also helps give focus to the various aspects of the people's cultural existence that each genre or text could be applied to.

The importance of generic classification of oral literature in contemporary scholarship cannot be over-emphasised. In this book, we have opted for academic generic classification of oral literature in order to contribute towards the study of oral literature as an academic discipline.

Oral narratives

The Embu and Mbeere oral narratives could be divided into seven sub-categories. These are myths, legends, aetiological stories, ogre stories, trickster tales, fantasies and ordinary tales. Although all the oral narratives share certain literary characteristics pertaining to the oral prose genre, each one has its own peculiarities as a sub-genre. Some of these peculiarities arise out of the function the sub-genre was created to serve within the society.

Myths

Myths are created out of events (usually imaginary) which happened in the remote past of a people. They are often based on the existence of unusual phenomena in the cosmos. The physical geographical environment is a particularly popular area for the creation of myths. The Embu and Mbeere myths are based on geographical features or aspects of human existence which are difficult to comprehend. The existence of impenetrable forests, huge mountains and rivers have provided these societies with bases for their myths. 'The Origin of Ndega's Grove' is a creative explanation of a geographical space which stood out from the rest of the environment because of the type of vegetation it harboured. It had huge trees forming a thick impenetrable grove while the rest was mere bush. 'The Origin of Death' explains a stage in human existence which is difficult to comprehend as it is a complete negation of living which is familiar.

Owing to the complex nature of the subjects which form the bases for myths, there are attempts in these oral narratives to bridge the gap between fantasy and the real world in order to facilitate comprehension. This would explain the personification of *Thagana* and *Tumbiri* in the story of this title in the Embu and Mbeere collection of oral narratives.

Legends

Legends are based on the lives of renowned figures in the history of a people. These figures are people who are known to have actually lived as members of the communities. To emphasise that these were actual people, many of the narrators of the Embu and Mbeere legends recorded in this book were at pains to identify clans or living people who had some blood relationship with the characters in their stories. However, although legends are stories of people who could be traced in the history of a people, the narratives are not historical accounts. They are imaginative or creative stories.

Over the years, the facts surrounding the qualities of these characters have been recreated according to the focus and artistic inclination of the narrator to fit with the functions each story is expected to serve. For example, in the legend, "Karwagi' in this collection, the detail that the warrior could hold a grown-up man in the air with one hand is a creative exaggeration to emphasise this man's strength.

Aetiological tales

Aetiological tales or "why narratives" give creative explanations about strange natural characteristics or behaviour of (usually) certain animals. These narratives have sometimes been confused with myths, but there is a significant difference between the two. Myths are more serious and deal with more complex and serious subjects than aetiological tales.

The Embu and Mbeere aetiological tales deal with commonplace subjects, such as why the hawk eats hens' chicks and why snakes live in holes. Although aetiological tales are not serious oral narratives, some of them may be used to convey social messages. A tale such as 'Why Frogs Have Flat Bottoms' sounds silly but can be used to warn against irrational gauging of one's strength against someone else in a variety of situations.

Ogre tales

Ogre tales revolve around a conflict or a problem brought about by interaction between human beings and ogres. In these tales the ogre is a major character but it should be noted that he is always depicted as an antagonist. In the ogre tales of the Embu and the Mbeere the point of contact between the ogre and the human being is often one which could be avoided. Some of the human characters are depicted as the authors of their own misfortune. For example in 'Karegi and the Ogre' the girl is given good security by the grandmother and all she needs is to keep quiet when the ogre calls her. But she is eager to reveal her hiding place to the ogre regardless of what she may have experienced from the ogre's inhumanity the previous day.

Notice that even in a story which evokes great sympathy for the victim from the audience, for example, in 'The Ogre's Wife', the victim is shown to contribute to her misfortunes. The pregnant woman is warned not to rest under the green shady tree near the river as this is where the ogres rest on their way home. Yet this is the very tree under which she chooses to lie down.

Trickster stories

Trickster stories revolve around cunning and trickery. A character (mostly animal) assumes a false personality in order to deceive others. Hence these tales are built on the conflict between illusion and reality. The victim's weaknesses such as gullibility and the tendency to put too much trust in other people, especially friends normally contributes to the subsequent misfortune.

Embu and Mbeere trickster narratives depict the victim of trickery as foolish. For example, in 'The Enmity Between Hyena and Hare', the reason Hare gives Hyena for the suggestion that they kill their mothers is not good enough to ordinarily convince the latter to take such a drastic action.

Sometimes the trickery boomerangs on the trickster such as in 'Two Friends Who Wooed the Same Girl' where the young man loses the girl to his friend through a trick to discredit the latter.

Hare is often the main character in trickster stories. At times, however, other animals do manage to trick him through carefully woven plots, such as in 'How Chameleon Defeated Hare'.

Fantasies

Fantasies are oral narratives in which people interact with supernatural beings and/or magical elements. In these stories, the human character is rewarded for good behaviour or punished for wickedness in a manner which belongs more to the supernatural world than to the natural human world.

In Embu and Mbeere fantasies, the supernatural world is usually represented by birds or old women such as in 'The Magical Bird'.

Ordinary tales

The stories classified under this sub-genre are based on ordinary events and day-to-day interactions between people living in the same community. In 'The Boy Who Was Eaten by the Lion' the boy meets a disastrous end for putting to ridicule his community's sense of responsibility over his security.

Oral poetry (songs)

The song is perhaps the most powerful genre of oral literature because of its versatility and communicability. It is distinguished from the oral narrative not only by its mode of performance and use of verse, but also by its extensive use of imagery and symbolic language. Song has permeated so many areas of Embu and Mbeere social existence that it requires somewhat extensive classification — into nine sub-categories. These are lullabies and children's songs, songs for childbirth and child-naming ceremonies, initiation songs, wedding songs, work songs, satirical songs, war poetry, political songs, and songs on cultural transition.

Lullabies and children's songs

Lullabies are sung by whoever is taking care of the baby — i.e., the mother, grandmother, elder sibling or any other child nurse. Children's songs are performed specifically by children at work or at play.

Some children's songs have messages of social significance; for example, the theme of wisdom acquired from age and experience in 'A Person Grows Old'.

Songs for childbirth and child-naming ceremonies

In Embu and Mbeere culture, the birth of a child is an important event for the whole community. It is an assurance of not only the continuity of the family lineage, but also an assurance of the continuity and survival of the community as a whole. This is the social context within which the songs in this sub-category are sung. They are sung at the arrival of a new baby, when confirming the name of the baby, and when taking gifts to the baby and the mother.

The people express their gratitude to the ancestors and the supernatural powers for the successful delivery of the baby, such as in 'The Baby Has Come Safely'. The people use endearing terms in thanking the mother for a job well done and encouraging her to care for the new member of the community. Notice how the baby is often referred to as 'our baby' thus confirming that he is not just an additional member of the family, but more importantly a new member of the community.

Initiation songs

Initiation is a rite of passage from one stage of maturity to another. The ceremony entailed is usually performed as a ritual. One of the major functions of poetry in the initiation process is to help the initiate attain physiological as well as psychological therapy. In addition to this, the themes in the songs instruct the initiate about what is expected of him in the stage after the completion of the ritual. A detailed analysis of the functions of poetry in the initiation process is presented in Chapter Three.

Among the Embu and the Mbeere, initiation takes two major forms: circumcision, which marks the end of childhood and the beginning of adulthood; and initiation of a man or woman when their children attain a certain age.

There is an abundance of initiation songs of which this book has recorded only a few. There are songs commenting on, and therefore encouraging, the bravery of initiates at a circumcision ritual; for example, 'Today is the Day We Shall Know the Coward'.

There are also songs reminding parents that they are to assume a more serious outlook towards life as their children move from one stage of life to another; for example, 'By which Look of Hair Will You be Swearing in Future?'

Wedding songs

Poetry has an important place in marriage ceremonies too. Indeed, a good number of participants at wedding ceremonies derive more enjoyment from the dance-drama the occasion offers than the sumptuous food served.

Among the Embu and the Mbeere, songs are sung from the time the dowry negotiations are going on upto the wedding day itself. Songs like 'Let Us Set Off' and 'Open for Them' play the role of knocking at the door of the future in-laws for marriage negotiations. The theme of respect for in-laws is a prevalent one in the songs sung at wedding ceremonies; for example, the song entitled "'Never Get Angry With the In-Laws'.

Through these songs, women find an opportunity to remind the society about the important role they play as the child-bearers in respect of the bride and groom; for example, "Let Me Be Given Some Before It Passes Along'.

Work songs

Work is perhaps the greatest inspiration for the song genre. There is a song for almost every type of work and people are always creating new songs out of new jobs or working situations. It is also true that work provides an opportunity for performance of satirical songs which may not be appropriate in other social contexts. In the collection of work songs in this book, it will be noted that songs related to working in the field, particularly those sung by women predominate. This reflects the fact that agriculture is the main occupation of the Embu and the Mbeere, and that women are a substantial majority of the labour force.

Satirical songs

Satirical songs use the literary qualities of the poetic genre to ridicule social weaknesses. Irony is the main literary tool used in these songs for satirical purposes. The two communities make great use of sarcasm and indirect references to laugh at those whose behaviour is deemed unacceptable. In 'I Will Sell My Daughter in Kilograms' for example, the singer pretends that he is the one who will sell his daughter, while in fact, he is using sarcasm to indirectly laugh at those who have commercialised dowry.

War poetry

War poetry is a sub-genre which is fast disappearing from Embu and Mbeere oral literture owing to the cultural changes that have taken place. However, poetry on war was either sung or recited. It was used as part of the warriors' exercises, for boosting the warriors' morale, for praising the warriors after a war (successful and unsuccessful), and for celebrating military success.

Political songs

The songs recorded under this sub-genre deal with issues of modern politics. In the pre-colonial and colonial period, political songs were limited owing to the absence of a centralised government as we know it in the modern times. The awe with which people occupying positions of leadership were held previously ruled out the existence of this category of songs.

Songs on cultural transition

As a creative expression of culture, oral literature is sensitive to any changes in human existence and social interaction. As people face new cultural and historical developments leading to the introduction of new elements in their culture, oral artists create new texts as commentaries on these changes. It is within this social context that this sub-genre emerges. In a song like 'They Are Asking for Her All Over', the oral artist makes a creative commentary on the effects of prostitution. A girl who takes up prostitution loses her physical and cultural place among her people.

Proverbs

The proverb is a genre that is nearly as versatile as the song. It is distinguished by its capacity to convey a message in a poignant manner while exercising great economy of language. Hence, a proverb can be defined as a terse creative aphorism or wise saying.

The success of the proverb as an oral literary genre depends on careful use of imagery and symbolic language. The depth of the underlying meaning in the interpretation as compared to the surface meaning makes it stand out as an understatement, or a statement with a great deal of hidden meaning. In fact the term *nthimo* (used for the Embu and Mbeere proverbs) implies "hidden meaning" arising from carefully selected or "weighed" language. They are relatively short; usually one metaphorical sentence.

The proverbs in this book have been classified into ten sub-groups: cautionary proverbs, proverbs on wisdom, proverbs on patience and perseverance, proverbs on kinship, proverbs on co-operation and communal life, proverbs on women, proverbs on men, proverbs on the socially and physically handicapped, proverbs on fate, and a general sub-group for general reflections on life.

A close scrutiny of these proverbs, as is indeed, the case with proverbs from other societies, will reveal that many proverbs could fit into more than one sub-group. A proverb such as 'The animal fated for destruction diarrhoea's during the dry season', could be classified as a cautionary proverb, a commentary on fate, or as a general reflection on life.

Riddles

A riddle is a question in the form of a statement or even a one-word hint for which concrete representation the respondent is called upon to identify. Riddles share stylistic qualities with proverbs — such as brevity, precision and metaphors. However, there is a significant difference between them. The proverb is more serious and is usually related to the human condition while the riddle is less serious and often performed at play and in a relaxed atmosphere.

Riddles are often grounded in a specific cultural and geographical milieu and a person who is alien to the culture may find it difficult to get the answer. For example, the riddle, 'I usually milk my cow while it is standing still', describing a bee-hive in Embu and Mbeere oral literature, would be difficult for a respondent who is not familiar with the type of honey production the statement refers to.

Some Embu and Mbeere riddles use ideophones instead of statements. Examples include the riddle represented by the sound as 'phew', whose answer is 'a pregnant woman'; and the one represented by the sound 'viu...viu', whose answer is "cows' tails". Such riddles are culture-specific, and respondent would have to be familiar with the sound system of the original language before even starting to guess the answers to such riddles.

Like other genres of oral literature, riddles are always being created out of new situations or prompted by the introduction of new elements into a given culture. For example, the riddle, 'Kenya is white on one side' (for a hen's feaces) must have been created recently after the introduction of formal education where there is map-reading, and also in the contemporary political situation where people are more conscious of belonging to a nation rather than to an ethnic community as before.

Puzzles

The Embu and Mbeere have no word for "puzzle". The term *ndai*, which actually means riddle is used to denote puzzles as well. The absence of a traditional term as well as the prevalence of puzzles (which are derived from new cultural elements) would suggest that the puzzle is a fairly new genre in Embu and Mbeere oral literature.

Interaction of genres

One of the aspects that pays tribute to the vibrancy of Embu and Mbeere oral literature genres is the way in which they interact with each other. Although each genre has its own etiquette, time and place of performance, there are points at which the genres meet. The oral narrative is a major point of confluence because of its ability to accommodate other genres, and its tendency to give them additional creative roles while at the same time strengthening itself aesthetically through them. Indeed, this is one of the reasons why the oral narrative is considered as "the mother of oral literature genres".

The oral narrative incorporates songs which are sung by some of the characters as the story develops. The song may be a device used by a character to disguise a certain happening in the story. In 'The Dance of Squirrel, Bush Cat and Young Girls', Squirrel and Bush Cat relay the message about Bush Cat's aching eyes through song. The song in this case disguises the crisis at hand so that the young girls cannot discover that Bush Cat is not as naturally handsome as they find him. It may be mentioned in passing that the song in this case serves a similar purpose as an aside in drama.

In some stories, the song acts as a propeller for the actions of characters or objects such as in 'My Father's Gourd' where the girl's song synchronises with the movement of the gourd and her own movements as she chases it. Elsewhere, the progression of the story largely depends on the song; for example in 'A Girl and an Ogre Named Kibugi', in which characters (including orgres) communicate through song. The song conveys emotions, helps relieve tension while at the same time propelling the story towards its conclusion thus making this narrative a type of oral literature musical. The song, therefore, interacts with the narrative in a way that strengthens the narrative aesthetically by infusing it with melody and a greater emotional quality.

The interaction between the song and the oral narrative does not stop at the incorporation of the song into the narrative. There are times when aspects of the narrative infiltrate songs. A historical event narrated in a story may be mentioned in a song. For instance, the period when Cierume was a chief in Mbeere is referred to in the song, 'A Great People'.

There are times when the name of a legendary character may be invoked in a song to inspire the singers; for example, the name of the above renowned woman is invoked in the worksong, 'Let Women be Supported' to inspire the women workers with determination. An interesting form of interaction between the song and the oral narrative is apparent when the song uses the narrative technique for certain didactic or aesthetic effects, such as in the song, 'They Are Looking for Her all Over'.

The nature of song also makes it easy for the genre to incorporate proverbs. The proverb for its part, interacts with the oral narrative when it is used to emphasise the moral of the story. This is evident in 'What Made Frogs to Lose Their Bottoms'. The moral of the story is that blind competition is disastrous; it is summarised by the proverb at the end, 'blind competition caused frogs to lose their bottoms'. This type of interaction between the oral narrative and the proverb can also be noticed in the story, 'The Girl Whose Children Were Eaten By the Ogre'. Here, the negative effects of deception are summarised in the proverb, 'That girl lost her arrow as well as her bird'.

Although the riddle is not incorporated into the main body of oral narrative texts as such, the two genres still have frequent interaction. During story-telling sessions, the riddle is used as a prelude to and for maintaining the audience's attention. In the more traditional times, there was no room for puzzles during story-telling, but it is now possible for one puzzle or two to be used as a means of punctuating the narrative session and maintaining the audience's alertness.

A puzzle is a problem presented in the form of a description or a pseudo-anecdote requiring the respondent to give a specific solution. Some puzzles are qualified by limitations or hints for the answer. A puzzle is longer than a riddle and often demands greater exercise of the respondent's wit. For example, the puzzle in this collection about a woman using a pumpkin to trick the monkey into returning the baby requires the respondent to think about the monkey's behaviour as well as the items in the hint which may have some connection with monkeys. Knowledge of the fact that monkeys like to imitate human beings and that pumpkins are some of their favourite foodstuffs is crucial for one to arrive at a solution to the puzzle.

A good number of Embu and Mbeere puzzles are based on cultural elements which were introduced recently, such as the one about a person having to lie in the middle of a busy road in order to quickly get to the mortuary. This puzzle must have originated more from an urban culture than from the Embu and Mbeere rural environment where, in some areas, one can go for a whole week without seeing a single vehicle. Although this puzzle was collected from Embu and Mbeere, it is a puzzle which is familiar to children from other ethnic backgrounds living in the urban areas.

Performance

Oral literature finds its expression through performance. Performance enhances unity among the performers and therefore underlines the fact that the art is essentially communal. Performance facilitates communication and thus gives oral literature meaning as a functional art. It is through performance that oral literature imparts serious messages and is able to entertain both the performers and the audience.

The verbal and performance attributes endow oral literature with a greater capacity to communicate sensitively, and where necessary, enhance the immediacy of the message.

Performance is not only a medium of expression, it is also what gives oral literature a life and an identity within the realm of art. Indeed, performance makes oral literature a living cultural heritage.

Embu and Mbeere oral literature shares certain performance characteristics with the oral literature of other African communities. However, there are aspects of performance which are peculiar to the two communities owing to their cultural peculiarities — i.e. certain fine artistic details which distinguish it from the performance of the oral literature of other communities.

This section aims at giving an insight into the modes of performance of the four major genres of oral literature. The performance of each genre is discussed separately. This is in recognition of each genre's different modes of performance, and different regulations and etiquette governing performance.

Oral narratives

Story-telling is one of the oldest arts among the Embu and the Mbeere. It is an art in which almost every member of the two societies must have taken part at one time or another. Stories were told in the evenings before and after the evening meal. It was taboo for anybody, children and adults alike to tell stories during the day. It was believed, for example, that if one told stories during the day, he would grow a nail on his bottom. Beliefs such as this one were used to encourage people to concentrate on work during the day and avoid the distraction of story-telling.

There were no hard and fast rules as to where stories were told. However, the etiquette was to hold the sessions in old women's huts. The participants would gather in a conveniently situated hut, which was often in a relative's home. As land demarcation and other elements of Western culture introduced nuclear-family types of homesteads, the venue for story-telling is shifting from grandmother's huts to mother's kitchen. Just as the grandmother did not necessarily have to be the biological mother of one's parents, the new venue does not have to belong to one's biological mother. Participants are free to join a group that is within a convenient distance.

Formulae

There are several formulae for starting and ending a story. The purpose of the starting formula is to attract the attention of the participants while the closing formula is for concluding the story and underscoring its overall message. The nature of the story guides the narrator in choosing the formula that will be most effective. The composition of the audience may also influence the narrator's choice of formula.

The commonest starting formula is for the narrator to say "Guciai rugano!" (Take a story!), to which the audience answers, "*Nitwecukia*" (We have taken). If the audience's response sounds low-key, the narrator may repeat the call-words more loudly and the audience will immediately understand that they are supposed to sound more lively and interested. So the second time the audience will answer more loudly and pay greater attention.

The first narrator in a story-telling session has a greater responsibility in attracting the attention of the audience. Instead of going straight into asking the audience to take a story, therefore, the narrator can start with a short riddling session and may throw a few riddles and either give the rest of the audience the freedom to respond or pick on particular individuals that are thought not to be alert. The narrator may also invite participants at random or selectively to contribute riddles for others to respond to. The starting formula and style changes as the session progresses; a narrator in the middle of the session may choose to go straight into the beginning of the story without having to call the audience to attention — if they are already attentive.

It may be noted here that although there is usually a lead player in organising the session, the dividing line between the narrator and the audience is very thin. Members of the group are free to take turns and tell a story. Listeners may contribute to the story by singing the songs in the story or by sounding the ideophones of animal characters.

The narrator's role

The ideal narrative oral artist is conscious of the social function of oral literature. While trying to win the audience's appreciation of the oratory, the narrator acts as a propagator of the society's moral values. Among the Embu and the Mbeere, there were leading narrators whose role was to inculcate social values. The narrators were both male and female, though the majority were female.

Besides being conversant with the society's moral code, the narrator also has to realise that he/she is a custodian of the people's culture, and hence be aware that while telling stories, he/she is in fact playing a role that is required of him/her by the society; in contemporary theoretical terms, he/she is a committed artist.

The ideal narrator is deeply conscious of the intrinsic role he is playing during the story-telling session. Since the stories he narrates have not been recorded in writing, he has to have a good memory in order for the narration to retain its authenticity even as new creative elements are being added in the course of the performance. It is important for the narrator to have the skill to organise his thoughts so as to give a cohesive message in each narrative. At the same time, he has to remember that he is dealing with art and, therefore, avoid preaching. The narrator also has to be alert to sustain the flow of the story when there are interruptions; interruptions are inevitable in story-telling sessions owing to the informal nature of the venue and the inevitability of someone seeking clarification. The narrator, therefore, has to be very patient if he wants the session to meet its goals.

The narrator's first duty during a story-telling session is to gauge the needs of his audience. He has to be sensitive to his audience so as to involve the members fully during the session. This sensitivity is reflected in his choice of material as well as in his narrative technique.

The themes of the narratives selected will vary according to the composition of the audience. A session which includes youths who are approaching will address themes related to marriage and parental responsibilities, such as 'A Young Man With Two Mouths' and 'Wamweru and Her Step-mother'.

The complexity of the stories will also differ according to the ages of the listeners. Hence, the sensitive narrator whose audience includes young children will choose stories such as 'Monkey and Crocodile' whose moral is easily understood and whose humour sustains the attention of youngsters.

The ideal narrator captures the attention of the audience at the beginning of the session and uses techniques which maintain this attention throughout.

Oral poetry

Embu and Mbeere oral poetry falls into two performance categories: recited poetry (recitations) and musical poetry (songs). None of the oral poetry is performed in a rigid or static position. Dramatisation is crucial to the performance of this genre.

Recited poetry

The poetry performed through recitation often requires a serious and sombre mood for the message to be communicated effectively. Poems whose effectiveness requires the invocation of supernatural powers — such as war, panegyric or praise poetry and religious poetry — fall in this group.

War and praise poetry such as 'Look at This Hero' and 'Let Me Count Your Ribs My Mother's Son' is recited and not sung. It is performed at ceremonies in which warriors are sent off to war or welcomed back from war.

The intervention of the supernatural is sought at such ceremonies. Hence, the mood is sombre and, therefore, warrants the choice of recitation over singing. At these ceremonies, the medicineman recites prayers making direct supplication to the supernatural powers for their blessings in the communities' military undertaking. The following is an example of a prayer session conducted just before warriors go off to war.

Medicineman: Whoever would dare touch
These young men of Gaciari
With a bad stick

May he be non-existent;
Say may he be non-existent.

People: May he be non-existent.

Medicineman: Say may he be non-existent.

People: May he be non-existent!

Similar texts which are recited rather than sung are those connected with oathing. For example, when a person suspected of murder denies the charge, there are specific poetic words he uses as he takes an oath to swear that he is not guilty.

Suspect: If indeed it was I (*takes concoction*)
               Who found that bad stick (*takes concoction*)
               Which ate Muruakithi (*takes concoction*)
               May I be eaten (*takes concoction*)
               By this concoction (*takes concoction*).

In each case, although it is not stated directly in the text, the supernatural powers are invoked to take part and give their blessings or judgement, depending on the intention of the performance. In these recitations, dramatisation is very important. Unlike modern dramatic performances where the performers have to rehearse before hand, in traditional performances the gestures and other forms of dramatisation came spontaneously and naturally without prior rehearsal. In some cases, such as the suspect's oath-taking cited above, the medicineman or other appropriate elder administering the oath might instruct the suspect in advance on when to take the concoction and when to say which words, but the actual gestures used in the course of the ceremony are spontaneous.

In the panegyric 'Look at This Hero' and 'Let Me Count Your Ribs My Mother's Son', the women's recitation is accompanied and indeed enhanced by dramatisation. Hand gestures such as pointing at the warriors are an important part of the ceremony. Ideophones and interjections are used for cheering the warriors who are at this time doing war exercises to show off their prowess in martial tactics. The women watch these exercises closely and decide when to make appropriate ideophones and interjections, such as "*aririririiti*!", "*ayia*!", "*niguo*!" (that's it) and "*one*!" (look).

Songs

Embu and Mbeere songs are performed on many social occasions such as initiation ceremonies, weddings, recreation and while people are carrying out various tasks. A soloist normally calls the tune and the other singers respond.

Body movements are essential to the performance of these songs. Each occasion and each song has its own peculiar movements, but the most popular ones among the Embu and Mbeere are the hips and bust movements for women and the torso movements for men. At weddings, women's erotic hip movements are used to tease the couple as a reminder that conjugal responsibilities must begin immediately after the conclusion of the festivities.

At young people's dances, most of the songs are performed by young couples. Here most of the movements are suggestive of love-making rhythms although the main idea is recreation rather than the implication that the couples should engage in such activities after the dance.

Worksongs are selected according to the type of job at hand. Hence, the type of song selected is usually the one whose rhythm can facilitate body movements which synchronise with the movements required to perform the task. The rhythm of a song such as 'Baby Stop Crying' lends itself easily to movements of rocking a baby, whether he is carried on the back or held in the arms. Similarly, 'You Woman Grinding Millet' has a rhythm which synchronises easily with movements required in grinding grain on the traditional grinding stone.

The soloist's role

The soloist, known as *mukui* in both Kiembu and Kimbeere, is a key player in the performance of songs. He is the equivalent of the narrator in the performance of stories. The role of the soloist is actually defined by the root of the name *mukui* which is *gukua*, meaning, "to call the tune".

The organization of the performance of song, whether at work or on other social occasions, depends on the soloist. He determines the choice of songs and the sequence that they should follow. He may consult with one or two of the performers and may have an assistant within the group, but the final decision is made by him.

As the person who starts the singing and sings certain verses on his own, the soloist should have a voice that communicates easily and is able to vary in order to be able to pitch the singing appropriately. He should also have leadership qualities so that the other performers respect his decisions.

The person most preferred for this role is the one who builds rapport with everybody in the community rather than the one who organises by bullying people.

As a custodian of culture, the soloist has poetic licence to comment on human behaviour and to fire the performing group into satirising social weaknesses. In this regard, the soloist has to be sensitive to his people's culture while respecting the etiquette of various performances. In satirical songs, for instance, the soloist decides whether to identify the victims of ridicule by name or by implication.

The soloist has certain special privileges in leading worksongs. While he calls the tune, he may "stretch his back", i.e., relax from the job just a little. However, on no account is he exempted from working. The soloist works like everybody else and so needs to be very alert to maintain the tempo in such a way that the song enhances rather than detracts from the activity at hand.

Proverbs

The performance of proverbs is peculiar in the sense that it is not anticipated but occurs spontaneously. Proverbs are uttered during formal occasions, such as traditional court cases and marriage negotiations or in informal social contexts such as a parent talking to his child or two friends conversing. In each case, the proverb is used to stress a point and the listener is therefore expected to be well-versed in the genre to understand the message fully. The opportunity to use the appropriate proverb presents itself naturally in the course of the interaction between people; the speakers do not have to plan in advance that they will make use of this rich genre.

There are, therefore, no formulae associated with the performance of the proverb. The only restriction is that a person cannot address a proverb to his senior; the communication through proverbs is usually from a senior to a junior or between equals. Hence, in marriage negotiations for instance, if the people who have come to ask for the girl's hand in marriage seem reluctant to pay the amount of dowry demanded, an elder on the side of the bride-to-be can retort that, "Giving birth is not the same as defecating!" Since these are agemates, a whole ammunition of proverbs may be thrown back and forth until the leader of the bridegroom's party says, "Today it's me tomorrow, it's you!" At this point, the bride's group may feel obliged to lower the bride-price in case some time in future, a young man from their side might send them to negotiate for a bride from the other side.

Sometimes old people take advantage of the power of the proverb as a tool of communication and it is not unusual for them to use proverbs to show off their oratorial skills. Conversing elders may throw proverbs at one another just to show off and to colour the conversation, hence performing the proverb for its aesthetic value more than for its didactic value.

In day-to-day interaction, older people frequently use proverbs spontaneously when communicating with the youth. Even in a simple case when, for example, a girl says to her mother that she is going out with her girlfriends as a cover-up for a young man, she might tell her, "Go, but remember that a traveller does not leave a banana roasting on the fire...Oh! And also remember that a person's best friend is the one who gives her the pregnancy that eventually kills her!"

Riddles

Embu and Mbeere riddles are performed either as part of story-telling sessions, or in the course of play. The riddle is a genre which is associated with children and, except in the context of story-telling, it is unheard of for adults to engage in riddling, however idle they may be. As a result, children are the master oral artists in the riddle genre both in the performance of old texts and in the creation of new ones.

Formula

Unlike the proverb which has no performance formula, the riddle has a strict mode of performance which must be adhered to even when the genre is interacting with the oral narrative. The following is the standard formula of the performance of Embu and Mbeere riddles:

Proposer:	Take a riddle.
Respondents:	We have taken.
Proposer:	I too have taken.
Respondents:	A riddle.

At this point, there is usually laughter from everybody on account of the absurdity of this riddle. The above riddle is really for warming up the session and making the performers alert. The real riddling session then begins as follows.

Proposer:	Take a riddle.
Respondents:	We have taken.
Proposer:	That which belongs to your grandmother and it is big.

The respondents try to solve the riddle one by one. Some respondents giggle with embarrassment because of the way in which poetic licence allows this riddle to have obscene implications. In the original language, the riddle implies that whatever belongs to the grandmother here is on her body. Some respondents might assume that it is a wound on the grandmother's leg. Many might think of her genitals, but feel too embarrassed to make such an obscene guess. After the respondents have given up, they request the proposer to tell them the answer and the session continues as follows:

Proposer:	What will you give me?
Respondents:	A house.
Proposer:	Oh! No!
Respondents:	Cianvuko

	(This is the name of a little girl who is among the respondents; she is offered as a bride to the proposer if he is a man. The idea here is to make the session as lively as possible, for instance by making offers which are funny or are likely to be rejected).
Proposer:	*Aai*! *Ika*! Oh! No! By the time Cianvuko grows up to be a bride, I shall have become curved or broken into two with age! *Nari*! *Ika*! Never! Oh! No!
Respondents:	We offer you cattle.
Proposer:	Whose cattle?
	(Respondents will offer herds in the neighbourhood until the proposer accepts one).
Respondents:	Kathambana's.
Proposer:	Keep your cattle! Do you think I am a beggar?
Respondents:	The cattle of Nthiga Muruamwosa (Nthiga son of Mwosa).
Proposer:	*Ayia*! *Ii*! Let them come, so that I can be drinking milk and a little blood! Oh! What did I tell you? The big one belonging to your grandmother — a shaven head.

At this point the respondents laugh at their failure to guess such an obvious thing while others sigh with relief that it is not the obscene answer they feared it was.

The riddling session continues with the participants taking turns as proposers until they get tired and they decide to stop, either through consensus or at the suggestion of the group leader.

Puzzles

As earlier mentioned, the puzzle is new in the oral literature of the Embu and the Mbeere. It is, therefore, not surprising that no etiquette has yet been developed for its performance.

There are times when a puzzle or two infiltrate into a riddling session but more often than not, this genre is performed while children perform a tedious job or walk long distances.

Chapter 3

FORM AND STYLE

Art is divided into three broad categories according to the mode of expression — i.e. visual art (or fine art), literary art (or creative writing), and performing art (music, dance and drama). The nature of oral literature is such that it can be put in both the last two categories.

Oral literature qualifies to be classifed as literary art because it uses language as its raw material. Like written literature, it depends on the creative use of language. But, whereas written literature uses writing as its medium of expression, oral literature depends on a combination of language and performance.

Each genre of oral literature has specific literary characteristics which distinguish it from other genres. Areas which offer points of contact and similarity between genres will however be noted and pointed out.

Oral narratives

Embu and Mbeere oral narratives are fairly short. Most of them can be narrated within a period of half an hour. The longer narratives often have songs and could take up to one hour depending on the narrator's inclination to audience participation. The brevity of these narratives is a deliberate technique which facilitates memorability.

Plot

The narratives have varying plots depending on the type of audience for which a particular story is intended. Narratives for very young children have simple, straightforward plots whereas stories for older children and young adults have more complex plots. The trickster story, 'Monkey and Crocodile' has a very simple plot. Crocodile tries to trick Monkey into being slaughtered in order that his heart may be used as medicine for the king of crocodiles. On the way to the crocodile world, Monkey learns about this trick and quickly thinks of a trick to save himself. In the end, Crocodile's

29

trickery boomerangs on him when he loses Monkey as his prey and has all his teeth knocked out in the bargain. This narrative is intended for young children and is, therefore, creatively pieced together in a simpler style than, say the legend Cierume' which has a more complex plot and spans a longer period of time.

Narrative techniques

Dialogue is an integral part of oral narratives. Its importance is such that it necessitates that human beings, and animals and ogres alike have the power of speech. The use of dialogue punctuates straight narration and makes the story more interesting. It adds life and credibility to the story and thus enhances communication of the message to the audience.

Dialogue is a powerful tool of characterisation as quite often characters reveal their personality traits through what they say and how they say it. 'The Origin of Ndega's Grove'. In this story, Ndega's stubbornness, which eventually leads to his downfall, is revealed in the manner in which he speaks and in what he says. Ndega even directly refers to his rebelliousness quite early in the narrative when he says ,"Today, today if I fail to take that girl home, I'll know my name is not Ndega the rebel!" This is the character's major personality flaw which eventually leads to his destruction, and it is most evident through what he says.

Repetition is used quite often in oral narratives. This could be the repetition of various elements in a narrative, such as events, actions, dialogue or songs. In the story 'A Woman and Hyenas', the hyenas' invasion of the woman's home is repeated several times in the story. Similarly, the song the woman uses to deceive the hyenas that she is not alone, is repeated until the hyenas discover that it is a trick and proceed to eat her up. Repetition emphasises major points in a story and helps to convey emotions.

Repetition is also used to weave events together in order to make a story coherent. In the story above, the woman's loneliness is emphasised by the repetition of the hyenas' visits. Similarly, the repetition of her song underscores the fear the hyenas instil in her. On the whole, repetition enhances the communication of the key message in the story, which is that a person who divorces himself from his community will have nobody to rescue him in times of great need.

Animal characters

In the oral narratives recorded in this book, animal names are used as proper nouns. Animals play roles similar to those played by human characters and in the stories populated by animal characters, animals are manipulated to represent human beings. This device is extremely effective in satirising human weaknesses. It must be noted here that its use is not peculiar to the oral literature of the Embu and the Mbeere, it is a style that features in other African oral literatures.

The use of animal characters enables the narrator to ridicule social follies while avoiding offending individuals who may be easily identified with negatively portrayed characters in the story. The device also helps to raise the audience's emotions in a controlled manner. In a story such as 'Monkey and Crocodile', Crocodile's threat on Monkey's life is condemned without making too many demands on the audience's emotions. The audience's pity for Monkey is aroused by revealing the danger in which Monkey is as he travels with Crocodile. However, the audience can emotionally cope with the danger better in relation to an animal victim than they would if a human character was in such a vulnerable situation. Similarly, when Crocodile loses all his teeth as punishment for his cruelty, the audience can afford to laugh, whereas it would be sadistic for them to derive humour from the plight of a human character in such a situation.

Humour is often successfully employed through the use of animal characters. Animals are easier and more acceptable to manipulate in absurd situations than human beings. The absurdity in the sewing of Bush Cat's eyes in 'The Dance of the Squirrel' Bush Cat and Young Girls' is humorous, especially to young audiences. However, the pain Bush Cat experiences as he dances with the girls he has won (through squirrel's artistry on the eyes) would be emotionally unbearable to the audience had a human character been used.

Animals are selected for various roles, depending on the characteristics associated with the particular animal, and are used as representative types to reflect social situations. The major animal characters in Embu and Mbeere stories are Lion, Elephant, Hyena, Hare, Goat or Gazelle, Monkey, Squirrel, Mole, Crocodile, Frog, Chameleon and Snake. Birds also appear in some stories. Dove, Hawk and Hen are some of the popular ones. All these animals are found in the Embu and Mbeere geographical environment. Their familiarity enables the audience to draw analogies between the animal characters and the human qualities the animals stand for.

Each animal character has specific attributes from the human world with which it is associated. Lion normally appears as the representative of leaders on account of the traditional role accorded to him as the king of animals. He is strong but not as intelligent as Hare. He is often ridiculed when he is tricked by Hare in stories where the power of wisdom over physical strength is emphasised.

Elephant symbolises might. However, Elephant is not given the place of a ruler. He often appears as a poor second to Lion because of his slowness and passive nature.

Hare is the traditional trickster. He is regarded as intelligent, but often uses his intelligence to fool others and profit from their foolishness. He fools everybody, big and small. Notice, for example, how he fools Lion and usurps the latter's power in 'How Hare Became Chief of Animals'.

Hyena, on the other hand, symbolises greed and selfishness. He is hated by both man and animals. These negative qualities, and the harm he causes others, makes him hated by animal and human characters alike. Notice, for example, how the existence of death in the world has been blamed on him in the story, 'The Origin of Death'. Hyena is stupid and often gets into trouble because of his single-track approach to relations with those around him; He views others mainly as a means of filling his stomach.

Crocodile, too, is regarded as selfish, malicious, calculating and cruel. He is hated because of his insensitivity to the suffering of others.

Snake on is seen as cowardly but cunning. It is interesting that he is sometimes seen wooing girls and succeeding in making them fall in love with him. In such stories, Snake plays the role of a young man who is outwardly smooth and utilises this trait to fool girls.

Chameleon is slow but cunning. Just as he does in his natural habitat, he camouflages his intentions to survive among those who are bigger and faster than himself. This character trait is illustrated in the way he wins a bride by tricking Hare in 'How Chameleon Defeated Hare'.

Monkey is most popular because he is seen as witty and humorous despite the fact that he steals people's crops. Perhaps, his close resemblance to man makes the Embu and Mbeere relate to him like a brother, albeit a mischievous one.

The smaller animals such as Bush Cat, Squirrel, Mole, Tortoise and Frog are easy sources of humour because of their physical features. Apart from their small size, their individual characteristics are aspects from which audiences derive a great deal of amusement. Bush Cat's large eyes, Squirrel's big tail, Frog's flat bottoms, Tortoise's uneven shell, and Mole's shyness are all objects of fun in oral narratives.

It is interesting that all animal characters are thought to be male, with the exception of Gazelle and Goat. These latter two play the role of mothers and are inactive except as symbols of motherly, tender, loving care. This marginalisation of females among the animal characters in Embu and Mbeere oral narratives is perhaps a mirror image of the two peoples' attitude towards women.

All birds except Hawk, Eagle and Vulture who are used interchangeably as symbols of greed, are friends of man. Some, such as Dove, are used as emissaries to carry messages in desperate situations. Hen is the bird equivalent to Gazelle and Goat in representing mothers in the bird kingdom, but she is portrayed as being stupid and absent-minded. In 'Why Hawk Eats Hen's Chicks', Hen loses Hawk's razor due to her single-track approach to life; she only thinks of looking after her children and is incapable of thinking of anything else.

In fantasies, birds symbolise the benevolence and the sense of justice of supernatural powers. In 'The Benevolent Bird', for example, a poor man is rewarded for his patience and mercy, but is later punished for greed and hardness of heart.

While affirming what is good and socially acceptable and hence furthering the didactic role of the oral narrative, the use of animal characters contributes to the aesthetics of these stories. The device facilitates dramatisation and adds life to the narratives. Animal characters enable the narrator to use gestures to imitate heir actions and also to make use of voice variation to reflect the different voices in dialogue. The device facilitates audience involvement when they at times join the narration and speak like the animals or sing the songs attributed to animal characters. In the final analysis, this stylistic feature contributes tremendously to the ultimate goal of educating the audience in an aesthetically appealing manner.

The ogre as a character

The ogre, known as *irimarimu* in Kiembu and *Irimurimu* in Kimbeere, plays an important role in Embu and Mbeere oral narratives. The ogre is thought of as an ugly creature. He is huge and frightening, but he often exhibits stupid behaviour. He is capable of changing himself into many different forms in order to attract human prey. Almost invariably, ogres are male.

The ogre's favourite camouflage is as a handsome young man since his favourite victims are women, especially girls of a marriageable age. Occasionally, they may appear disguised as very old women in order to attract children, but they always revert to their normal grotesque form after they have caught their prey. It is interesting that in the ogre world, there are no females; ogres always have to fool human females whom they imprison as wives.

Ogres symbolise evil, danger, selfishness and the threat to life. They eat human beings; and this anti-social behaviour symbolises inhumanity in the form of cruelty and exploitation. Occasionally, ogres represent well-deserved punishment, such as in the narrative 'Mutema Kianda and his Son Gacau Mundu'. In this narrative, ogres symbolise all the forces of evil against which man is powerless.

Suspense is a dominant stylistic feature in ogre tales. First, there is the suspense the audience experiences when it is made to wonder whether a certain character is an ogre, or whether some action taken by a human character may lead to the protagonist's confrontation with the ogre. This kind of suspense can be noticed in 'The Young Man With Two Mouths' and 'My Father's Gourd'. There is also the suspense the audience experiences after the ogre has caught his victim. The audience experiences fear for and anxiety over the victim's safety before the victim is eventually saved from the ogre's clutches. Notice this kind of suspense in 'A Girl and an Ogre Called Kibugi' which is enhanced by the use of song.

Most Embu and Mbeere ogre stories end with the release of the victim from the ogre's trap. Even where the victim has been eaten by the ogres a way has to be found to get him out of the ogre's stomach. In 'A Girl and an Ogre Called Kibugi', the girl's father, at the suggestion of the ogre, cuts the ogre's little finger and the girl comes out followed by all the people the ogre had eaten before. However, there are cases where the victim has to die for the message to be communicated. In 'My Father's Gourd,' the girl has to die to warn the audience against the senseless pursuit of worthless things.

Oral poetry/songs

Embu and Mbeere oral poetry consists of songs and poems intended for recitation. Most of these poems are fairly short, but their performance time is sometimes stretched through the use of repetition. For example, the circumcision song, 'The Child Has Become Just the Way His Mother Was' consists of the title - sentence alone, but is extended into a whole song through repetition.

Repetition is central in Embu and Mbeere oral poetry. A stanza may be repeated to form a whole song as in the above example, or certain words or sentences within a song may be repeated several times. In a work song such as 'All Strength Will Be Eaten by Ants', the sentence, "It is better to cultivate" is repeated before stating the importance of cultivation. The repetition is aimed at emphasising the importance of the job at hand so that the work party does not slacken. The repetition emphasises the sense of purpose in their job: their goal is to save children from starvation, as stated later in the song.

In some cases, the songs are punctuated by refrains such as in the song, 'Let Women Be Supported', which is punctuated by the refrain:

Iyai uu let women be supported
The women of my age set are supported diligently
With millet gruel
Seconded by fermented milk from a gourd

In these poems, the artists make use of contrast, imagery and rich vocabulary.

War recitations are full of elevated language that raises warriors almost to the level of demi-gods. For example, in the war recitations entitled, 'Look at This Hero' and 'Let Me Count Your Ribs My Mother's Son', the warrior is contrasted with the slow-footed bride and then described as an explosive to emphasise his strength and hence express the confidence the community has in him as their defender. The lines, "Let me count your ribs my mother's son/The way you were counted by the hedges" express the reciter's creative interpretation of the warrior's experiences on the battlefield. They refer to the hardship and starvation that the warrior has had to endure at the battlefront; he has grown so thin that his ribs are sticking out and can actually be counted. While he was fighting, the warrior's only friends were the hedges behind which he hid from the enemy's lethal weapons.

Satire pervades Embu and Mbeere oral poetry so much so that this book has taken cognisance of this fact and grouped songs under the classification, satirical songs. The most common techniques through which satire is achieved in Embu and Mbeere oral poetry are sarcasm and exaggeration. In 'A Girl Being Sold in Kilograms', the artist exaggerates the situation when he says that the girl is being weighed in kilograms the way beans for sale are weighed. Through this exaggeration, the song ridicules the various reasons given to support high bride-price. The artist is being sarcastic when he says that he will sell his daughter in kilograms, going as far as giving reasons as to why he should charge fees for his daughter. He is actually ridiculing those who use the introduction of the money economy and consequent economic inflation to commercialise bride-price. In 'Nyaga Son of Gituro Woos All Women', exaggeration is used to ridicule promiscuity and callousness in male-female relationships.

The question and response form is very popular in Embu and Mbeere songs. This facilitates the orderly participation of various people in the performance of these songs. The questions are usually in the form of challenges and each challenge has a response to it. The song, 'You Woman Grinding Millet' is created in this form whereby children pose challenges to the woman who is grinding and she responds as she continues grinding. Notice this question-and-response form also in the wedding song, 'Whose Honey is This?' and in the female initiation song entitled 'With Whom Shall I Dance?'

There are paralinguistic stylistic devices used in Embu and Mbeere oral poetry whose effect can only be fully appreciated in the original language and through performance. These aspects include rhythm, consonance, assonance and ideophones. The children's musical game, 'Rain Pour Down We Play in the Puddles' is one of the very rhythmical poems whose effect can only be fully appreciated if performed. As will be noticed even in the translated version of this poem, rhythm is achieved through repetition, ideophones and exclamations. In some songs, rhythm is achieved through consonance, such as in the song, 'Come or I Come' where the sound "*ka*" is repeated, especially in the refrain "*uka kana mbuke!*"

Certain vowels are repeated to create a certain mood in Embu and Mbeere songs. A good example of the use of this device is in the female initiation song, 'You Woman Cutter'. In the original version of this song, the vowel '*i*' is repeated to create an emotional effect. This is the sound which is most conspicuous when one is crying. Its repetition, therefore, gives the initiate who has to sing it immediately after her operation, a chance to release emotions built from the pain she has just experienced.

Embu and Mbeere songs frequently use ideophones as punctuation or for rhythmic and melodic effect. The most common of these are "*ii*", "*uui*", "*rariyu*", "*aiya*", "*uiya*", "*iyiai*", "*oyio oho*" and "*hmn*". Women use the ululation "*aririiriiiti!*" to convey great excitement or joy. Although some ideophones and ululations have been recorded in some of the songs in this book, it is difficult to record a text from a performance with exactitude when writing. In some cases, there is no fixed form of a text as the performers have the freedom to manipulate it and incorporate ideophones when and where they deem fit. Further ideophonetic effect is provided through musical accompaniments, or by whistling and using other appropriate noises in the course of the performance.

Proverbs

Embu and Mbeere proverbs appear in the form of short precise statements conveyed through symbols, metaphors, allegories and hyperboles. Sometimes they are stated in reference or as a conclusion to a narrative which the listener is expected to be familiar with. The effectiveness of each proverb depends on how appropriate it is to the social context in which it is used. In order to make each proverb effective in its own right, several stylistic devices have been used over the ages in the creation of these proverbs, the most outstanding of which are discussed below.

Economy of language is the most conspicuous in proverbs. The sense of the proverb is compressed into as few words as possible, with some proverbs consisting of two or three words in the original language. For example, 'Love means trouble' (6) and 'Devils hate jokes' (23). The proverb, 'He who waits does not arrive' (28) consists of only two words in the original language. This has been achieved by defying the rules of grammar and using poetic licence to create a rich word from the verb "to wait". The created word "*mbeterera*" is a noun in the context in which it is used in the proverb and it implies, "waiting" as a noun or "he who waits". In some cases, the brevity is achieved through the omission of the subject of the action and/or the object in the proverb. The proverb, 'If you see it silent, it has swallowed' (73) goes even further in the attempt to economise on words. The omission of subject and object makes the proverb consist of three words in the original. The snake that has swallowed and the prey that has been swallowed are only implied. The proverb, 'If it shines too much it misses someone to bask in it' (161), which has twelve words in English, only has four words in the original. Here, the prefix used for the sun has been joined with the act of shining, "*ringiara*", and also by joining the act of basking in the sun has been joined with he who basks. Word economy facilitates quick communication and emphasises the immediacy of the advice conveyed through the proverb.

Proverbs commonly employ imagery in the form of metaphors, similes, symbols and personification, for clarity. Some similes are comparisons between objects which belong to completely different zones. For example, the comparison between a mother and the stomach in 'Whoever is advised and controlled by his mother is like the one who is controlled by his stomach' (223), and 'A fool is like a beehive' (120). On the surface, the comparison may appear far-fetched but the cultural attitudes towards the object of comparison give logical clues to the implications of the proverb at deeper level.

Metaphors are formed from common activities or objects which are easily found in the Embu and Mbeere environment. Animal husbandry, farming and making ropes for tying farm produce are common activities. Hence, the audience of proverbs such as numbers 9, 16, 61, 34, 151, 303 and 346 which are created from metaphors taken from these activities, are expected to relate to the message easily.

Among the Embu and the Mbeere, the use of imagery created from filth is a popular way of sharpening proverbs as satirical tools against human weaknesses 'He who befriends the beetle is brought presents of dung' (40), 'A rhino hates its own faeces' (175), and 'If you step on faeces with one foot, step on it with the other one as well' (91) are illustrations of this fact.

The animal world is a fertile source of symbols in the creation of Embu and Mbeere proverbs. Animals used are found in the environment and are therefore easy to relate to. The elephant is used as a symbol of might (proverbs 30 and 143), the hyena as a symbol of greed and malice (22 and 45), and the snake symbolises hidden or subtle danger such as in 'Do not disturb a snake in its own hole' (21). The use of symbolism in proverbs is a very effective way of satirising unacceptable behaviour and helps communicate the message sharply and vividly.

Quite often, inanimate objects are personified such as in the proverb, 'The pot laughs at the potsherd' (10). Some very witty personification can be seen in the proverb, 'The mouth that ate the grain is the same one that asks what shall I plant' (34). This proverb is both satirical and humorous. The mouth has been personified twice to represent the person who consumes the grain with his mouth and uses the same mouth to beg for seeds to plant. Personification makes proverbs concise and the message they contain, unforgettable.

Allegories have been used in proverbs to good effect. Human beings, birds as well as animal characters are used in allegorical proverbs such as 'They cheated you at the market but you blamed the path as you walked along it' (375), 'The despised is the one who killed the lion' (262), and 'The eagle was brought down from the sky by greed' (17). There are allegorical proverbs which refer to well-known oral narratives and usually have animal characters; for example, 'Copying others caused frogs to lose their bottoms' (31) and 'Two smells (from roasting meat) caused the hyena to break its legs' (45).

Proverbs also employ negative statements to communicate their message. Some examples are: 'One who has a well does not need to go to the well' (102), 'The umbilical cord is not a sweet-potato vine' (163), and 'He who refuses to help an orphan does not prevent the day from dawning' (276). The negative form adds to the effectiveness of these proverbs by giving them a categorical tone and hence making them more persuasive.

Hyperbole or exaggeration occupy an important place in Embu and Mbeere proverbs. Their use is evident in proverbs such as these: 'A person who has a brother is never beaten to death' (173), 'People who have no unity are killed with one club' (188) and 'The eagle gives birth to a dove' (372). Hyperbole or exaggeration creates a shock effect and therefore makes the listener think about the message communicated through the proverb.

There are other stylistic devices used in Embu and Mbeere proverbs which are not as recurrent as those discussed above, but which are equally important in contributing to the effectiveness of the texts. These are parallelism, repetition and consonance. Parallelism is used particularly in sounding very serious warnings; for example in the cautionary proverbs, 'The curse from a living person is worse than that from a dead person' (97) and 'They dance at the coward's home and mourn at brave person's home' (99).

Repetition is normally used as a clever and artistic way of reminding the listener about some important fact of life, such as in the proverbs, 'He who does not know does not know that he does not know' (137), and '*Uteci u eci u*'(Whoever does not know this knows that) (138). Consonance adds to the memorability of the proverbs, and in some cases, the device is used for satirical purposes. Notice, for instance, the use of consonance in the following proverbs in which the Embu and the Mbeere satirise themselves: '*Mumbeere ndaugaga mbaura nwa augire mbaika*' (A Mbeere person never says help me put this load down he only says help me lift this load (185) and '*Muembu ndeci marumua aici maimwa*' (An Embu person remembers only when he is denied something but does not remember when he is given (186).

Riddles

Riddles are created from familiar objects in the environment. Natural phenomena such as thunder and rain are suitable material for the creation of riddles. Parts of the human body, such as a woman's breasts, whose characteristics are presumed to be strange, are used for humorous effect. Riddles always take the form of questions and answers.

The questions in these riddles take different forms. A riddle may be posed as a statement giving a hint for the object around which it revolves such as, (3) 'Two identical hills', (A woman's breasts) and (16)'A restless straight person' (A naked herdsboy).

The commonest form of statement for the riddles is the one where the question is posed in a way which describes an action as a hint to the answer; for example, 'You always swallow it but you never get satisfied' (Saliva), and 'I have built my house on a hill' (the nose (8)). Some riddles are posed through an actual question, for instance, 'Who are these people who passed here singing?' (bees), (38) and (39) 'Where are those people in black coats going for a circumcision ceremony?' (black ants). Notice that the humour in the riddles posed through the description of an action depends on the dramatisation.

Negative statements also feature quite commonly in Embu and Mbeere riddles. In these riddles, the emphasis is on the negative part which is the hint to the answer. For instance, 'I have slaughtered a buffalo but I have not filled one hand' (hair) and 'Where I slaughtered the white goat never misses white colour' (ashes). Occasionally, parallelism is used in the creation of these riddles, 'Where I am coming from there is a road but where I am going there is none' (snail).

An interesting type of riddle is that which appears in ideophonetic form such as '*Whooo*!' (a pregnant woman), '*Keregece*' (ten cent pieces), and '*Ngiriri ngiriri*' (bicycle). The riddles in this form are culture-specific in the sense that the ideophones are derived from the linguistic systems of the people's language and would make little sense to people who are not familiar with Kiembu and Kimbeere. In the case of '*Whooo*!'

38

(15), the behavioural patterns of the people are also important. This is the sound made by a very tired person, especially a woman weighed down by a heavy pregnancy load.

Most riddles depend on imagery. The imagery is selected from many areas of the Embu and Mbeere environment. These are from agricultural activities, such as 'My garden has been harvested by an animal which has no footsteps' (77); architecture, for instance, 'I have built my house on a hill' (8), and, from the type of landscape in which they live, for example, 'Two identical hills' (3). In some cases, the riddles stretch poetic licence to extremes and use imagery suggestive of obscenity. 'A girl wrestling with her father' (82) has incestuous connotations and yet, the answer is quite harmless (The small grinding stone and the big grinding stone). In the latter case, the riddle exploits poetic licence to create suspense. The listener is kept in suspense when his thoughts toy with the taboo areas in human relations, but is greatly relieved to learn that the answer to the riddle is far from taboo.

Puzzles

Most Embu and Mbeere puzzles are presented as short anecdotes. All the puzzles in this book appear in the form of anecdotes with the exception of numbers 12 and 14. The anecdote presents a problem which the respondent attempts to solve using the hints given. Many of the situations alluded to in the posed puzzles are absurd, exaggerated and somewhat unrealistic. However, the creativity used persuades the respondent into thinking that the puzzle presents a desperate situation for which a solution must be found to save the characters involved.

A sense of urgency tricks the respondent into ignoring the absurdity and making the necessary effort to save the situation. This urgency is presented, for example, in the puzzle in which a cock is desperate to find a convenient place to lay an egg (3). The desperation created by the fragile nature of eggs and enhanced by the mention of fire and a large expanse of water tricks the respondent into forgetting that cocks do not lay eggs. This is the aim of the puzzle. The use of these devices helps to sensitise the audience, hence facilitating the role of puzzles as a genre of oral literature.

Chapter 4

THE SOCIAL FUNCTIONS OF ORAL LITERATURE

Oral literature is intricately related to the social environment of the people who create and perform it. As the creative expression of a people's culture, it manipulates language to express their values, beliefs, traditions and entire worldview. No culture is static; culture develops alongside the progression of history. A culture's dynamism is sustained by man's ability to adapt his attitudes and practices to changing circumstances. Oral literature is a powerful tool for facilitating this cultural dynamism. By sensitising society and commenting on human behaviour, oral literature not only helps society redefine its concerns, but it also contributes towards social regeneration.

Oral literature is a performed art. Through performance, oral literature facilitates human interaction thus strenghthening not only the state of being but also the social intercourse between an individual and his fellows. In this way, it fosters good relations among people living in the same environment.

The universe is a complex phenomenon and human beings need to understand it in order to build a comfortable niche for themselves within it. Oral literature attempts to explain the cosmos and man's existence in the universe. It helps people to understand the natural environment and their place within this environment. By contributing to the creation of order on the physical, social and psychological levels, the art helps human beings to develop a sense of belonging in their day-to-day existence in an otherwise mysterious universe.

The aesthetic nature of oral literature provides human beings with an avenue through which to channel and develop their creativity. As they perform or attend performances of oral literature, they are entertained and at the same time given a chance to test their creative prowess. In this process, they gain confidence in themselves as members of their natural and social environments.

Oral literature also makes an important contribution to contemporary written African literature. As a record of the history and culture of the African peoples, oral literature gives the modern African writer not only a backbone, but also an identity for his art. Oral literature makes a significant contribution to African cosmology in contemporary African creative writing thus enabling it to meet the objective expressed by Gabriel Okara when he says:

I think the immediate aim of African literature is to put into the whirlpool of literature the African point of view, to put across how the African thinks.*

In the final analysis, oral literature is to society what oars are to a boat. It facilitates a society's movement through the waters of historical progression. As a reservoir of a people's culture, oral literature gives society a sense of direction and self-confidence. Through articulating society's hopes and aspirations, oral literature acts as a pillar on which human beings can lean in the course of their day-to-day activities and also in their historical development.

This chapter discusses the social functions of Embu and Mbeere oral literature, genre by genre, based on the assumption that each genre has a unique contribution to make towards the ultimate goal of making the social environment a better place to live in.

Oral narratives

Although the performance of the oral narrative takes place in a relatively relaxed atmosphere, it is taken very seriously as a didactic tool and as an art that contributes tremendously to the survival of the people in the geographical and social environment. The narratives help to explain the mystery of the world and unravel the nature of being. In the day-to-day existence of people, the cultural values expressed in the narratives act as the yardstick against which the society's moral standards are measured.

Myths and legends

Myths such as 'The Origin of Death' help people to cope with the nature of existence; this myth explains the origin of a phenomenon which human beings find very difficult to accept. It is difficult to accept that life, with all the struggle and joy that living brings, is destined to end. It is important that the explanation offered by the narrative brings in the decision of a supernatural being thus endowing the situation with a seriousness that is beyond human control. Human beings, represented by animal characters, are made to take the blame for this *status quo* and are therefore persuaded to accept its consequences. Notice also the way in which the narrative explains the situation as an irreversible decree of the supernatural thus forcing human beings to accept it as a *fait accompli*.

Narratives help to establish and explain the relationship between people and the natural world. The myth of the origin of Ndega's grove and that of the separation of Thagana and Tumbiri Rivers explain the existence of unusual and awe-inspiring geo-

---

*A. Roscoe, *Mother is Gold* (Cambridge: Cambridge University Press, 1971).

41

graphical phenomena. It should be noted here that these stories were created in the period when the societies concerned lived in an environment that was not developed, full of impenetrable forests and rivers that could only be crossed with unreliable make-shift bridges. Apart from helping people express their curiosity about the unusual aspects of the natural environment, such myths helped ease the people's fear of such features, hence facilitating society's harmonious co-existence with nature.

The myth, 'How Embu and Mbeere Separated' helps to explain the kinship bond between the two ethnic groups in a way that shows their closeness as well as their differences as social units. This myth contributes towards the people's understanding of their origins and hence gives them a sense of identity. Moreover, human beings the world over have been interested in the question of identity. It is this question that the myth addresses for both the Embu and the Mbeere.

From the foregoing examination of the function of Embu and Mbeere myths, Jung and Kerenyi's contention that :

A myth is a statement about society and man's place in it and in the surrounding universe. Myths are ways of explaining paradoxes, the paradoxes of social order within extra-social chaos, of the relationship of authority to power and the universe.*

Like myths, Embu and Mbeere legends have specific social functions. In the first place, these legends are creative records of the people's history. They provide creative links between the present and the past. A legend such as 'Kamunge son of Njeru Mutunyi', records the society's resistance against slave trade, one of the worst forms of oppression suffered by African peoples at the advent of colonialism. Kamunge's bravery is emphasised as a way of encouraging the youth to follow his example in circumstances which demand militant action. Similarly, the legend 'Cierume' teaches the people, particularly to women, the need for determination and a sense of purpose. The legend is aimed at inspiring women to emulate Cierume's strength of character by emphasising that courage and determination are not the preserve of men. Hence these legends reaffirm strong personality traits as seen through the deeds of renowned historical figures.

Legends are not restricted to stories created around positive historical figures. They include stories of people who were well known for contravening the expected moral codes. Like legends on positive historical figures, these legends about human weak-nesses serve a social function. They are aimed at discouraging social evils and misde-meanour. A legend such as 'Ndindika son of Mbarari and Nyaga son of Karaga' is a recreation of the story of two notorious Embu thieves which condemns stealing and parasitic dependency on other people. The legend discourages this kind of behaviour by warning that the consequences of such behaviour are excommunication, and even death.

---

*Jung and Kerenyi, *Introduction to a Science Mythology* (London: Routledge and Kegan Paul, 1970).

Ordinary tales

The ordinary narratives in this book are subdivided into three categories: stories on communal life, trickster stories and ogre stories, teach the accepted etiquette and norms of the Embu and the Mbeere.

Stories on communal life emphasise the need to nurture interdependence between an individual and the other members of his community; communalism is preferred to individualism. In the story, 'A Woman and Hyenas', people are warned on the consequences of detaching themselves from one's community and leading the life of a hermit. The woman experiences extreme loneliness and has nobody to come to her aid when she is confronted with danger. She dies a terrible, painful and demeaning death as food for hyenas because of divorcing herself from the community. The story entitled 'Mutema Kianda and His Son Gacau Mundu' condemns the tendency of the rich to despise the unsuccessul. Mutema Kianda regards other people as flies and so undertakes a difficult journey, together with his son, to search for a deserted land with no flies where they can slaughter their cattle and enjoy the meat without having to share it with anyone. The moral of the story is that everyone, including the rich, needs the co-existence offered by communal living arrangements. Mutema Kianda is blind to the fact that wealth is not synonymous with self-sufficiency. He may have the cattle, but without other people's co-operation, he cannot have the fire with which to roast the meat. Premature death is the inevitable punishment of the wealthy who have a condescending attitude towards other people.

Trickster stories teach the importance of distinguishing between external appearances and the inner motivations for survival in the social environment which condition people's behaviour. In 'Monkey and Crocodile', there is a sharp contrast between the way in which Crocodile relates to Monkey and his true intentions. On the surface, Crocodile is friendly and considerate to Monkey. This is illustrated in the way he offers Monkey a ride on his back to cross the river. But deep down, Crocodile is selfish, inconsiderate and calculating. His real intention is to lead Monkey to his death so that his heart may be used to treat the Crocodile king. The story further assures people that through wisdom and quickness of thought, they may thwart the malicious intentions of others and survive. This is illustrated by Monkey's wit and alertness which save him from Crocodile's machinations.

As discussed in the previous chapter, the ogre, through his man-eating habits, symbolises evil and cruelty in human beings. The ogre also represents the dangers lurking in the geographical and social environment. Hence, *ogre stories* teach society about the value of caution in dealing with people, and in one's movement in the physical world. In order to avoid confrontation with these dangers, individuals are taught to avoid moving around carelessly, acting thoughtlessly, judging people from external appearances and ignoring the advice of those with whom one lives.

In the story, 'My Father's Gourd', thoughtless pursuit of ideas is criticised. The girl's chase of the gourd at the expense of her safety is a thoughtless obsession which leads to her death. 'Kiondondoe and the Orgre' points at the consequences of not heeding advice. From 'The Young Man with Two Mouths', youths of marriageable age learn the importance of looking beyond appearances in judging personalities. The girl who eventually gets imprisoned as the ogre's wife is misled by the ogre's mask of good looks at the dance. She is so infatuated with these good looks that she can neither see the two mouths the other girls see, nor hear the ogre's warning song that he is an animal and not the handsome young man she thinks he is. In other words, she is both blind and deaf to the true personality of the ogre.

In Embu and Mbeere ogre stories, it is quite common to have a story in which the victim has been led into a confrontation with the ogre desperation rather than thoughtlessness or carelessness. An example is 'The Ogre's Milk', in which the two girls end up being eaten by the ogre for drinking his milk during a famine. Notice that before the girls take this course of action, they have tried other legitimate ways of finding food and failed. They have traversed distant lands in search of work to no avail. Such a story is used to remind the audience about the dangers inherent in the physical world. This lesson is emphasised in the conclusion to the story: "Now all the people co-operated in killing the ogres in the land. They then warned their children to avoid visiting deserted villages."

Besides their didactic role, Embu and Mbeere oral narratives serve the function of entertaining the audience because of their aesthetic qualities. There are humorous narratives used for entertaining the audience and relieving tension at story-telling sessions. A story such as 'The Dance of the Squirrel, Bush cat and Young Girls' entertains the audience through the absurdity of stitching Bush cat's eyes for the sake of courting dancing partners. Even stories with serious moral lessons contain aesthetic features which add to the entertainment of the audience. For example, the songs in 'A Girl and an Ogre Called Kibugi' give the audience the opportunity to relieve tension by participating in singing.

The story-telling session provides a social forum for people to meet and relax from the stresses of daily life. As will be seen later under functions of oral poetry, a social event that brings people together helps foster good relations between members of the same community. In this regard, the story-telling session enhances healthy relations between the participants.

Oral poetry

Poetry is a central pillar in the life of the Embu and the Mbeere. Almost every sphere of the people's existence is given rhythm and the breath of life by poetry. Its importance as part and parcel of life is introduced in an individual's life right at birth.

The whole celebration of the arrival of a baby is facilitated by poetry. Women sing as they await the birth of a baby and after the delivery, they congratulate the mother through song. In a way, poetry acts as an anaesthetic during the delivery of children in Embu and Mbeere. Poetry soothes the mother as she goes through the motions of labour. The melody from the singing of so many other women also gives her psychological comfort that she is not alone; through song, the other women seem to actually share the labour pains with the one giving birth.

Poetry is also used to welcome the baby into the world. Immediately after the birth, before the umbilical cord is cut, the women ululate four times for a boy and five times for a girl. They chant,

> *"Aririririiiti!*
> *Aririririiiti!*
> *Aririririiiti!*
> *Aririririiiti!*
> *Aririririiiti!"*

The variant ululation for male and female children is significant. Here, poetry is used to not only announce the gender of the newborn child, but also to assign him or her a status within that community. Hence, a boy is assigned a higher status than his female counterpart since, as discussed in Chapter One, the Embu and the Mbeere are patriarchal societies.

At the child-naming ceremony, poetry is used to underline the fact that the child belongs to the community as a whole and not only to his immediate family. In the song entitled, 'The Mother of a Child is not One', the women sing:

> The mother of a child is not one
> The mother of a child is not one
> Co-wife bring clothes
> Aunt bring water
> It is God's own blessing.

From this moment on, a child is initiated into a poetic world. If he is sick, the medicineman invokes the gods and the ancestors to assist in the healing process using poetry. When he cries, he is soothed with poetic lullabies. As he grows older, the child uses poetry to amuse himself during play-time, and later joins adults in using it to express emotions.

Some children's songs provide entertainment and rhythm during games. A significant number of these songs serve a dual purpose. A song such as 'Whoever Has Farted' entertains because it is funny, and at the same time inculcates good manners in the child. Similarly, the grazing song 'We Shall Lead Them' helps boys pass time and kill boredom while out in the bush herding livestock. However, it also passes a serious message about gender relations. From the song, the boy learns that his status is higher than that of a girl and that as a man, he has the responsibility of defending his people.

Children use songs to express emotions and vent frustrations. In 'Elephants You Licked Salt', children use animal characters to hit at the adults who ignore their needs. Whenever a child cries, complains the singer, he is given the breast to suck. To the singer, this is just a tactic to silence the child and ignore his deeper need for the adult's companionship. The child expresses his sense of loneliness through the image of being abandoned in "hyenas' dens".

An interesting children's song that plays a dual role is the lullaby, 'Baby, Stop Crying', The child-nurse (an older sibling or a young relative of the baby's mother) uses the rhythm of the song to soothe the baby who is probably strapped on her back. At the same time, she lets off frustrations through the words "child of big mouth". In the original language, there is a double meaning expressed in these words; they refer to both the baby and its mother. The baby has a big mouth because he cries all the time and bothers the child-nurse, while his mother has a big mouth because she is fond of scolding the child-nurse about the way she handles the baby in her absence. Through poetry, the child-nurse is able to hit at those who keep her from joining other children at play and do not seem to appreciate her efforts.

Among the Embu and the Mbeere, poetry is used by adults to express emotions. Women, who form the majority of the workforce in Embu and Mbeere, use poetry to express their frustrations about this *status quo* such as in the song, 'This Year I Shall not Dig'. They use the genre to voice the ironical situation in which they find themselves, whereby they shoulder the responsibility of feeding the family. During famines, they sometimes have to go far from home to work among foreign people for grain to feed their families. Yet, if anybody has to starve because of food shortages, it is the women.

At weddings, women use poetry to demand recognition in society for the important role they play in delivering children. This demand is apparent in the following excerpt from the song, 'Whose Honey is This?'

> Let me be given some as it passes along
> This brew belongs to child we delivered
> You men! We know you were hiding while we were delivering
> We are the owners of that child
> Let us be given some as it passes along.

Quite often, women take advantage of the poetic licence availed by this genre to express their dissatisfaction with their social marginalisation. The song 'Kanyanya Let Me Push You Along', for example, enables women to comment on a fundamental practice in which their role as parents is often taken for granted. When a girl is married, the dowry is paid to the father and the mother's contribution in bringing up the bride is hardly acknowledged. The singer is using the song to send an emissary to her son-in-law asking for compensation for her role in delivering his bride; a role that has not been hitherto recognised since all the dowry has been given to the girl's father and male relatives.

46

The woman decides to send this message through someone else rather than do it directly since the great respect between a woman and her son-in-law in Embu and Mbeere culture forbids a close meeting between them. In fact, in the days when there was plenty of bush, if one of the parties happened to be walking along the path and noticed the other approaching from the opposite direction, he or she would duck into the bush to avoid a face-to-face meeting. In sending this message through someone else, the singer is showing her respect to her son-in-law and to the culture of her people.

It is also significant that the bride's mother chooses the bridegroom's mother as her emissary. As the mother of the target recipient of the message she is closer to him than anybody else and is therefore, likely to gain his audience easily. Finally, as a fellow woman and agemate, the bridegroom's mother will definitely understand the situation and empathise with the bride's mother. In approaching the issue this way, therefore, women use the song genre to criticise the *status quo* and to enhance solidarity with each other, not only in an indirect and creative manner but also in a way that respects the culture of their community.

At work, women use the song genre to comment on the *status quo* and to cement their solidarity. This is illustrated by the songs they sing at work parties. It is true that many of the work songs are aimed at facilitating the job at hand and preventing boredom. The musicality in the songs creates rhythm for the task and enhances the unity of the work party. However, some of the words in the songs are used to underline the importance of unity and co-operation between the women at a level that is higher than that of the job at hand. The song, 'Let Women be Supported' articulates the solidarity women view as necessary for their survival in a society where they have to work extremely hard.

Men also take advantage of the possibilities of oral poetry to express solidarity with each other. Some of the songs sung by the male initiates during seclusion, after circumcision, are aimed at cementing their relations with one another. The word "brother", used by initiates to address each other should be viewed in this light. New adult initiates regard each other, as brothers and handle their social responsibilities together. In the song, 'I Thought It Had Been Postponed', the initiates refer to themselves as "battalions" and as "young warriors linked by the same secret". Such expressions underscore the solidarity the initiates view as necessary for them to carry out their duty as defenders of their communities.

Oral poetry is also used to enhance communal solidarity in times of war or political crisis. The songs the warriors sing as they perform exercises in preparation for war help strengthen the bonds between them. The war recitations which women use to praise their warriors boost the latter's morale and re-assure them that the rest of the community is behind them and appreciates their efforts.

In the colonial era, the Embu and Mbeere used the song genre to react to new human relationships and to express their dissatisfaction with the new form of government. Oral poetry gave the people a channel through which they could express their reactions to a situation which presented new working conditions as well as unconventional human relations.

Many of the songs from the colonial era are protest poetry, i.e protests against colonial oppression. The song, 'They are Being Weighed by Force' protests against forced labour on European settlement farms. It attacks all the evils inherent in this system, such as exploitation, alienation of people from their families, and even loss of lives. 'Kagoce and the Deep Waters' is a protest as well as a praise song. The song acclaims the bravery of a man named Kagoce who openly questioned the colonialists on the issue of forced labour. Apart from encouraging Kagoce in his political campaign, the song was an indirect way of sensitising people on the oppressive nature of forced labour and urging them to rise up against it.

'Sons of Mbeere are the Soldiers' voices the people's protest against the forced conscription of Mbeere young men into the colonial army. Since these unwilling conscripts were not trained in the use of the new weapons, they ended up doing odd jobs such as cooking, which were regarded as unmanly. The song reacts to this situation with bitter satire as seen in the excerpt below:

Soldiers have gone marching ii!
They write letters
And the letter is read
And it says good morning
I am just sending you greetings
And I shall come at the end of the year.
White men are no joke!

The letter is personified to satirise the situation where an inanimate piece of paper now substitutes a husband and a father.

The conscripted men are not spared the satire either. They are ridiculed through the repetition of "Soldiers oh! Soldiers oh! Soldiers ... Soldiers have gone marching". The song comments on the emasculating effects of the conscription when it refers to the young men as the "uncircumcised sons of Mbeere".

Satirical songs are used to ridicule and, therefore, correct misdemeanour. If a person within a community is known to engage in unacceptable behaviour, a satirical song is composed to ridicule his actions. Notice how openly the real identity of the offender is revealed in some of the songs such as 'Nyaga son of Gituro Woos All Women'. The song, which ridicules the promiscuity of a man, leaves the audience in no doubt as to the identity of the culprit. It does not stop at naming him as "Nyaga", because this is a fairly common name in Embu and Mbeere, but goes further and repeats that the cassanova is none other than Nyaga son of Gituro. The direct identification of the culprit is very effective in discouraging bad behaviour in both the culprit and in prospective offenders.

The oral poetry genre enables the Embu and Mbeere to react to drastic cultural changes. The people express their reactions through satirical songs; for example, the effect of the introduction of the money economy on traditional practices is given some attention in 'A Girl Being Sold in Kilograms'. The song ridicules fathers who take advantage of the tradition of paying dowry to enrich themselves by making exorbitant demands on those who marry their daughters. The song argues that it is as if the brides-to be are now being evaluated alongside commodities for sale such as beans. Through the use of satirical songs, the people are able to comment on cultural disintegration. The people's shock at the introduction of prostitution is expressed through the song, 'They are Asking for Her All Over'. The song comments on prostitution as an evil way of life which alienates women from the traditional values of their communities causing them to lose self-respect and preventing them from playing their traditional roles as wives and mothers.

Curiously, funeral songs and dirges are markedly absent from the Embu and the Mbeere oral poetry. That the dead were thrown into the bush without much ceremony rather than being buried, would only partly explain why the two communities do not have dirges. It would still be expected that these two peoples would mourn the loss of the members of their communities through the expressive genre of oral poetry. But perhaps, the absence of such poetry has more to do with the fact that among the Embu and the Mbeere, poetry celebrates life, whether in joy or in sadness, and that this kind of perspective would exclude death from the celebration as it negates life. However, the work song 'All Strength Will be Eaten by Termites' alludes to death and gives the social attitude towards death.

Lastly, as mentioned earlier, the poetry genre acts as a link which fosters good relations between people. During ceremonies such as initiation, the communties use dance as a therapeutic experience which cleanses them psychologically as well as physically and hence prepares them, not only for the ritual, but also for a renewal of their existence in ushering in a new generation of adults into the society.

Proverbs

A proverb could be regarded as the nutshell in which a people's philosophy, worldview, wisdom, values and attitudes are encapsulated. Deep messages are contained in each proverb and almost every proverb plays multiple social roles. Proverbs, especially about human relations, are didactic. They broaden one's outlook on life, sound warnings against dangerous courses of action, and correct behaviour through satire without inflicting personal injury. They also facilitate the conveying of messages which are difficult to communicate directly and can be used to buttress a point of view. The two communities use proverbs to fan themselves when the weather of life is too hot and oppressive, or as a walking stick to prop them in uncertain times. This genre, which consists of brief creative statements known as proverbs, is an anchor that sustains society in its day-to-day handling of life.

Embu and Mbeere proverbs teach about cultural values and human relationships. The value of communalism is underscored in the proverb 'People from the same village rescue each other from the fangs of a hyena' (201). The proverb encourages neighbourliness between people in the same community, but another warns that 'Marriage ties with neighbours creates enmity' (205). The latter teaches that even if people live in the same community, they nevertheless should be wary of very close ties because frequent interaction may breed ill feelings. It may be noted in passing that for almost every Embu and Mbeere proverb, it is easy to find another which seemingly contradicts it. This should be viewed as a strength rather than a weakness in the genre. It is a characteristic that enables proverbs to remind human beings that everything has a limit and that one should avoid excesses.

Proverbs are sharp cautionary tools used to caution people on a wide range of life experiences and human relationships. They are like the stick in the proverb, 'If a person wants to dig out sweet potatoes, he uses a sharp digging stick' (55). Through a careful choice of proverbs, one can warn about a whole range of human experiences. A warning about the need to look beneath the surface in assessing situations and in dealing with other human beings is sounded by proverbs such as, 'People usually cross the river where it sounds loudest' (72) and 'If you see it (snake) silent it has swallowed' (72). The need to relate to people according to their temperaments is emphasised by the proverb, 'Devils hate jokes' (23). There are clear cautionary messages in proverbs on areas of human interaction which are normally seen as beneficial rather than a loss such as 'Love means trouble' (6) and 'A person's best friend is the one who gives her the pregnancy that eventually kills her' (1).

Embu and Mbeere proverbs instruct people on economic survival through warning against bad planning as in, 'The traveller does not leave a banana roasting on a fire while he goes on his journey' (11). 'If you cook two pots of food at the same time, one of them gets burnt' (66) cautions against handling too many things at the same time and encourages quality as opposed to quantity of work. On the other hand, if a person fails because of bad planning, he is expected to face the reality as recommended in the proverb 'If you step on faeces with one foot step with the other one as well' (91).

A proverb such as 'Spreading a bed properly does not guarantee peaceful sleep' (289) contains a great deal of wisdom. Normally, people engage in certain tasks or projects expecting to reap direct and immediate fruits from their labour. Yet, quite often, experience has shown that hard work or dedication is not always commensurate with the rewards. The proverb above broadens one's outlook on life, but also helps people bear the disappointment of not being rewarded for their hard work.

Embu and Mbeere proverbs are used to ridicule bad behaviour in a poignant but indirect manner. Unlike songs, proverbs do not identify the culprit of bad behaviour. Their satire thrives on the use of imagery and metaphorical language. Greed is often satirised by the use of proverbs that emulate images of animals and birds associated with dirty eating habits. For example, 'The eagle was brought down by greed' (17) warns about the destructive consequences of greed. Satire acquires full expression through personification such as in the proverb, 'The mouth that ate the grain is the same one which asks, "what shall I plant"' (34). This warns against eating without thinking about the future.

The two communities' wisdom of ages is couched in their proverbs such as 'Death has no promise' (295), which directly and precisely states the fact that death does not make an appointment with its victims on when it will come. This is evident throughout human experience. The question then is, why should a proverb state what is an obvious fact?

Owing to human beings' love for life, people find it difficult to accept the proximity of their lives' end even when they are critically ill. The proverb therefore reminds people that as they enjoy life, death is always close by, and that it is therefore important to take the necessary precautions just in case it is one's destined time to die.

The proverb genre is very effective in communicating social attitudes. Quite a significant number of Embu and Mbeere proverbs communicate the two communities' attitudes towards certain subjects and certain sections of society. The communities' attitudes towards fate, fortune and misfortune are expressed in proverbs such as, 'A person's share is never inherited by someone else' (288). This proverb is used to comfort and encourage people to continue struggling when they are tempted to give up because their equals have made greater achievements than them. The proverb reminds people that their share of success will come in its own good time because none of their successful equals could have possibly taken what was destined to be their good fortune. On the other hand, if the unsuccessful person's problem is that others have succeeded through his efforts, the proverb, 'Whoever starts making a rope is not the one who finishes it' (303), which means that fortune can be fickle, reminds him that this is only natural.

The proverbs which relate to the socially and physically handicapped such as 'The person under the tree is the one who knows what ants feed on' (277) solicit people's sympathy towards the less fortunate. If one happens not to have experienced disability and tends to despise people assuming that it is their fault be handicapped, one is reminded that 'to lead an unhappy life is not one's wish' (258).

There are proverbs which specifically encourage people to assist those who are worse-off than themselves; for example, 'While you are giving millet to birds, give also the chicken to eat' (261) advises people to give their surplus resources to the less fortunate rather than throw them away. This proverb is linked to the belief that there are blessings in assisting those who are handicapped.

There is a significant number of Embu and Mbeere proverbs which amplify some important beliefs related to the people's attitude towards the handicapped such as 'Do not laugh at a cripple before he passes by and while you are still alive' (259). This proverb is linked to the belief that if you laugh at a handicapped person, you will suffer disability or give birth to a handicapped child.

Embu and Mbeere proverbs convey the communities' attitude towards men and women and the social expectations of both. They can be used as Parameters of examining gender relations; men are regarded as strong in contrast to women, who are regarded as weak. This is reflected by the proverbs, 'If men are defeated, women dare not attempt' (239), and 'If a he-goat cannot overturn, would a she-goat manage?' (239).

Women are regarded as the cause of men's downfall, and there are proverbs which caution against a woman's influence on her son or on her husband; for example, 'Whoever is controlled by his mother is a fool' (224) and 'One who steals with an uncircumcised boy is happy when he gets circumcised, but one who steals with his wife is only relieved when she dies' (235).

Although it would not be right to draw a clear-cut line and argue that all proverbs on women are negative and all proverbs on men are positive, the vast majority of proverbs give a negative portrayal of male and female characters refer to women. Furthermore, there are proverbs which are used to justify traditions which favour men at the expense of women, and others which show complete disregard of women's feelings as human beings in the face of these traditions. The proverb, 'There is no cock which serves only one hen' (256), favours men over women because it justifies polygamy without regard to women's reaction to this tradition where two or more women are forced to share one man. In fact, there is a condemnatory proverb in reference to women in this situation and which is insensitive to their feelings: 'Two wives are two pots of poison'(221). These proverbs serve as agents of socialisation in the community with regard to expectations of men and women.

In spite of the discriminatory nature of some of these proverbs on women, the Embu and the Mbeere have often found the genre to be a very effective tool in judging cases which involve male-female relationships. Such cases are, for instance, where a young man is accused of making a girl pregnant and he denies in order to avoid the responsibility of marrying her or maintaining the child.

As proverbs are normally used only among equals or by a senior to his junior, it is the elders who use proverbs to probe or counsel the young couple or to argue with each other about the two sides of the case before them. Hence to probe the girl to talk about an otherwise embarassing subject about how she got pregnant, the elders might say, 'What is stored in the heart is removed through talking' (53). And to the young man who wants to evade the responsibility which comes with his enjoyment, the elders would say, 'Sweetness finishes teeth' (70). In defence of the young man, the elders representing him can state that the girl is equally responsible for the outcome of the relationship by reminding the elders representing the girl that, 'If you tell your sister to sit decently and she refuses you should laugh at her' (237). If there is room for reconciling the two young people and counselling them to opt for marriage, the elders will conclude with 'Two hands wash each other' (213).

It should be noted here that up to the present time when most cases in Kenya are judged in modern courts under common law, there are quite a number of cases or aspects of cases which are found to be better handled by community elders because of certain intricacies touching on tradition. Besides the foregoing example, cases involving land, succession and divorce are also adjudged in a like manner. Proverbs have been found to be most useful in a adjudicating cases because of their precision in articulating arguments and supporting deep arguments based on tradition.

Riddles

Riddles are perhaps the most misunderstood genre of oral literature. For a long time, scholars of oral literature have dismissed riddles as a genre that does not deserve serious academic consideration. This misunderstanding is based on the major strengths of the riddle rather than its weaknesses as a genre. Riddles are tremendously entertaining and for this reason, they have appeal for children and adults.

Ruth Finnegan finds it necessary to apologise for the inclusion of a section on riddles in her study of oral literature when she says:

It may be surprising to find riddles included in a survey of oral literature. However, riddles in Africa have regularly been considered to be a type of art form, albeit often of minor and childish interest, and have long been included in studies on oral literature.*

However, riddles are a serious genre of oral literature and it would be a misnomer to dismiss them as an art form of "minor and childish interest". Charles T. Scott is perhaps the only oral literature scholar who comes closest to recognising the need to re-examine the inferior place into which the riddle has hitherto been relegated when he says:

The status of the riddle as a minor genre of folklore can probably be attributed to several rather widely held conclusions about riddles in general. One is that their primary function is mere entertainment or amusement. A second is that they are most often associated with the genres of children rather than with the presumably more serious preoccupations of adults. A third conclusion is that their content and language tend to focus predominantly on concrete, homespun details rather than on the more abstract features of human relations and behaviour which one expects, for instance, in proverbs and aphorisms. Doubtless, there is considerable accuracy in these conclusions, but there is also no doubt that each of these conclusions can be challenged as valid generalisations.**

---

*Ruth Finnegan, *Oral Literature in Africa* (Nairobi: Oxford University Press 1976) p. 426.
**For a detailed study, see "The Song as an Expression of Solidarity for Embu and Mbeere Women", in Ciarunji Chesaina, *Perspectives on Women in African Literature* (Nairobi: Impact Asssociates, 1994) pp. 29–44.

Embu and Mbeere riddles serve important social functions. Apart from their entertainment function, these riddles are didactic and as such have a significant role to play in the socialisation of children. For both adults and children, Embu and Mbeere riddles are effective as mental exercises to keep people alert for effective communication. These riddles are also useful as reflections of accepted norms and etiquette. Like proverbs, riddles provide a channel through which people can marvel at cultural change.

In the socialisation of children, riddles are important in cognitive development. They help children develop their imaginative powers by providing them with problems which exercise their minds. Because these riddles are based on items found in the children's environment and culture, they provoke children to be alert about the world around them and therefore, develop the habit of being observant. Owing to their creative qualities, such as the use of imagery, riddles provide an interesting teaching method.

There are many Embu and Mbeere riddles which teach about the material culture of the people. The round hut which was an important part of the traditional architecture among the Embu and the Mbeere features frequently in riddles such as in 'A hut with one pillar' (45) and in 'Go that way and I go this way we meet at the slippery place' (73).

Through riddles, children are made aware of the economic culture of the people. The two major economic activities of the Embu and the Mbeere, agriculture and pastoralism, are reflected in the constant reference to crops and livestock in riddles. (For illustrations see numbers 44, 47, 51, 54, 55 and 77 for agriculture and numbers 20, 23, 28, 29, 44, 81, and 101 for pastoralism).

Riddles are also used to teach about human relationships, accepted etiquette and norms in the society. For example, the respect a man owes his elder brother and the respectable distance between a man and his daughter are alluded to in 'My father has been knocked down by my younger paternal uncle' (83) and 'A girl wrestling with her father!' (82) respectively. Wrestling is a very common game between boys, that is, between children of the same sex and age. The two riddles give children a chance to ridicule situations in which the social norms seem to have been flouted and then sigh with relief when the answers to the riddles reveal that it is not human beings who are involved, but the axe and a tree in the first case; and the small and big grinding stones in the second.

As is the case with proverbs, it is quite common for riddles to play multiple roles. The two riddles, for example, teach about human relations and economic activities; they also help children to learn how to associate ideas with concrete objects. They are important in the education of children because of their uncomplicated form and their straight-forward question-and-answer performance technique. They form a genre which offers children a chance to be participants and not merely audiences. Children are at ease with this genre from a very early age. It would therefore follow that riddles contribute to children's education during their formative years and in a way, enable them to develop confidence in themselves and in the world around them. If it is true that children are the adults of tomorrow, riddles perform a crucial social function in preparing culturally integrated members of the future society.

The social function of Embu and Mbeere riddles is not limited to the education of the young; they serve other functions which are relevant to adults. Some riddles express cultural attitudes and remind people of the accepted norms and behaviour. A riddle such as 'When will your obese sister get married?' (95) expresses the people's negative attitude towards girls who delay marriage. The description of the unmarried girl, even her association with the round and obese grain store, warns girls who have attained the age of marriage about the scorn they will suffer if they delay taking up their role as wives.

Similarly, a riddle such as 'An uncircumcised boy up a tree' (22) which tends to equate the red-bottomed monkey with an uncircumcised boy also expresses a cultural attitude and would appeal to adults as well as children. Uncircumcised boys are associated with dirt and unacceptable childish behaviour. Among the Embu and the Mbeere, calling a man an uncircumcised boy is one of the worst insults imaginable. This riddle warns men against engaging in any behaviour which might cause them to be equated with the red-bottomed monkey.

Riddles enable adults to comment on and ridicule unwarranted situations. One such situation the two societies have been able to ridicule through the use of riddles is the colonial situation. The riddle 'Eitieitie!' (21) describing the English language as the language of monkeys and 'A white man peeping through the window' (94) specifically ridicule the colonial masters. In Embu and Mbeere, it is an insult to call a person a monkey (nugu or ntheeru in the two languages). It means that the victim of the insult is not a full human being and that he is stupid. The first riddle is used to insult the colonialist and hence call to ridicule his treatment of Africans. The second riddle also insults the colonialist by comparing him to mucus. There is an implication here of the white man being seen as scum; something disgusting that should be thrown away. In a sense, therefore, these two riddles were used as a means of silent resistance against colonial domination.

Many items introduced during the initial contact between Africans and Europeans have become subjects for riddles. These include money (63), matches (65,67), cups (72), metal cooking pots (68), bicycles (69), motor cycles (70) and the aeroplane (64). Riddles in such cases enable people to comment on and marvel at the introduction of new material culture. Notice the humour people derive from some of these objects, such as in the personification of the cup and in describing the noise made by a motorcycle as similar to farting.

Riddles entertain both adults and children. They also help to sharpen their wits and exercise their mental faculties of adults as well as children in story-telling sessions. Riddles are entertaining because their style provokes humour and laughter. The entertainment value of riddles has been often erroneously underrated. In societies such as the Embu and Mbeere, where an individual has to struggle so hard for his survival and

55

that of his family, entertainment comes in as an important form of relaxation to refresh people and make them more productive in their struggle for survival. In this regard, riddles have as high a value as any other genre.

Puzzles

Many of the social functions of puzzles overlap with those of riddles discussed above. However, there are some fine differences owing to the literary uniqueness of the two genres. For example, the unravelling of some of the puzzles depends more on common sense than on familiarity with the culture from which they come. There are others which, like riddles, are culture-specific; for example, number 4; about the woman, her baby and a monkey. A puzzle such as this one serves the purpose of teaching about the culture of the people while at the same time boosting peoples's observation skills.

Embu and Mbeere puzzles are performed with the main purpose of entertaining the participants and passing time. Many of these puzzles are humorous in form and in the challenges they pose to participants who try to unravel them. The participants are entertained, for instance, by the absurdity of the situations presented and by the equally absurd suggestions offered in attempts to unravel the puzzles. Notice this absurdity in number 8, where a boy wants to marry his father's mother because the father married the boy's mother.

The various subjects from which puzzles are created make it possible for human beings to joke about subjects which are normally taken seriously as well as those which are awe-inspiring. The puzzle about a man having to lie down in the middle of the road in order to speed up his arrival at the mortuary (10) jokes about death in an absurd kind of way. Such puzzles help people to cope with the fact of difficult phenomena such as death.

Owing to their use of ambiguity, and the incongruity between the problem and the answer solicited, puzzles provide the participants with a forum for mental exercise. Although the main participants in puzzle sessions are children, the complexity of some of these texts offers an avenue for sharpening the wits of young and more mature adults. A good example of this is where the respondent has to figure out how to help a goat, sweet potato vines and a leopard cross the river in such a way that the goat does not feed on the vines and the leopard does not eat the goat (1).

Lastly, like riddles, Embu and Mbeere puzzles help people to comment on the introduction of new material culture. Notice, for example, the way in which the puzzle about using a syringe to suck orange juice for healing a critically ill patient helps people to marvel at the wonders of modern technology and modern medicine.

PART TWO: LITERARY TEXTS

Chapter 5

NG'ANO — NARRATIVES

Myths

Uria Embu na Mbeere magaukanire

Tene tene muno mbere ya aa uma matari aciare Embu na Mbeere maari mundu na muruang'ina. Maaturaga vamwe, makarithia vamwe, wana indo ciao ciari ciao itakugarukanua. Andu acio maturaga wa vamwe.

Riu Embu, nimarivaga Mbeere muno. Mumbeere ndangiagambire riria Muembu akwaria. Wana irio rimwe muembu niwaricaga Mumbeere amuroretie akamuva we avaa. Mbeere atuiririte Embu "Mbari ya Karega" niundu wa uumu wa kiongo, nake Embu agatuira Mbeere "Mbari ya Yura" niundu wa kurikwa urii-ri.

Riu indi imwe Embu na Mbeere nimatuire kiathi marue mbaara yao ithire. Muthenya wa mbaara wakinya, Mbeere maukire na miti nao Embu magiuka na nviu ithondeketwe igekara ta miti. Mbaara iria yari vandu vau! Mbeere yarivua-i! Embu matindikire Mbeere nginya Kiethiga nao Embu makithii gutura Muthiru.

Vau nivo Mbeere mambiririe gutura kundu kwa muthanga gutaumaga irio, nao Embu magiaka kuria gukuvi na mutitu kuumaga irio .

How Mbeere and Embu separated

Place of origin : Thau (Embu)
Narrator : Stephen Njokera (Male; 75 years)

Long long ago before our grandfathers were born, Embu and Mbeere were brothers. They lived together, looked after their livestock together, and even owned property jointly.

Now the Embu used to beat the Mbeere very often. A Mbeere person could not utter a word when an Embu person was talking. There were even times when an Embu person could eat food while a Mbeere was just watching and only give him some when he himself was full. Mbeere

59

people had nicknamed Embu people, "The Clan of Rebels" because of their stubborness, while the Embu had nicknamed the Mbeere, "The Clan of Famine" because of their being denied food.

Now, one time, Embu and Mbeere made a date to fight and finish all their conflicts. Now on the day of the fight Mbeere brought sticks as their weapons while Embu brought swords disguised as sticks. The war which was fought! The Mbeere were beaten! The Embu pushed the Mbeere until Kiethiga, while the Embu went to live in Muthiru.

That is when the Mbeere started living in the sandy land where crops cannot grow, while the Embu built their homes near the forest on productive land.

* * *

Kiumo kia Gititu kia Mwene Ndega

Ava ava nambari iiria, vaaria, vaaria, ava ava ukionaga Kiamuvove, vaaria uguo ukionaga Riakirathi, vai runji ruai mathiga.

Riu runjiri ruu, nivo Nthara ethambaga. Na Nthara aai mwana mwari mwaro ma. Mwari ngatha wavenagia tá nthoroko. Angiathekire, njerumi yaikanua kau! We! Gutii mwari wai angiruga Nthara.

Riu Ndega-i nake kwa arithagia kathakari kai rutere rwa runji. Riu Nthara akithamba Ndega akimwona akiuria. "Mwari uuria ukwithamba vaaria ugukenga ta ruru niru nuria u? Kanthii ngamwone."

Ndega agikinya na varia mwana mwari aari akithira niurire. Akimucaria muthanjeri agitura. Amutura agicioka Ng'omberi ciake. Muthenya ugituka atamwona ringi wa akiinukira.

Ruyuri Ndega agicioka wa vau kathakari wana ng'ombe ciake. Akirithangia we. Waindi kariua gakinya varia gatagati, Nthare uuria ringi, akithamba runjiri ruria. Ndega akivita akiuga, "Umunthi uyu narega kwinukia uuria mwana mwari! Nwanga ndetagwa Ndega Muregi!"

Wa Ndega agitiga ng'ombe iricaga akinyururuka egiritanitie ana mati akithii ethithite akungite ki. Akiumirira mwana mwari "muku!" "Mwana mwari akivugura. Nake Ndega akimukethia akimuria, Mwana mwari ketheka!"

Mwana mwari akimuria, "Kwokunvavukia kwokwenda atia?"

Ndega akimwira, "Taundu ukwithitha ninie, kwa ngwenda tuthii nawe kuuria gwakwa ukandugagire!"

Mwana mwari akitheka na nthoni uria ari mathekaga. Ndega ona uguo akimwenda muno. Akimwira, "Kwa ngwenda tuthii nawe utuike muka wakwa. Witagwa atia?" Mwana mwari akimwira:" "Ndii ritwa."

Ndega akimwira, "Ucio ti undu. Ritwa ngagucariria. Andu enyu..." Mwana mwari akirugira uvoro akimwira, "Twathii nawe, ndukanae gukamburia andu etu."

Ndege akimwira, "Ndigakuria."

60

Makithii wa makiambiriria gwikara vamwe, muthuri na mwongia. Magiikaara, magiikaara. Mwongia agwica kugia ivu. Nake Ndega niundu woria amwendete akimuthinjira mburi noru ma. Ndeterera mwana aciarua ta mutugo niundu Ndega ekaga uria akwenda. Ritwa Ndega riaumite vau va umu wa kiongo wa Ndega. Ndega Muregi!

Riu-i Ndega wa akiara rutara, wa akiambiriria gwokeria muka tunyama turia twai tunoru. Ingi wa indi Ndega agutinia kanyama egue kana ni kaviu: 'Vurio!' I mwongia akuthara kanyama!

"Ngagwitaga Nthara, muvuria uyu!" Vau nivo ritwa Nthara riaumire.

Riu Nthara akinyia indi yake agiciara kavici getagwa Irugi. Gagikura, gagikura. Gagituika mundu mugima. Irugi atiuka mundu mugima nina akimwira, "Thama."

Irugi akithama akithii gutura weru, navau vetagwa Thau. Akigurana agiciara kavici getagwa Ireri. Riu munthi umwe Irugi agiuka kuthokeria nina nethe guku mucii. Makirete njovi nyingi ma. Ingi mutici Thau ni kwa uki?

Ndega akunyua njovi akuriwa ndio. Nthara wakimuria, "Kwotangundagia njovi?" Ndega akimuria, "Ta undu watua gwitia njovi-i andu enyu makarete ri?"

Nthara akimuria, "Kinthi ndiagukanirie ngikwira ndukae gukamburia andu etu?" Ndega akimwira, "Ndingienda kwigua ukimbira ndigakurie andu enyu. Thii wire andu enyu mathokie!" Nake Nthara akimwira, "Uretia ithoki ria andu etu? Nukuriona!"

Wa Nthara akira Irugi, "Mundani njira mwinuke!"

Irugi wa akimunda njira na andu ake, wa makinuka.

Nthara akimunda kwina kigaru. Akiiviuria nviurio. Arika kwina kigaru mbura nayo ikigamba "Puuu!" Ikiura! Ikiura! Ikiura! Kamucii ka Ndega wana ng'ombe ciake, ikiurira na indo ciake cionthe ikinyua nthi. Riu vau vakigia iria inene muno. Vagicioka vakimera miti vakigia gititu kinene muno. Wa andu magigitwira ritwa, Gititu kia Mwene Ndega.

The origin of Ndega's grove

Place of origin :   Kagaari (Embu)
Narrator   :   Jesse Njeru (Male; 75 yrs)

Here here; that side just there. Here here overlooking Kiamuvove, just here overlooking Riakirathi, there was a river of rocks.

Now at that river, that is where Nthara was bathing. And Nthara was a really beautiful girl. A beautiful girl whose skin shone like pigeon peas. If she laughed, the gap in her teeth! You listen! No girl could surpass Nthara in beauty.

Now Ndega on his part, he was herding his animals at a bush near the river. Now, while Nthara was bathing, Ndega saw her and asked, "Who is that girl bathing who is shining like something out of this world? Let me go and see."

When Ndega reached where the girl had been, she had disappeared. He looked for her among the reeds but he could not find her. When he failed to get her he went back to his cattle. The day passed before he could get her again, so he went home.

The following day, Ndega went back to the same bush with his cattle. He grazed them for a while. When the sun was sitting in the middle of the sky, there is Nthara again, bathing in the

61

same river. Ndega swore, "Today, today if I fail to take the girl home! I'll know that my name is not Ndega the Rebel!"

So he left the cattle grazing and descended, hiding by the bushes. He went hiding, bending dead silent. He just shot out before the girl, muku! The girl turned. Ndega greeted her, "You girl, receive my greetings!"

The girl asked him, "What do you want that you frighten me so?"

"Although you are hiding from me, I just want to take you with me to my house so that you can be cooking for me," Ndega said.

The girl laughed shyly, the way girls usually do. When Ndega saw that, he loved her very much. He told her, "What I want is for you to come with me and become my wife. What is your name?"

The girl told him, "I have no name."

Ndega told her, "That is nothing. I shall look for a name for you. Your people..." The girl cut him short and said to him, "If I go with you, never ask me about my people! What have I told you? Don't you ever ask me about my people!"

"I shall never ask you," Ndega assured her.

They went and started living together as man and wife. They lived together, they lived together. The wife got pregnant. And Ndega, because he loved her so much, slaughtered a goat for her; a very fat goat. He did not wait for the child to be born because Ndega used to do as he pleased. The name Ndega originated from Ndega's stubbornness. Ndega the Rebel!

Now Ndega prepared a rack and started roasting the choice pieces of fat meet for his wife. No sooner had he cut a small piece of meat to check whether it was ready than, Vurio! Didn't the woman snatch the meat? Ndega told her, "I shall be calling you Nthara, you snatcher!" That is where the name Nthara came from.

Now when her time came, Nthara gave birth to a boy called Irugi. The boy grew up, the boy grew up. He became a grown-up. When Irugi became a grown-up, Nthara told him, "Migrate!"

Irugi migrated and went to live in the scrubland in that place called Thau. He married and got a boy called Ireri. Now one day, Irugi came to pay his father and mother a visit. They brought with them a lot of beer indeed. Oh, don't you know Thau has abundant honey!

Ndega drunk the beer until he was completely drunk. Nthara told him, "Won't you give me some beer?" Ndega asked her, "Now, while you are asking for beer, when will your people bring some?"

Nthara asked him, "Didn't I forbid you to ask me about my people?

Ndega told her, "I wouldn't like you to tell me not to ask you about your people. Go tell your people to bring beer!"

And Nthara told him, "Do you really want my people's beer? You will see it now."

Now Nthara told Irugi, "Set off and go home." Irugi set off with his people and went home.

Nthara started dancing kigaru. She swung herself and swung herself. As she danced, the rain sounded, puuu! It rained and rained and rained and rained. Ndega's home and his cattle, his goats! Ndega was drowned with all his property. He disappeared. Now there, was filled with a huge lake. And then trees grew and eventually there was a huge grove. And the people named it Ndega's Grove.

* * *

62

Uria gikuu kiambiririe

Nyamu ino igwitwa nviti, kwokuga ni kindu kiaro? Nto! Nto! Nto! Nviti ni kindu gicuku muno! Nviti ni nyamu i rwetho, iyendete na ningoroku muno!

Tene tene muno-i, kwai Nviti na Nvuko. Ati ndui? Nviti na Nvuko. Riu andu nimekarire makiyuria, "Angwa nu tugutuma kwa Mwene Njeru akamenye andu magekagwa atia makura?"

Wa magicurania magitua matigatume mundu umwe. Makiuga nimatuma andu aya, airi. kenda umwe angiremererwa, uria wingi athii na mbere. Wa magitua matume Nviti na Nvuko.

Nviti na Nvuko ciakinya Kirinyaga, kuuria iguru kwa Mwene Njeru, ikimutariria ndumiriri cia andu. Mwene Njeru akithikiriria agiciira niaituma wa cioiri woguo ciatumitwe ni andu. Agiciira ndumiriri yake iria igakinya mbere nwayo ikavingia watho wake. Uvoro uria ugakinya mbere nwaguo ukavinga.

Nviti ikinengerwa ndumiriri ya gikuu nayo Nvuko ikinengerwa ndumi riri ya mwoyo. Ta nyamu ino ciamate njira iciokie ndumiriri cia Mwene Njeru kuuria nthi.

Kubu! Kubu! Kubu! Ikithii, rimwe riiganene rimwe itiganite. Ciakuviviria nthi, Nvuko ikiambiriria kuviavia ikinyie ndumiriri yayo mbere ya nviti. Iking'arang'aria. Ikithii. Wa igikinya mbere ya Nviti.

Yakinya ikivanda ivaririe kuvecana uvoro. Ikinogorora. Ikithua kiongo. Ikiyuria, "Angwa mbirirwe atia?"

Ikithua kiongo ringi, ikiambiriria, "Mbirirweee... Mbirirweee....Mbirirweee.." Nvuko itai iratumbukania uvoro, Nviti igikinya wekiuga:

"Kinthi tuiirirwe andu makura makucage magaikua na vau nja ndicage?"

"Kinthi tutiirirwe uria Mwene Njeru amirire:

"Ayia! Ini! Mbirirwe andu makura maigagwe na vau nja kenda makariukaga!" Thina niati Nvuko ikiuga uguo maundu mai makuvitana. Uvoro uria wavecanitwe ni Nviti at̲andu makucage wai ukuvingua. Riu Nviti, ni mundu uria ukuthwire. Ni mundu uria ungigucariria kirii ugakua.

The origin of death

Place of origin : Gakwegori (Embu)
Narrator : Kaunju wa Gacugo (Male; 81 yrs)

This animal called Hyena, do you think it is a good thing? *Nto! Nto! Nto!* Hyena is a very bad thing! An animal which is jealous, loves itself and is greedy beyond measure!

Long long ago, there was Hyena and Mole. What did I say? Hyena and mole. Now people reflected and asked themselves, "Who can we send to Mwene Njeru, God, to find out what should be done to people when they grow old?"

So they thought and decided they should not send one person. They said they would send two people so that, in case one of them was unable to continue, the other one would. So they decided to send Hyena and Mole.

Hyena and Mole, when they reached Kirinyaga, up there the home of Mwene Njeru, they explained to him the people's message. Mwene Njeru listened and told them he would send both of them just as both of them were sent by the people. He told them that the message which would arrive first would be the one to be confirmed.

Hyena was given the message of Death while Mole was given the message of Life.

Kubu! kubu! kubu! They travelled sometimes together, sometimes one ahead of the other.

When they neared Earth, Mole started hurrying so as to deliver his message before Hyena. He went. Kubu! Kubu! Kubu! Mole hurried for sure.

He arrived before Hyena. On arrival, Mole stood upright in readiness to deliver his message. He stretched himself to relax his muscles. He scratched his head, and asked himself, "Now what was I told?'

'I was told ..ee.. I was told...ee... I was told...' Before Mole had uttered the message, Hyena arrived and said, "Were we not told that when people grow old they sould be dying and then be thrown outside for me to eat?"

Oh! Yes! I was told that when people grow old they should be kept outside so that they can come back to life!" he sad.

But by the time Mole said that, the decision had already been made. The news that had been delivered by Hyena had already been confirmed.

Now Hyena is the person who hates you. He is the person who could look for an opportunity to bring about your death.

* * *

Thagana na Tumbiri

Tene tene muno runji rwa Tumbiri na rwa Thagana ciari mundu na muruang'ina. Riu Thagana na Tumbiri mendanite muno muno. Mararaga vamwe na makithii vandu gutii watigaga uria wingi.

Riu utuku umwe Thagana na Tumbiri nimatuire kiathi makathii rugendo vamwe ruyuri. Makirana, "Niturara wa vamwe na ruyu tukathii wa vamwe na tukarugama wa vandu vamwe."

Makigucanira na makimama. Nwati irauko undu uria wai wa kumakania niati Thagana akiramuka ethire tumbiri amutigire tene. Riu Thagana niwarakarire muno muno. Aaarakara akivita, "Tinie watiga we Tumbiri? Nawe tondu niwandiga urata wetu wathirira ava. Kuuma riu tutikagia ndugu ringi. Wana gwakua ndui!" Arikia kuuga ciugo icio, Thagana amundire njira akitherera na mwena ucio wingi. Niundu wa marakara make, Thagana athiire agikururagia miti iria yai njirari akimikuuaga nginyagia iriari riria inene.

Kuuma indi iyo, nyunji icio cioiri wana akorwa ciumite vamwe Kirinyaga, ithereraga igaukanite. Kwiragwa ati ungikira manji ma Tumbiri na ma Thagana gitururi kimwe nwa gukua kingikua. Gutwikaga ati rumena rwa nyunji ino ni runene ati mundu angikia

64

maguru runjiri rumwe acioke amarikie ruria rwingi atanai muniaru, ni gutwarwa angitwarwa.

Thagana (Tana) and Tumbiri (Engare Uaso-Nyiro)

Place of origin : Gitituri (Embu)
Narrator : Sarah Geteria (Female; 70)

Long long ago, River Thagana and River Tumbiri were brothers. Now Tumbiri and Thagana loved each other very much. They slept in the same house and whenever they went anywhere, neither went without the other.

Now one evening, they made a plan to undertake a journey together the following day. They said to each other, "Let us sleep together and tomorrow, let us travel together and let us stop at the same place."

They came to an agreement and then slept. However, in the morning, what was surprising was that when Thagana woke up, he found that Tumbiri had left him ages back. Now Thagana got very very angry. In his great anger he swore, "Isn't it me you left, Tumbiri? Since you left me, our friendship has ended here and now. From now on we shall never be friends again. Whatever happens!"

After saying those words Thagana set off and started flowing furiously in the opposite direction. Owing to his anger, he uprooted all the trees which were in his way as he flowed down and carried them, eventually depositing them in the big ocean.

From that time the two rivers, although having the same source on Mt. Kenya, flow separately and in different directions. It is said that if you take water from Thagana and mix it with water from Tumbiri in the same gourd, the gourd will break. People believe that the enmity between these two rivers is so great that if a person dipped his feet in one river and then, before drying off the water, he puts the feet in the other river, he would drown.

* * *

Aetiological tales

Kiria Giatere Ciura Matina

Ciura tene ciari nyamu mbaro muno tondu ciari na matina. Ciekaraga manjiri na rimwe igekara nthi nyumu.

Indi imwe nikwagire na thina muno niundu wa mbura kurega kuura. Mbura yarega kuura gukigia na yura inene muno ria irio wana manji ma kunyua magitura.

Riu ciura niciathinirue muno ni twana turia twari tunini twatura gia kunyua. Yura nirianenevire muno nginya ciura iria nene ikiambiriria kuria tuura turia tunini. Twana twarirwe nginya tukithira tuonthe vururi-ri ucio.

65

Vuva ya kavinda kanini mbura niyaciokire ikiura. Gukigia manji meganu wana irio nacio ikimera yura rikithira.

Ciura ciona uria manji mecurite na uria vururi wavuite, ikiambiriria kwirira uria ciarire ciana igiciria gutikaura. Ikiambiriria kuruga kuu mivurori iria yecurite manji ikinaga, "Narire mwana ngiugaga mbura ndikaura."

Iria ciingi ciai na kuu ithimari wana iria ciai nthi nyumu wanacio ikiambiriria guciokia, "Wananie, wananie, narire mwana ngiugaga mbura ndikaura."

Ciura niciathiire na mbere na kwina nginya igitungana vamwe. Rwimbo niruacacire muno nginya rukigia na mukui. Mukui ainaga, "Narire mwana ngiugaga mbura ndikaura."

Nacio iria ciingi igaciokia, "Wananie, wananie, narire mwana ngiutikaura."

Riu rwimbo ni ruakinyirie vandu rugicaca muno nginya ciura ikiambiriria gucindana. Wa kiura gikaruga nakio kiria kingi kiona murugire wakiria kingi gikageria kuruga muno gucinda kiu. Wa kiura kiaruga gikagamba nthi, meke! Kiria kingi kiona gikaruga nakio gikagamba nthi, meke! Ciura ciathiire na mbere na kwigerekania nginya ikimendeka vuva cionthe ikiura matina.

Mwigerekanio watere ciura matina.

What made frogs to lose their buttocks

Place of origin : Kiritiri
Narrator   : Mwitungi Nyaga (Female; 80yrs)

Long ago, frogs were beautiful animals because they used to have buttocks. They lived in the water and sometimes, they lived on dry land.

A time came when the land was struck by great poverty because of drought. It failed to rain for a long time until there was a great famine. Even drinking water could not be found.

Now frogs were troubled very much by the young children because they had nothing with which to feed them. Now when the famine became unbearable, the big frogs started eating the small frogs. The young frogs were eaten until there were no frog's children left in the land.

After a short while, it started raining. Now there was plenty of water and even crops grew, and the famine was a thing of the past. When frogs saw how abundant water was and how beautiful the land looked, they started regretting for having eaten their children believing that it would never rain again. They started jumping in the flooded rivers singing:

I ate my child thinking that it will never rain!"

The other frogs which were in the wells and even the ones which were in the dry land started replying:

"Me too, me too, I ate my child thinking that it will never rain."

The frogs continued singing until eventually they met at one place. The song and dance became so involving until it got a soloist. The soloist sang:

66

"I ate my child thinking that it will never rain."

And the other frogs replied,
"Me too, I ate my child/thinking that it will never rain."
The dance went on until it eventually became a competition between the frogs. Each frog would jump and then the other frogs, seeing how that one jumped, would try to jump higher. When each frog jumped it would drop down with a thud, *meke*! Whenever the next frog saw this it would jump even higher and also drop down, *meke*! Now the frogs continued competing with each other until they were flattened completely, losing all their buttocks.

Foolish competition caused frogs to lose their buttocks.

* * *

Kiria giatumire Ngiti iturage na andu

Tene tene muno Ngiti na nyamu cionthe cia kithaka ciaturaga vamwe mutitu-ri wari vakuvi na itura rimwe. Nyamu icio cia kithaka ciaturaga vamwe waro muno. Ciarutaga wira vamwe wana nginya gucaria irio ciacaragia wa vamwe. Undu uria warakaragia nyamu nyingi ni gukuma kwa Ngiti. Ngiti niyakumaga na vinya muno utuku nginya igata nyamu iria ciingi toro.

Riu muthenya umwe-ri, nyamu icio cia kithaka nicieciririe uria ingika itige kuthinagua ni inegene ria Ngiti. Ikithii kwi athamaki acio, Munyambu na Gitang'a ivange uria ingika.

Muvango uria wavangirwe ni wa kuraga Ngiti. Munyambu ukivewa wira wa gucema Ngiti utuku na kumiuraga yamama.

Utuku gatagati, Ngiti imamii, Munyambu niwamicemire imiurage. Niguo ucio Munyambu, kavora kavora, niguo ucio Munyambu. Wakinya vari Ngiti, ukiminyita nayo Ngiti ikivonoka.

Riria Ngiti yamenyire ati ii thina-ri, yamundire njira ing'aritie iturari riria ria andu riai vakuvi na kithaka.

Andu meetura maari marikanitie na kumama, nwati riria meguire inegene ria Ngiti igikuma, makiramuka mone ni ndui kiu kiagambaga uguo. Andu maramuka, nimaverwe uvoro wonthe ni Ngiti na ikimera mangimitethia kumigitira ndikauragwe nayo nwa imatethie. Kwoguo andu magioca ivanga na macoka makithii kwingata nyamu icio ciendaga kuuraga Ngiti.

Riria andu maciokire mucii nimarikanire na Ngiti imariragire micii namo makamiva irio na uturo. Kuuma muthenya ucio, Ngiti ituraga kwa andu imariragira micii nao mamivecaga uturo na irio.

67

Why Dog lives with people

Place of origin :   Ivurori (Mbeere)
Narrator   :   Mwitugi Nyaga (Female; 80 yrs)

Long long ago, Dog and all the wild animals lived together in a forest which was near a certain village. Those wild animals lived together very well. They worked together and even went out to look for food together. The only thing which used to disturb the animals was Dog's barking. Dog used to bark too loudly at night, disturbing the other animals while they were asleep.

Now, one day, the wild animals wondered how they could solve the problem of the noise from Dog's barking. They went to their leaders, Lion and Leopard, to decide on what to do. Now the decision that was made was that of killing Dog. Lion was given the job for stalking Dog and killing him in his sleep.

In the middle of the night, while Dog was sleeping, Lion went silently to kill Dog. There is Lion, slowly slowly, there goes Lion. When Lion reached where Dog was, he caught Dog but Dog slipped out.

When Dog knew that he was in trouble, he set off and ran to the village near the forest where people lived. The villagers had already slept, but when they heard the noise of Dog's barking, they woke up to see what was making that noise. Now, when the people woke up they were told the whole story by Dog and he also told them that if they helped him, he would help them in turn. So people took machetes, knives and axes and went to chase the animals which wanted to kill Dog.

When the people got back home, they made an agreement with Dog that he would guard their homes for them and they would feed and house him. From that day, Dog lives with people, guarding their homes for them, and people in turn provide Dog with housing and food.

* * *

Kiria gitumaga Nvungu iricage tuciu twa Nguku

Indi imwe tene Nguku na Nvungu maari urata munene muno. Maturaga vamwe na maundu monthe mao mekaga vamwe.

Riu Nvungu ari na kienji giake kiari kiugi muno gia kurenga ngunyu. Ngunyu cia Nvungu ciari cia kuneneva narua muno kwoguo ndaari angikara atai na kienji. Muthenya umwe Nvungu niwathiire gucaria irio agitiga Nguku amenyagirire tuciu twake tondu nwa indi ari ikuthandura matumbi make. Mvungu niwatigire Nguku kienji giake amenyagirire. Nguku nake niwakenirue ni uguo na akira Nvungu, "Ayia! Wana nwatakwa ukumenyaga. Nigwiyuragia na ngoro uria ningika ndinatinie tukunyu twa twana tutu twakwa na menje turia twina njuiri nene!"

Nvungu nake akiira Nguku, "Watua gutumira, menya ndukandere niundu niwici uria ngunyu ciakwa ikuraga na karugi. Kanthii tondu nina ivenya inene muno. Riria Nvungu athiire Nguku agiciria ke ambe agacaririe ciana irio mbere ya gutwenja na

68

gututema ngunyu. Nguku wa akiriganirwa ni kwiga kienji mbere ya kuthii. Acoka acaririe kienji gigitura. Akira twana tumutethie gucaria, nwati "ng'u!" kienji gitioneka."

Riu riria Nvungu aukire, ataarirua ni Nguku uria maundu mathiire, akiuga, "Nwa kienji giakwa ngwenda!"

Nguku ageririe kumukaira akimwiraga ti guta ateere kienji na kwenda Nvungu akirema. Nvungu aarakarire agioca indo ciake cionthe akithama. Akithii, Nvungu atigire era Nguku akaricaga tuciu twake nginyagia riria akamuciokeria kienji giake.

Kuuma indi iyo Nvungu itindaga ikiria tuciu twa Nguku nayo Nguku itindaga ivuragia nthi igicaria kienji kia Nvungu. Kuuma muthenya ucio Nvugu ndianarenga ngunyu na ni gitumi cii nene uguo.

Why Hawk eats Hen's chicks

Place of origin : Gitituri (Embu)
Narrator   : Sarah Geteria (Female; 70)

Sometime long ago, Hen and Hawk were very good friends. They lived together and they did all their things together. Now Hawk possessed a very sharp razor for cutting his nails. Hawk's nails used to grow very fast and so he could never stay without a razor.

One day, Hawk went to look for food and left his razor with Hen. He asked her to look after it in his absence. Hen was very happy about this and told Hawk, *"Ayia* It is as if you knew. I was wondering in my heart what I would do to trim my children's nails and shave the ones with long hair!"

Hawk told Hen, "If you use it, don't lose it because you know how quickly my nails grow. Let me go as I am in a great hurry."

When Hawk left, Hen decided to look for food for her children first before shaving them and cutting their nails. Hen forgot to keep the razor before she left. When she returned she looked for the razor but could not find it. She told her children to help her look for it, but, where! The razor was nowhere to be seen.

Now when Hawk came back and Hen explained to him how the situation was, he simply said, "All I want is my razor!"

Hen tried to plead with him not to think she lost the razor intentionally but Hawk was adamant. Hawk became so angry that he gathered all his property and left. But before he left, Hawk told Hen he would be eating her chicks until the day she would return her razor.

From that time, the hawk always eats the hen's chicks and the hen always scratches the ground looking for the hawk's razor. From that day, the hawk has never cut its nails and that is why they are so long.

* * *

69

Kiria gitumaga Njoka iturage irinari

Tene tene muno Nduru na Njoka maari urata munene muno. Nduru nake aari na mwari wake ngatha. Riu mwari ucio nimagire urata na Njoka nginyagia Njoka ikithii kuuria uthoni kwi Nduru igure mwari-we.

Indi ya kugurana Njoka ndiari na indio cia kurairia Nduru. Riu ikiuria Nduru etikire Njoka ike uviki igacoka kuraiya vuvari. Nduru niwetikire na mwari akigurua ni Njoka akinathii gutura mucii wayo.

Muthenya umwe Nduru niwathiire guceerera muthoni-we na kugiira rurayio. Nduru niwarugirwe iruga inene nati etia Njoka rurayio niyaregire naruo.

Njoka yarega na rurayio Nduru niwarakarire muno nginya akiambiriria gutetia Njoka na mbaara ikigwa vo. Mbaara yaruirwe nginya Nduru agitivua muno ni Njoka agikua. Nduru agikua atigire aruma Njoka akimira igaturaga marinari na wana yaumira muthenya nwa nginya igacokaga irinari utuku.

What makes Snake live in a hole

Place of origin :   Ishiara (Mbeere)
Narrator   :   Mucanje Kimore (Male; 90 yrs)

Long long ago, Squirrel and Snake were great friends. Now squirrel had a very beautiful daughter. The girl became such good friends with Snake that Snake went to ask Squirrel to allow him to marry his daughter.

At the time of the marriage, Snake did not have any property to give to Squirrel as bride-price. So he requested Squirrel to allow him to marry his daughter and pay the bride-price later. Squirrel agreed and his daughter was married by Snake. She went to live with Snake at his home.

One day, Squirrel went to pay his son-in-law a visit and to collect his bride-price. He was welcomed with a sumptuous feast, but when he asked Snake to give him the bride-price, Snake refused. Squirrel got very angry when Snake refused to pay the bride-price. Squirrel quarrelled with Snake until a fight erupted. The battle was fought so fiercely that Squirrel was badly hurt and died. Before Squirrel died, he cursed Snake and told him he would be living in a hole and that even if he came out during the day he would still have to go back into the hole at night.

* * *

Legends

Karwagi

Karwagi aai mundu wi vinya muno. Embu rionthe gutii mundu ungiarugire Karwagi na vinya. Angiagwatire mundu nwa kumukiriria na iguru na njara imwe.

Thina ya Karwagi yai imwe tu; irio. Irio ciaricagwa ni Karwagi! Nwa muka waici!
Muka wa Karwagi aarugaga nyungu imwe nene ya irio cia murume wenga. Ucuru
naguo, muka ucio akiaga, agakia agekira wa Karwagi kigina.

Uvoro uria wai mwaro muno wa Karwagi niati ndaai uthu na mundu. We ndatumagira
vinya yake na kunyamaria andu. Vinya yake yai ya kuruta wira. Gucimba na kurima
muvonia munene muno wai ta kubucia kwi mundu ucio wai vinya wetagwa Karwagi.

Karwagi

Place of origin :   Gakwegori (Embu)
Narrator   :   Kaunju wa Gacugo (Male; 81 yrs)

Karwagi was a very strong man. In the whole of Embu nobody was stronger than Karwagi. If he
caught a man, he would lift him up in the air with one hand.

The problem with Karwagi was only one, food. The food Karwagi used to eat! Only his wife
knew. Karwagi's wife used to cook one big pot of food for her husband alone. And as for porridge,
the wife used to grind and grind. She would then put Karwagi's share in the big gourd.

The good thing about Karwagi was that he had no enmity or ill-feelings towards anybody. His
strength was for working and not for destroying others. Digging a very big piece of land was like
closing an eyelid to that strong man called Karwagi.

* * *

Mbogo wa Ikou

Mbogo wa Ikou aai mundu wecikene. Nwati ndecikene ni waro wake. Ecikene ni ucuku
wake. Mbogo wa Ikou aai murogi. Vandu va gutumira wara wake na kuroria andu ta
ago aria engi, we wira wake wai wa kuraga andu na urogi wana ciama.

Mundu uyu ti Mbogo wa Ikou aai mwiyendi. Amenete ago aria engi muno. Ago a
Embu, Mbeere wana nginyagia Ikamba, engi muno mathirirue na urogi ni Mbogo wa
Ikou. Mundu mugo angietirwe Embu guca kuragurira andu, ucio ni wa kuragwa ni
mbogo wa Ikou. Ekaga uguo akaiga kindu gatagati ka njira iria mundu mugo ucio
akenukira. Akevita akauga, "Angigakinya mucii gwake kana auke Embu ringi, noriwa
ni kaurugo gaka."

Na nwaguo mundu mugo ucio ndaai anginuka ai muoyo. Mbogo wa Ikou amenete
andu onthe. Wira wake waai wa kuragana. Ndaai ciana ciake kana andu ao niundu
amauragite onthe.

Riria Mbogo wa Ikou akwire, gutii mundu ungiavutirie indo ciake. Gutii mundu
ungiendire kuringithanua nake. Mbogo wa Ikou agairwe ni nviti nicio ciarire indo ciake
akua.

71

Mbogo son of Ikou

Place of origin :   Kirigi (Embu)
Narrator   :   Paul Gatema (Male; 70 yrs)

Mbogo son of Ikou was a famous man. But he was not famous because of good deeds. He was well-known because of his bad deeds.

Mbogo son of Ikou was a witchdoctor who specialised in killing people. Instead of using his art to heal people like other medicinemen, his work was to kill using poison and witchcraft.

This man known as Mbogo son of Ikou was very selfish. He hated other medicinemen very much. The medicinemen of Embu, Mbeere and even Kamba, most of them were finished by Mbogo son of Ikou. If a medicineman was invited to Embu to come and heal people, that one was a victim of murder by Mbogo son of Ikou. What he used to do was to place something in the middle of the path the medicineman would follow on his way home. Then he would swear and say,"If ever he gets back home or comes to Embu a second time, may I be killed by this concoction!"

And indeed such a medicineman would never make it back home alive.

Mbogo son of Ikou hated everybody. His work was to kill. He did not have children of his own or close relatives because he had killed all of them. When Mbogo son of Ikuo died, nobody dared touch his property. Nobody would have liked to be associated with him. The successors of Mbogo son of Ikou were hyenas; they were the ones who ate his property when he died.

* * *

Gakinda wa Mugwe

Gakinda wa Mugwe aai mundu mwende na mutie muno. Endetwe muno ni aka na ciana. Gakinda wa Mugwe aai mundu mugo munene wa mirimu ya ciana. Murimu wa ciana uria ungiaremire Gakinda wa Mugwe gutii mundu mugo wingi ungiavotanire naguo. Aici miti yonthe ya mirimu ya ciana. Nwakio gwake gutatiraga ciana na mang'ina.

Gakinda wa Mugwe aai mundu mutie muno na mwende muno. Undu uria wake wamakirie andu ni umwe. Riria Gakinda wa Mugwe akwire, andu nimamakire muno ni kwona urogi indori ciake. Mamakire niundu matieciragia mundu tocio wavoragia ciana nwa avote kurogana.

Gakinda son of Mugwe

Place of origin :   Kagaari (Embu)
Narrator   :   Jesse Njeru (Male; 75yrs)

Gakinda son of Mugwe was a man who was greatly loved and honoured. He was loved especially by women and children.

Gakinda son of Mugwe was a great medicineman. He specialised in healing children's diseases. Any children's disease which defeated Gakinda son of Mugwe could not be healed by any other medicineman. He knew all the herbs which could heal children's diseases. That is why his homestead was never without children and their mothers.

Gakinda son of Mugwe was loved and honoured very much. The thing about him that shocked people was just one. When Gakinda son of Mugwe died, people were shocked to see poison among his property. They were shocked because they never expected a man like this who used to heal children could keep something that could kill.

* * *

Ndindika wa Mbarari na Nyaga wa Karaga

Ndindika wa Mbarari na Nyaga wa Karaga maai aii acuku muno. Aii aya airi magendaga vamwe na maiaga vamwe.

Undu uria wai mucuku muno wa Ndindika na Nyaga niati wii wao ndwai wa indo ciingi tiga indo cievu. Indo cievu tu! Undu uria wingi mucuku wa andu aya airi niati mai averia muno muno. Mangiethiririe kamwaongia gakiruga methirwe ni njovi makwendaga nagatii nayo, nwa nyungu mateguraga makathii makamivecana mavewe njovi.

Ndindika na Nyaga nimathiicaga kithakari varia kavici kararithia makaia mburi. Makathinja magokia nyama makaria. Matiatigaga kindu. Makathii na ruuo makaruvecana makundue njovi.

Undu uria wai wa magegania niati Ndindika wa Mbarari na Nyaga wa Karaga matiaiaga na nthitho ta aii aria engi. Ika! Aya airi maiaga gituri na muthenya maroretue ni andu.

Mangiavirirwe cirari wa wii, mai na ugi wao wa kurega gwitikira mavitia mao. Nyaga aurua kiuria augaga, "Ndingiaria munyanyawa ataritie!"

Nake Ndindika angierirwe arie, uugi wake wai wa gucinurana. Akaruma muthitangani akamwira, "Niuga nimbiite mburi ciaku ninie ngurithagiria?"

Niundu woguo rionthe Ndindika nwawe warivagua.

Wa rionthe ciira yatua mundu uria mwie arivwe, ithe wa Ndindika niwe warivagwa tondu muvici ndamakagua ni maundu ta mau. Riu indi niyakinyire ithe wa Ndindika akinogua ni kurivwa tondu wa uturika wa muvici. Aatete indo ciake cionthe niundu wa uturika ucio wa muvici.

Munthi umwe athuuri nimatuire Ndindika arive indoiria aiite watoria kwamenyeretwe. Namo metho monthe makiroria ithe wa Ndindika. Nwa kurugama ithe wa Ndindika arugamire akigwata Ndindika akiira athuuri, "Ndethiai kugwata uyu mwana muturi. Umunthi nirio ngumuraga niundu ninakinya muthia wa kurivua niundu wa uturi wake. Ndikariva mathiri make ringi! Nimenda akua na njara ciakwa!"

Ndindika egua uguo akira ithe, "Ndukethinie na kunyita. Wananie ni mukinyiu muthia. Mbikira rurigi ngingo, ninevecana."

Ithe wa Ndindika amwikirire mukanda ngingo akimucuria mutunduri wai vau agikua. Nginyagia umunthi, vai mugumo uria wacokire kumera varia vai mutundu uria Ndindika acurirue.

Riu nimuria Nyaga wa Karaga nake athiire ku? Ndindika akua, Nyaga nake ndai angitura. Auragirwe ni yura na ivoru. Mukwa Nyaga aurire Gikuu. Augire we ndangikara na mundu murume akirivagira mathiri ma wii.

Ndindika son of Mbarari and Nyaga son of Karaga

Place of origin : Kirigi (Embu)
Narrator : Jonah Kamisi (Male; 60 years)

Ndindika son of Mbarari and Nyaga son of Karaga were very notorious thieves. The two thieves went everywhere together and they always stole together.

The worst thing about Ndindika and Nyaga was that their stealing activities were not aimed at acquiring property. Theirs were thefts to satisfy their stomachs; just things for the stomach! The other thing that was so bad about these two was that they were wicked and they punished other people. They were very insensitive. If they found an old woman cooking and their aim was to obtain the beer and drink, which the old woman did not have, they would remove her pot from the fire, throw away the food and take the pot to exchange it for beer.

Ndindika and Nyaga would even go as far as the bush where a boy was grazing animals. They would steal a goat and slaughter it. Then they would roast the meat eat and take the skin and exchange it for beer. They never left anything behind.

The most puzzling thing about Ndindika son of Mbarari and Nyaga son of Karaga was that they never stole in secret like other thieves. These two thieves stole during the day when people were watching them, in a carefree manner.

If ever they were taken before a court of elders, they had their own cunning way of denying their crimes. If Nyaga was asked a question, he would say, "I can't talk before my companion talks!"

As for Ndindika, if he was asked to speak, his trick was to snap at people. He would insult the claimant and ask him, "You say I stole your goat; am I the one who herds your goats for you?"

It follows then that every time, it was Ndindika who used to be fined. Whenever Ndindika was fined, it was his father who paid because Ndindika never cared about such things.

Now, a time came when Ndindika's father got tired of paying for his son's misdemeanour. He had lost all his property in the course of paying for his son's debts. One day, the elders concluded, as often that Ndindika should pay for property he had stolen. As usual, all the eyes looked at Ndindika's father. Ndindika's father suddenly stood up, held Ndindika, and told the elders, "Help me hold this wicked child. Today is when I shall kill him because I have reached the end of paying for his wickedness. I shall never pay for his debts again. I want him to die by my own hands!"

When Ndindika heard that, he told his father, "Don't trouble yourself by holding me. I too have reached the end of my tether. Put a rope on my neck. I have surrendered!"

74

Ndindika's father tied a rope around Ndindika's neck and hanged him on a *mutundu* tree which was nearby. Up to this day, there is a *mugumo*[1] tree which grew later on the same spot where the *mutundu* tree on which Ndindika was hanged.

Now you are wondering what happened to Nyaga son of Karaga. After Ndindika's death, Nyaga was not going to live. He died of starvation and loneliness. Nyaga's wife ran away to Kikuyuland. She said she would never live with a man for whom she would have to pay debts incurred in the course of stealing.

* * *

Kamunge wa Njeru Mutunyi

Kamunge wa Njeru Mutunyi aai njamba nene ya ita na mutongoria munene wai mwende ni andu onthe a Embu. Kamunge endetwe ni andu muno muno nginya makamwinagira:

> *Kamunge wa Njeru Mutunyi*
> *Urorathimwa*
> *Kamunge wa Njeru Mutunyi*
> *Urorathimwa*
> *Kamunge wa Njeru Mutunyi*
> *Mwene Njeru akwige matuku mengi!*

Andu mendete Kamunge muno niundu niwatharikagira nthu ciao. Andu nimaici Kamunge ai vo matingithinua ni nthu. Nthu ingiathithikire Embu, Kamunge nioca mbutu yake mathii matai na guoya, marue mengate nthu iyo kuraca muno.

Kamunge endetwe ni andu muno niundu niwe wamenyagirira Aembu indi iria Arabu maukaga kugura njogu cia maguru mairi cii ngombo.

Riu indi imwe Arabu nimaukire kugura ngombo Nembure. Kamunge ocire mbutu yake akimitongoria makirua mbara nene muno. Indi iyo Kamunge niwavotirwe nwati andu nimakenirue muno ni uria erutanirie. Na ringi niwonirie Arabu Embu ti ria mathe. Arabu mamenete Kamunge muno na mamwiraga:

> *Kamunge wa Njeru*
> *Niukamenya munthi umwe*
> *Kamunge wa Njeru*
> *Munthi umwe nwokamenya!*

Arikia kuvotwa Kamunge erire Embu rikarage rivotorete indo cia mbaara. Arikia kuuga uguo akivangania mbutu yake ringi. Akira njamba ciake cia ita ciivite ati itikavuruka nginya riria Mwarabu agatiga kugura Muembu.

---

1. Mugumo is a sacred fig tree.

Arabu nao mai andu augi na acovu muno. Mekaga uguo, magauka ati ni miguongo ya njogu marenda kugura. Marikia kugura miguongo, makera aria mamenderia mamave andu. gakundi a kumonia njira macoke macioke. Andu acio mathii kwonania njira mathiicagwa nao na matiacokaga.

Rui Kamunge niwecikene vururi wa Embu kuonthe. Ndaicikene wa kwao Ngandore kuonga. Indi imwee mundu wa kuuma Kagaari niwauragire mundu. Aurire wa akithii kwithitha gwa Kamunge. Gwa Kamunge wa Njeru mutunyi nwakuo onire kwaro gwa kwithitha.

Wana riria Kamunge athuire andu aria manyariraga aria engi, niweguire ntha niuria mundu ucio amuthaithire. Kwoguo akimuthitha gwake.

. Mundu ucio ekarire gwa Kamunge ciumia nyingi. Ai kuu, ndangianyuire njovi na arume aria engi ni gwitigira ndagakunyanirwe. Njovi yake yai yake na Kamunge wenga.

Riu munthi umwe andu a mundu uria wauragitwe nimathiire gucaria mundu ucio muragani. Megua ati ethithite gwa Kamunge, nimamakire muno muno. Marigirwe muno uria Kamunge njamba ya ita yai igweta uguo yavotete kuthitha muragani. Makiuga mathii gwi Kamunge mamwire mamunengere muragani ucio mamuike uria ekire mundu wao.

Mundu umwe Mumiru wetagwa Gatumu niweguire uria kwathii. Akigua Kamunge akira andu acio, "Wana mungimwoca. Ni mundu mucuku muno guku kuonthe gutii mundu maaragia nake. Wana njovi ndukona akinyua na arume aria engi."

Mumiru uria ti Gatumu egua uguo aking'aria akiira mundu uria muragani, "Ta ngundia kavia kamwe ka njovi nanie ngwire kaundu."

Mundu ucio muragani nake agiciokia, "Thii! Nie ndiaragia na Amiru!"

Gatumu akigeria wa ringi akimwira, "Ngundia kavia kamwe nguire kaundu negua."
Muragani akimwingata wa ringi.

Riu rirua nario rikithua. Kamunge wa agiuka na andu aria macaragia muragani. Akithii akimwira, "Ta uka nina kaundu ngwenda gukwira."

Mundu uria akiuma vau nja. Akira Kamunge, "Kwina njovi uka twambe tunyue."
"Nari! Twambe twikare nthi. Njovi tukanyua ringi."

Andu aria macaragia mundu ucio maai vuva ya Kamunge. Maukire magikira mundu ucio rurigi ngingo makimukururia makithii nake.

Gatumu egua uria kwathii akira mundu uria na kimini, "Uguo toguo. Tethua ni njovi yaku. Ngwirire gwi kaundu ngwendaga gukwira ungundie gacovi warega. We wi mundu gitegua!"

Ruu niruo rugano rwa Kamunge wa Njeru Mutunyi.

Kamunge son of Njeru Mutunyi

Place of origin :   Kirigi (Embu)
Narrator   :   Jonah Kamisi (Male; 60 yrs)

Kamunge son of Njeru Mutunyi was a renowned warrior and a great leader who was loved very much by everybody in Embu. Kamunge was loved so much by people that they used to sing for him:

Kamunge son of Njeru Mutunyi,
May you be showered with blessings
Kamunge son of Njeru Mutunyi
May you be showered with blessings
Kamunge son of Njeru Mutunyi
May Mwene Njeru, our God
Grant you a long life!

The people loved Kamunge so much because he used to fight their enemies. People knew that while Kamunge was around, they would never be troubled by enemies. If enemies encroached on Embu land, Kamunge would lead his warriors and they would fight fearlessly until the enemy was pushed far far away.

Kamunge was loved by people because he was the one who protected Embu people when the Arabs used to come to buy two-legged elephants as slaves.

Now, one time some Arabs came to buy slaves at Nembure. Kamunge took his battalion and led it in a very fierce battle against the Arabs. In this war, Kamunge was defeated but people were very pleased with his efforts. He also showed the Arabs that Embu people were not a joke.

The Arabs hated Kamunge very much and they used to tell him.

Kamunge son of Njeru,
One day you will know.
Kamunge son of Njeru,
You will see one day!

After he was defeated, Kamunge told Embu people to stay on guard all the time. He told them to be armed and ready for war all the time. After saying this, he re-oranised his army. He then told his warriors to swear that they would never rest until the day the Arabs would stop buying Embu people.

The Arabs were very cunning and very bad. They would come and say they wanted to buy elephant tusks. After buying elephant tusks they would tell those who had sold to them the elephant tusks that they needed a few guides to show them the way and that they would later send these back. The people who went with the Arabs as guides never came back.

Now Kamunge was famous all over Embu. He was not renowned only in his neighbourhood of Ngandori. One time, a man from Kagaari killed another. He fled and went to hide at Kamunge's home. The home of Kamunge son of Njeru Mutunyi is the only place this man saw as the best refuge.

Although Kamunge hated people who persecuted others, he felt pity for this man because of the way he pleaded for help. So he gave him refuge and hid him in his home. That man stayed in Kamunge's home for many weeks. While he was there, he never went drinking with other men for fear of being betrayed. His beer was only for him and Kamunge.

Now one day, the relatives of the murdered man went hunting for the murderer. When they heard that he was hiding at Kamunge's home, they were greatly shocked. They failed to understand how Kamunge, a great warrior and leader, could hide a murderer. So they decided to go to Kamunge and ask him to give them that murderer so that they could do to him what he had done to their relative.

A Meru man called Gatumu heard what went on. He heard Kamunge telling the people, "You can take him. He is a very bad man. In this whole neighbourhood, there is nobody he talks to. Even beer, you can't see him drinking with other men."

So the Meru man called Gatumu, after hearing this, ran to the murderer and told him, "Give me just a hornful of beer and I shall tell you something."

The murderer replied, "Go away! I don't talk to Meru people!"

Gatumu tried again and told him, "Give me just a hornful of beer and I shall tell you something I heard."

The murderer chased him away again. Eventually, the sun set. Kamunge arrived with the people who were looking for the murderer. He went and told him, "Come I tell you something I want to tell you."

The man went out in the yard. He told Kamunge, "There is beer, come we drink first." Kamunge told him, "No! Let us first sit down. We shall drink beer later."

The people who were looking for the murderer were behind Kamunge. They came, put a rope round the murderer's neck and dragged him away.

When Gatumu heard what happened he told the murderer in Kimeru, "That's it! You can seek help from your beer. I told you to give me a sip of beer so that I tell you something and you refused. You are a person who never listens to others!"

That is the story of Kamunge son of Njeru Mutunyi.

* * *

Mwenda Mwea

Mwenda Mwea aai mundu mugo na murathi wai igweta muno. Aaturaga guku Thau. Wanavaria aaturaga na guku mbere ya Gititu kia Mwene Ndega; Mwenda Mwea aicikene miena yonthe iria irigiciritie Gititu Kia Mwene Ndega. Mundu angiaugire aumite Thau, Gicere, Kyeni kana va Kagaari nwati ethirwe ndeci Mwenda Mwea, Mundu ucio nwanga muthani.

Mwenda Mwea arathire maundu maria mekikire kiambiriria kia ukoroni. Guekikire uu.

Munthi umwe, mundu wetagwa Kanyange niwatwarire muvici kwi Mwenda Mwea. Endaga Mwenda Mwea amwire kana ugurani wa muvici wai murathime. Riu mundu na muvici makinya, Mwea aamamukire na urume na urata watoria amenyerete.

Arika kuthikiriria thina iria yaretete andu acio, Mwenda Mwea akinyita mburi yake yetagwa Giceru akithikiriria. Mburi ikiania. Mwenda Mwea akinyita mburi ringa nayo mburi ikiania. Mwenda Mwea akithikiriria waro wa akinainia kiongo.

Riu maundu makinya vau, Mwenda Mwea erire Kanyange ere muvici ndakagurane mugongo ucio wingi. Akiuga uviki ucio wai wa mutino. Muvici nake akigua nai muno na akigiwa ni kieva, "Kwa gutai kigongona kingithegutia mugiro ucio?" Kanyange akiuria Mwenda Mwea.

Mwenda Mwea amwirire magauka munthi wingi na indo na muvici nimaukire maretete indo iria metitue ni Mwenda Mwea. Riu vau Mwenda Mwea aveverere muvici wa Kanyange kaundu akimwira aige kaundu kau thiri matuku make monthe.

Arikania na maundu mau mogurani Mwenda Mwea anyitikire akiambiriria kuratha, "Nimona njoka mbiru yukite, yukite kuuma Naikuru, ivitukirire Embu ithiite, ithiite, ithiite, ithiite ... nwati tutikethirwa vo indi iyo. Ngethirwa nithithite na mburi yakwa Giceru. Giceru tukikethitha? Mburi ikiania.

"Nimona giconi giceru kia muromo wethaga giukite, giukite, giukite. Nimona giconi kia muromo wethaga kiumbukite giukite na guku; giukukite, giukite... Nwati gigikinya tutikethirwa vo. Ngethirwa nithithite na Gicheru wakwa. Giceru tutikethitha?" Mburi wekiania.

"Nimona ng'ombe cietu ithiite cionthe; itavitwe ni andu atune. Mundu wi ndegwa niendwa amithinje riu. Nimona tukirivirua Rukanga. Nwati maundu mama magikikia, thue tutikethirwa vo.

Ngethirwa nithithite na Giceru. Giceru tutikethitha?" Mburi wekiania.

Arikia kunuga maundu mama monthe Mwenda Mwea niwaririre.

Miaka minini yathira, ng'ombe nyingi niciatavirwe ni athungu.

Mwenda Mwea

Place of origin :   Thau (Embu)
Narrator   :   Nthia wa Geteria (Male; 70)

Mwenda Mwea was a famous medicineman as well as a seer. He lived here in Thau. Although he lived beyond Ndega's Grove, Mwenda Mwea was well-known all over the areas surrounding Ndega's Grove. If anybody claimed to be from Thau, Gicera, Kyeni or anywhere in Kagaari but did not know Mwenda Mwea, then that person was a liar. Mwenda Mwea foresaw all that happened in Kenya at the beginning of the colonial era. It happened like this:

One day, a man called Kanyange took his son to Mwenda Mwea. He wanted Mwenda Mwea to tell him whether the son's forthcoming marriage would be blessed. Now when father and son arrived, Mwenda Mwea received them with sternness mixed with friendliness as was his habit.

After listening to the problem at hand, Mwenda Mwea touched his goat known as Giceru, the White One, and listened. The goat bleated. Mwenda Mwea listened carefully to the bleating and shook his head. At this point, Mwenda Mwea told Kanyange to tell his son not to marry a woman from the opposite ridge. He said the marriage would portend evil. The son was very upset.

"Isn't there a ritual you could perform or a sacrifice you could give to ward off this evil?" Kanyange asked Mwenda Mwea. In response, Mwenda Mwea told Kanyange to bring several items for further divination on another day.

On the appointed day, father and son came back with the things Mwenda Mwea had asked for. This time Mwenda Mwea whispered something to Kanyange's son and told him to keep it secret thoughout his life.

After he had finished with this marriage problem, Mwenda Mwea went into a trance and began foretelling the future.

"I see a black snake coming, coming from Nakuru, passing through Embu and going, going, going going.... But we shall not be there at that time. I shall be hiding with my goat, Giceru. Giceru, won't we be hiding?" The goat bleated.

"I see a white bird with a metal beak coming, coming, I see a bird with a metal beak flying this way, coming, coming.... But by the time it arrives we shall not be there. I shall be hiding with my Giceru. Giceru, won't we be hiding?" The goat bleated.

"I see all our cattle gone. Plundered from us by red people. Whoever has a bull, he had better slaughter it now.

"I see us being beaten at Rukanga. But when these things happen, we shall not be there. I shall be hiding with my goat, Giceru. Giceru, won't we be hiding?" The goat bleated.

After he had finished saying all these things, Mwenda Mwea cried.

A few years later a lot of cattle were plundered by the British.

* * *

Cierume

Cierume aari mwongia wecikene muno muno niundu wa umiriru wake na urume wake. Mwongia uyu ti Cierume aciarirwe Mbeere. Athungu magiuka Mbeere na Embu, Cierume aari arikumenyekana muno muno ari munene na mutongoria wa mbaara.

Guku Mbeere na Embu gutiari mwongia ungikuviviria gwikara ta Cierume. Wana nginyagia Ikamba, Gikuu na Miru, nwanga ongia airi tu mangiringithanwa na Cierume. Mwongia wa mbere ni uria wetagwa Ciokaraine wa murwa Barungu Mumiru na wa kairi ni Mugikuu uria wetagwa Wangu wa Makeri. Ongia aya oiri nwao mangiringithanua na ciiko cia Cierume cia utongoria.

Ritwa ria Cierume riragwa riaumire ritwari ria mundu murume, ati mundu muka wekarii ta mundu murume. Nwati nie ngitaura ritwa riri, nwambugire ni ritwa ria kumana na urume niundu mwongia aari urume muno.

Undu uria wambere wai wa magegania wa Cierume ni ati guku Mbeere tutingiathukirue ni nthu ari vo. Ika! Cierume aruaga mbaarari na urume. Mwongia uyu wana ndaruaga na ruviu kana uta na migui. Ika! We Cierume aruaga na mubaria uria ongia mainaga nyimbo naguo. Ucio niguo atumagira na agatoria nthu cionthe cia Mbeere.

Ngo ya mbere ya Cierume ndathondekerwa ni mundu kana akithondekera. Ika! Ngo ya mbere ya Cierume arutire mbaarari. Ni kuruira amiruire. Kiai ta kiveo kia umiriru wake.

Ekire uguo, kwari Mwikamba umwe wathinitie Mbeere muno. Mwikamba ucio wa rionthe angiathithukire Mbeere na mbutu yake, kurivwa kuria Ambeere marivagwa! Andu ma Mbeere makucaga engi mangiathithukirwe ni Mwikamba uyu. Cierume ndaari wa mathe; auragire Mwikamba ucio na mubaria wake na njara ciake. Mwongia acokire ngo ya Mwikamba ucio niyo yai ta kiveo giake niundu wa kuthengutiria Ambeere nthu iyo yaremete arume onthe. Ngemi iria ciaugirwe kundu guku! We!

80

Mbaara iyo na ciiko cia Cierume mbaarari iyo niciatumire igweta riake rimate muno. Ciana na andu agima ma Mbeere na Embu, nginyagia Ikamba na Miiru gutii utegua ritwa na ciiko cia Cierume.

Riu, kuri undu umwe wa thina indi cionthe mundu muka arigutuika njoria kana ari kuthamaka gatagati ka arume. Undu uyu ni ta rwetho kana mugongo umwe kwigua na ati mundu muka niwacindana na arume.

Niundu wa Cireume kuthii Mbaarari na gutoria muno muno wana gukira arume, andu amwe nimegucaga rwetho. Amwe wana megucaga nai nwa undu wa utongoria wa Cierume. Amwe megucaga nai nwa undu wa kwona Cierume akithii na akaria ivoto na aumiriritie micemaniori ya arume. Mutikumenya mue guku gwetu micemanio itwire iri ya arume atheri?

Riu andu amwe nimambiririe kuthekerera Cierume. Aria engi makaugaga maundu ma kumunyuriria.

Indi imwe mundu umwe niwaririe ta akunyururia Cierume akiuga, "Arume mwanona ruru avai? Ati aka nimarima mekarii nthi ta arume! Micemaniori ya arume matingitira! Riu mwongia uyu ugwitwa Cierume niatwonia atia? Ruru! Mitugo yake ya gukararania na arume na kurua ta mundu murume niyagutwonia uria tutwire twikaga ni nai. Eee! Ingi ndatwire nathue arume tucoke gwikaraga micii, tukirugaga wana tugiciaraga ta aka!"

Cierume ndagamba kiugo. Agwatire mundu murume ucio, akimuriva nginya akimwonia urume wake niwa mana. Ndivo iria Cierume arivire mundu ucio! We! Kwa avonokirue ni andu aria maai vakuvi.

Riu nao andu Mbeere yonthe nimakinyirwe ni ndeto icio. Kuumagia indi iyo, gutiri mundu wanacioka kuruma Cierume kana kumunyururia. Aciokire agitiwa muno gukira mbere, na agituika mutongoria wa bururi mutie muno.

Cierume anai mumenyekanu, athungu nimaukire guku bururi wetu. Riria makinyire Mbeere mauria uria wathanaga varia Cierume atwire, augire niwe waari munene. Kwoguo Cierume agituwa civu wa kuu.

Mbeere kuonthe na Embu kwonthe, gutiari civu mundu muka wingi tiga Cierume. Guku kuonthe gutiari mwongia wingi civu tiga Cierume. Na nwa ciiko ciake cia gutethia mugongo wa Mbeere ciatumire wana andu metikire atuike munene wao indi ya ukoroni.

Cierume niwekarire kavinda kanene wa wathanga ari civu. Riu ari civu, Cierume niwamenyerere na gutethia andu make muno. Muno muno Cierume atethagia andu make na kumaririria micemeniori iria methagirwa nayo na ndici na macivu maria mengi.

Undu umwe Cierume ekirire vinya muno micemaniori iyo ni wa kwaririria andu make matige kuthinua na mawatho maria athungu maretete. Uvoro umwe waturitie Cierume ni uria Ambeere matumagirwa ni athungu ta kindu gitari vata. Ta uvoro wa Ambeere kuvirwa na vinya kuuria macambari kurimira Athungu matigite micii yao, ucio waari undu waturagia Cierume muno. Cierume ndaari angigua guoya akira ndici anari muthungu ati maundu mau maari macuku. Cierume kai ndetigirite nginya athungu! Indi imwe wana niwarakarire nginya agita ndici kivici niundu wa mawatho make ma kunyamaria Ambeere.

Riu indi imwe ndici niwetire macivu monthe ma Embu na Mbeere mucemanio Kirimari. Riu nivakinyite vandu macivu mamwe makiguira Cierume rwetho niundu aari mundu muka nwati niwakirite arume engi na utongoria wake. Nimavangire uria mangivota kurutithia Cierume unene.

Mekire uguo makigia ndundu ya macivu arume onga. Makivenia Cierume ati ndici augite mucemanio ucio niuthiiwa ni andu monthe mai nduuru. Ati ndici augite macivu monthe mathii matai nguo.

Cierume nake wana ethirwa aari mwongia wari urume ndaari aturite nthoni. Mwongia uyu ari mundu muka watiitwe ni andu na wanake agetia. Riu ndangiari angiyonania nduuru yake tondu onire ucio ni undu wa nthoni na mundu niwagirirwe gutia mwiri wake uria atiitwe ni andu aria engi. Kwoguo akira macivu mau mengi arume mathii onga we ndangithii nduuru. Akigeria kwira macivu mau matigetikane na watho ucio makirega. Cierume enyitire nthunu akiuga, "Ndwire nimwiraga andu aya athungu matwathaga na mawatho ma gutunyarira. Aya ni andu maturiku muno. Mwi mwegua andu magima makirwa mathii nduuru? Mwi mwegua guku tukira munene arute nguo tumwone nduuru? Thiii nduuru mue mwethirwa mwi ivici ta kivici kiu kimwitite mucemanio wa giko! Nie ndingikinya mucemanio tocio!"

Uguo niguo macivu mau arume mendaga. Mendaga Cierume ndakathii mucemaniori niguo moone kamweke ga kumwigirira maundu macuku kwi ndici arutwe uciivu. Macivu mau matumanire na nthitho nguo ciao ithithwe vandu navau mbere. Riu makiambiriria rugendo rwa Kirimari rwa mithenya iiri tondu rwai rwa maguru, mambiririe matari nguo. Uguo niguo mavenirie Cierume ati mucemanio wai wa nduuru. Makithii magikirira nguo varia ciathithitwe.

Makinya Kirimari merire ndici Cierume araugire we ndangikinya mucemanio wititwe ni kivici. Ndici egua ugo akirakara. Riu Cierume ndaari vo eyariririe wana aigiriwa maundu macuku atia. Ndici aukire wa akivuta Cierume uciivu.

Mwongia uyu wetagwa Cierume wana ethirwa niwavutirwe uciivu na njira iyo, igweta riake niundu wa utongoria wake ritianathira.

Niwathiire na mbere na gutiwa na kuririkanwa ni andu. Nginyagia umunthi andu nimainaga na makagana uria Cierume aari mwongia mutongoria mumiriru na mutie muno. Ritwa ria Cierume na igweta riake niritethagia aka ma Mbeere na Embu kumiriria na gwika maundu mao na umiriru matagukua ngoro.

Cierume

Place of origin : Ishiara (Mbeere)
Narrator : Grace Wanjeru (Female; 70)

Cierume was a woman who was very famous because of her perseverance and bravery. This woman known as Cierume was born in Mbeere. By the time the British came to Mbeere and

Embu, Cierume had already established herself and become renowned as a leader of her community and a great warrior.

Here in Mbeere and also in Embu, there was no woman who could come close to having those attributes which Cierume had. Even among the Kamba, Kikuyu and Meru, it is only two women who can be compared to Cierume. The first of these two women was a woman named Ciokaraine daughter of Barungu from Meru. The second one was a Gikuyu woman named Wangu wa Makeri. These two women are the only ones whose qualities of bravery and leadership can be compared to those of Cierume.

It is said that the name of Cierume originated from the term "*mundu murume*", meaning "a man". However, my interpretation of this name is that it is a name which alludes to bravery. According to me, its origin is the term "*urume*" which means "fierceness" or "courage" because this woman was extremely courageous.

The first thing that was wonderful about Cierume is that here in Mbeere, no enemy would have dared attack us while Cierume was around. Oh, no! Cierume used to fight in war alongside men. This woman, in fact, did not even fight with a sword or a bow and arrows. Oh, no! She used to fight with a stick, the type of stick which women used when performing traditional dances. That is the stick Cierume used and she used to defeat all the enemies of Mbeere people.

Cierume's first shield was not made for her by anybody. Oh, no! The first shield Cierume used, she brought back from the battlefield. She fought for it. It was like a prize or a reward for her courage.

It happened like this. There was a Kamba warrior who had troubled Mbeere people very much. Any time this warrior and his battalion invaded Mbeereland, the suffering which Mbeere people experienced! Mbeere people died in large numbers whenever this warrior invaded our land. Cierume was a serious person and had a sense of purpose; she killed this Kamba enemy with her stick and with her own hands. This warrior's shield was the prize Cierume got for her brave act. She took it and it was the one she used thereafter whenever she went to war. The shield was the prize Cierume got for killing the enemy who had defeated all the men. This act called for great celebration. The whole land was filled with ululation. Oh, yes!

Cierume's fame spread far and wide on account of this feat, and many of her actions. Her fame rang through out Mbeere and Embu. She was known even among the Kamba and the Meru. There was nobody who did not come to hear about the character and deeds of Cierume.

Now, there is one problem which always arises whenever a woman succeeds or becomes a leader among men. This problem arises from jealousy and some people feel unhappy if a woman succeeds where men have failed. As a result of Cierume's victory in the battlefield, succeeding particularly where men had failed, some people were jealous of her. Some people had ill feelings towards her just because of her outstanding qualities of leadership. Others were unhappy to see Cierume talk articulately at meetings whose membership was predominantly male. Don't you know that in this land of ours meetings have always been exclusively for men?

Now some people started ridiculing Cierume. Others actually started abusing her. One day, a man made fun of Cierume and ridiculed her saying, "Oh! My fellow men, have you ever seen wonders like these? Oh! These days women cultivate seated down like men. They never fail to turn up at men's meetings! What kind of picture is this woman called Cierume showing us? Oh! My goodness! By arguing with men and fighting like a man, she is trying to question our traditions. She is trying to show us that the way we have handled our affairs from time immemorial is wrong. Ah! Let her tell us men to start looking after homes, cooking and even bearing children like women!"

Cierume never uttered a word. She simply got hold of that man and beat him up until she showed him that his manhood was nothing. The beating that man received! Ah! He was only saved by people who were around.

Now, the news of this incident travelled far and wide in the whole of Mbeereland. From that time, nobody dared tease or ridicule Cierume. The respect people had for her became even greater. Her fame as a strong leader increased.

While Cierume had already established herself as a leader, the British came to colonise our land. When they arrived in the neighbourhood where Cierume lived and enquired who ruled there, Cierume said she was the ruler. So the British made her the chief. In Mbeere and Embu, there was no woman chief except Cierume. The whole of this land there was no woman chief except Cierume. This was a well-deserved position. She won it because of her unquestionable qualities of leadership and also because of her great concern for the welfare of Mbeere people. This is what made the whole community consent to her being made a colonial chief over them.

Cierume ruled as chief for a long time. Now, while she was chief, she guarded and helped her people to the best of her ability. She was very outspoken at the meeting of all the chiefs and the District Commissioner. She was always on the side of the people at these meetings.

One thing that Cierume worked very hard to change was the tendency of the colonial government to enforce laws which undermined her people's welfare. Cierume was very bitter about the way the British used her people as objects or as useless beings. For instance, she was against the system of forced labour whereby Mbeere people were forcibly taken to work in the white settlers' farms, leaving their families with nobody to care for them. Cierume had no fear telling the white District Commissioner that this kind of treatment was wrong. Cierume feared nobody, not even the white man! At one time, she was so indignant that she called the District Commissioner an uncircumcised boy because of instituting laws which were oppressive towards the Mbeere people.

Now, at one time the District Commissioner invited all the chiefs of Mbeere and Embu to a meeting at Kirimari*. During this period, some chiefs were getting jealous of Cierume because of the way she towered over them at meetings and yet to them, she was a mere woman. So they plotted on how to get her deposed.

In their conspiracy, the male chiefs lied to Cierume that the District Commissioner had ordered all the chiefs to attend the meeting naked. They told her that the District Commissioner had decreed that this was a meeting with a difference because it was a meeting in the nude.

Although Cierume was courageous, she did not engage in acts which indicated lack of self-respect. She would never have done a shameful thing like revealing her nakedness to people. She believed that a person ought to respect herself the way she was respected by other people. So she told those male chiefs to go to the meeting on their own because there was no way she would attend the meeting nude. She tried to persuade those chiefs to rebel against such a ruling but they refused to listen. Cierume held her arms akimbo and said, "I have always told you that these white people who colonized us rule us through oppressive laws and that they are very wicked people. Have you ever heard us tell any of our leaders to take off his clothes so that we can see his nudity? Go naked you people if you are uncircumcised boys like that uncircumcised boy who has called this dirty meeting!"

Kirimari literally means "up the mountain". This is the present Embu town.

That is what these male chiefs wanted. They wanted to trick Cierume so that she failed to attend the meeting. They had earlier on planned on how they would accuse Cierume falsely with matters which would anger the District Commissioner so much that he would depose her as chief. Now, when they set off for the two-day journey to Kirimari on foot, they were naked. That is how they tricked Cierume into thinking that it was a meeting of nudes. However, they had sent people ahead carrying their clothes. They travelled until they reached where the clothes were hidden and got dressed.

When they arrived at the meeting, these chiefs told the District Commissioner that Cierume had said she could not attend a meeting which had been convened by an uncircumcised boy. When the District Commissioner heard that, he was very angry. Now Cierume was not there to refute these allegations or to defend herself. So the District Commissioner immediately stripped Cierume of her chieftaincy.

This woman known as Cierume, although she was deposed from her colonial chieftaincy, her fame as a leader did not come to an end. She continued being respected and remembered by people. Up to today, people still sing praise songs to Cierume. They sing how she was a well-respected courageous female leader. The name of Cierume and her fame still helps Mbeere and Embu women by inspiring them to manage their affairs fearlessly and with determination.

* * *

Stories on communal life

Rwimbo rwa Nduru, Gikaa na eritu

Tene ri, kwari Nduru na Gikaa na nyamu ino ciiri ciari urata munene muno. Muthenya umwe Nduru na Gikaa nimeyovire waro muno makithii rwimbori rwari na aari mengi muno.

Riu Nduru aari na aari engi muno ma kwina namo. Aari monaga Nduru ari mwaro muno nati Gikaa ndanona mwana mwari wanai umwe wa kwina nake. Rwimbo rwathira, Gikaa na Nduru nimenukire kwao mucii.

Makinya mucii Gikaa akiuria Nduru kiria gitumire aari maura niwe.

Nduru erire Gikaa etikire atumwe metho manyivanyive na mathii rwimbori ringi aari makamwinia. Gikaa niwetikire atumwa metho ni Nduru.

Kivwai kiu Nduru na Gikaa nimathiire ringi rwimbori. Indi iyo Gikaa niwonire aari engi muno a kwina namo. Aari kwa macindanaga kwina na Gikaa. Gikaa niwambiririe guturwa ni metho kuria atumitwe. Riu wa makinaga na aari Gikaa akiambiriria kwinira Nduru.

Ii! Ninguturwa Nduru,
Nduru ni metho makwa Nduru,
Nduru maria undumite Nduru, Nduru
Niundu wa rwimbo Nduru.

85

Nake Nduru agicokia:

Umiriria woguo Gikaa, Gikaa
Twine na aari Gikaa, Gikaa
Ii ndumiririe Gikaa, Gikaa
Twine na aari Gikaa Gikaa.

Aari maria mainaga na Nduru na Gikaa maugaga ni rwimbo maraina, umwe agakua uria wingi agacokia. Matianamenya ni metho maria matume maaturaga.

Gikaa niweyumiririe nginya rwimbo rukithira nati makinya mucii niwerire Nduru amutumure metho mau. Nduru nake agitiira gikaa akimwiraga, "Gikaa avai nimonire uria uugi wakwa ugutethirie? Ngutumire metho nginya aari makwenda muno!"

Gikaa niwakenire muno ainua ni aari nati niwerire Nduru amutumure niundu we ndangiaturire na metho matume na magaturaga wa rionthe. Nduru niwamutumurire nake agikara wana metho make mari manene.

The dance of Squirrel, Bush Cat and young girls

Place of origin : Kiritiri (Mbeere)
Narrator : Karigi Maketho (Female; 70 yrs)

In the olden days, there lived Squirrel and Bush Cat. These two animals were great friends. One day they decided to attend a dance which had been organised in their village. The two animals adorned themselves very well and went to the dance.

Now Squirrel became very popular with the girls. They wanted to dance with him. The girls found Squirrel very handsome but Bush Cat did not get a single girl to dance with. When the dance was over, Squirrel and Bush Cat went back to their home. At home Bush Cat asked Squirrel why the girls refused to dance with him. Squirrel told him that his eyes were too big and they frightened the girls away.

Squirrel told Bush Cat to let him sew up his eyes so that they could be a bit smaller. Squirrel convinced Bush Cat that if he agreed to this plan, all the girls would want to dance with him at the next dance. Bush Cat agreed and Squirrel stitched up his eyes.

Now, in the evening, the two friends attended the dance once again. That evening, Bush Cat was very popular with the girls. They were competing to dance with him. Eventually Bush Cat started feeling pain on his eyes. So while he was dancing he started singing.

Ii! Oh! I am feeling pain, Squirrel, Squirrel
On my eyes, Squirrel, Squirrel.
The eyes you sewed up, Squirrel, Squirrel
Because of the dance, Squirrel, Squirrel.

And Squirrel would reply:

Persevere just like that Bush Cat, Bush Cat
We dance with these girls, Bush Cat, Bush Cat
Ii! Oh! You just persevere Bush Cat, Bush Cat.

The girls who were dancing with Squirrel and Bush Cat assumed that the two friends were just singing as part of the dance. They thought one was acting as a soloist and the other one representing the general performers. They had no idea that Bush Cat's stitched eyes were paining.

Bush Cat perserved until the dance was over. However, when he got home, he told Squirrel to undo the eyes. Before unstitching the eyes, Squirrel boasted to Bush Cat saying, "Bush Cat, did you see how my intelligence really helped you? I stitched your eyes until all the girls were flocking to you!"

Bush Cat was happy to have danced with the girls but he insisted that Squirrel undo the stitching because he could not bear the pain in his eyes. Squirrel unstitched the eyes and Bush Cat lived the rest of his life with large eyes.

* * *

Mwongia na Nviti

Tene tene muno, kwari mwongia watuire iturari rimwe. Indi imwe andu etura nimarikanire mathame. Mwongia ucio nake akiuga ndangithama. Augire we ndagutinda akithinua. Riu riria mwongia ucio atigirwe ari weka, niwarwarire kironda kiai kinene muno. Agicoka miaka yathira mingi agikura. Riu kuu nikwamerire miti mingi gugituika ithaka itheri na mititu mitheri.

Muthenya umwe nviti niciaukire kuvingurithia mwongia imurie. Nwati mwongia niweguire nviti mbere. Acigua akiina na mugambo munene:

Aria mumamii ii
Ukirai mwoce nviu
Nviti iguicaii ii
Nviti niikuvivirie ii.

Nviti ciegua rwimbo ruu ikigua guoya ikiura.

Nviti ciaukaga wa mutheya gutuiria mwongia na kumenya uria mekaraga nake. Riu niciekarire nginya ikithigana. Ikimenya kwa mwongia einithagia gutii mundu mekaraga nake; ekaraga wa weka. Nviti niciamenyire mwongia ucio ndaari na muthuri kana na mwana.

Muthenya umwe nviti niciaukire kuria mwongia.

Nake akiambiriria kwina.

> *Aria mumamii ii*
> *Mutiukire mwoce nviu*
> *Nviti igucaii ii*
> *Nviti niikuviriria ii.*

Nviti nacio igicokia ikina:

> *Mwongia uri mucii uyu*
> *Nitumenyete uturaga weka*
> *Na kironda kia muthumo*
> *Umunthi ndungivona ii!*

Nviti ciarikia kwina uguo ciatonyire, ikinyita mwongia uria, ikimuria wonthe wana mavindi.

Mutura weka akucaga wa weka.

A woman and hyenas

Place of origin : Ivurori (Mbeere)
Narrator : Mwenda Njeru (Female; 80 yrs)

Long long ago, there was a woman who lived in a certain village. Once upon a time, the villagers decided to migrate to another land. That woman decided she was not going to move. She said she did not need to be bothered.

Now when the woman was left alone, she developed a very big wound on the leg. After many years, she also grew old. Then in that area, trees and bushes grew so that the whole neighbourhood was bush and forest.

One day, hyenas came to force the woman to open the door so that they could eat her. However, the woman heard the hyenas before they got to the door. So she sang in a loud voice:

> You sleeping ones
> Wake up and take up your swords
> Hyenas have invaded us
> The hyenas are at the doorstep.

When the hyenas heard that song, they were afraid, so they ran away. The hyenas used to come every day in order to find out with whom the woman lived. Now they investigated very thoroughly and found out the woman's secret. They found out that the woman just sang to disguise the fact that she lived alone; she did not live with anybody. The hyenas knew the woman had neither a husband nor children.

One day the hyenas came to eat the woman. The woman sang:

You sleeping ones
Wake up and take up your swords
Hyenas have invaded us
The hyenas are at the doorstep.

The hyenas replied:

Woman in this house
We have realised you live alone
And you have a big wound on the leg
Today you cannot escape!

After completing their song, the hyenas broke into the woman's hut and ate her up, including her bones.

A person who lives alone dies alone.

* * *

Mutema Kianda na Gacau Mundu

Mutema Kianda ari mundu mutongu muno. Ng'ombe ciake ciari nyingi muno gukira cia andu onthe a itura. Riu Mutema Kianda niwagurire mwongia umwe akimuciarira kavici getagwa Gacau Mundu.

Indi imwe andu engi nimavangire uria mangiuraga Mutema Kianda niguo moce ng'ombe ciake. Andu acio mavangaga na mwongia wa Mutema Kianda. Riu makivanga Gacau Mundu niweguire kwoguo akithii akira ithe ti Mutema Kianda.

Mutema Kianda ekire uguo akiuraga mwongia ucio wake wa akira Gacau Mundu mathame. Matuire nimathama na ng'ombe icio cionthe mathii makairire weru utari ngi kana nvungu. Makivura ng'ombe wa makimunda njira.

Makithii, makithii. Makinya vandu vangiturua makiuria atiri, "Weru uyu wii ngi kana nvungu?"

Ngi ikigamba, "uuu."

Makithii, makithii. Magikinya vandu vengi makiuria woguo, "Weru uyu wii ngi kana nvungu?"

Magitura macokio kwoguo makimenya kuu nikuo magutura maricagire ng'ombe ciao kuo matai na mundu ukumavoya.

Nimathinjire ndegwa. Undu uria wai wa thina niati gutiai vandu mangiavoire kamwaki ga gwokia nyama ciao. Nimathinikire magicaria mwaki. Mathinikanga indi ndaca, nimonire gatogo gagitoga varaca. Makimenya vau nivo makuthii kuvoya mwaki. Mutema Kianda akira Gacau Mundu athii akavoe mwaki vau.

89

Akinya kanyombari kau gatogaga mwaki, Gacau Mundu ethire kamwongia gagituma kiondo. Mwongia agigakundia ucuru. Agicoka akirwa eyocere mwaki. Akuamiriria gwoca mwaki agitikirwa ni nthakame nati ndamenya yauma naku. Agioca mwaki akivirira ithe. Mwaki ndwakana.

Mutema Kianda akimenya ke athi agire mwaki wingi. Akinya gwa kamwongia karia, akirwa eyocere mwaki nati ndakarorie itara. Akiroria itara akiona nyama cia andu icuritue kuu itara. Riu Mutema Kianda akirakara agioca gicinga kinene muno akiringa kamwongia gakigirika. Kamwongia gagikua gakiruma Mutema Kianda gakimwira anake agakua uguo.

Mutema Kianda ndakinyia mwaki atai mukuu. Gacau Mundu nake na ng'ombe magikua wario. Ucio niguo wai muthia wa Mutema Kianda na mucii wake.

Mutema Kianda and his son Gacau Mundu*

Place of origin : Ivurori (Mbeere)
Narrator : Mwitugi Nyaga (Female; 80 yrs)

Mutema Kianda was a very rich man. He was richer than all the people in the land. He had more cattle than anybody in the neighbourhood. Now Mutema Kianda married a woman who bore him a son named Gacau Mundu.

At one time, some people plotted to kill Mutema Kianda so that they could take his cattle. These people conspired with Mutema Kianda's wife. Now while they were plotting, Gacau Mundu overheard so he went and told his father.

Now, what Mutema Kianda did was to kill his wife and migrated with his Gacau Mundu. They decided to move with all the cattle to a land where there were no flies or hawks. So they beat their cattle and set off.

They went, they went. When they reached a place which looked as if it could be inhabited they asked, "Does this land have flies or hawks?" Flies replied, " *Uuu!*"

So they went again and went and went. They reached another place and asked, "Does this land have flies or hawks?"

There was no response so they knew that this was the place where they could settle with nobody to bother them while they were eating their meat.

They slaughtered a bull. The biggest problem was that there was no place for them to get a little fire to roast the meat. They really searched for fire but in vain. After undergoing many problems, they saw some smoke from afar. So they decided that was where they were going to beg for fire. Mutema Kianda told Gacau Mundu to go beg for fire from there.

When he arrived at that hut where the smoke was coming from, he found an old woman weaving a basket. The old woman gave him some gruel. Then he was told to get some fire for himself. As he was bending to get the fire, some blood dripped on him but he did not know where it came from. He took the fire and took it to his father. However, they did not manage to light the fire.

Mutema Kianda — an extraordinary name which literally means "one who cuts the valley".
 Gacau Mundu – an unusual name meaning "a human calf".

Now, Mutema Kianda himself decided to go and get some more fire. When he arrived at the old woman's place, he was told to get some fire but not to look up at the rack above the fireplace. He looked up and saw some human flesh hanging on the rack. Mutema Kianda got angry, took a log of wood from the fire and hit the old woman with it until she fainted. Before she died, the old woman cursed Mutema Kianda and told him that he would die the same way.

Mutema Kianda did not reach where he was to light the fire before he died. Gacau Mundu and the cattle died at the same time. That was the end of Mutema Kianda and his family.

* * *

Wamweru na ng'ina munini

Indi imwe kwari na muthuri wagurite aka airi. Aka aya mairi matiegucanaga. Mwongia wa Kairi aari mwitii, muveria na wi wiru mwingi muno.

Riu mwongia wa mbere niwakwire agitiga kaana gake kamwiritu getagwa Wamweru. Mwongia wa kairi wanake aari na keritu gake getagwa wa Wamweru. Twiritu tuu twetagwa undu umwe tondu twaciaritwe ngina wa ithe wao.

Riu niundu wa wiru wake, mwongia ucio wa kairi niwavangire uria angiuraga kaana ka mwiruwe. Ithe wa twana aai akuthii thavari. Mwongia ekire uguo akinja irina riari iriku muno. Agicoka agituma kaana gake vandu gatikone agikia kau kengi irinari. Arikia gwika uguo mwongia ucio niwathikire Wamweru akinenuka mucii.

Riria Wamweru ucio wingi aciokire, auria kuria mwari wao athiire, mwongia ucio amwirire athiire kwa ucuwe.

Mithenya yathira karundo, Wamweru niwambiririe kumaka na aambiriria gucaria mwari wao. Akithii na vau mugundari akinaga uu:

Wamweru wetu
Wathiire ukindiga niki?
Riu vava arete kauki
Tukaria nau?
Wamweru ii! Wamweru ii!
Wamweru wetu!

Kaana karia kaari irinari nako gacicokia na kamugambo gaceke gakiina uu:

Wamweru wetu
Nyanya munini
Niwaminjire irina
Akinthika ni mwoo
Wamweru ii! Wamweru ii!
Wamweru wetu!

Muthuri ucio niwacokire akiuma thavari. Acoka Wamweru akimwira uria ng'ina athikire Wamweru ucio wingi ai mwoo. Wavau, wavau muthuri ucio makithii na mwari makithikuria kaana kau kai kathike. Magikava maguta ma ng'ondu gagitavika ithetu rionthe riria karite kai irinari.

Rui muthia, muthuri ucio akiuraga mwongia ucio wa kairi niundu wa gwika giiko kiu gicuku muno gia kuthika mwana ai mwoo. Vuvari muthuri ucio agitura na gikeno muno na ciana icio ciake ciendanite muno.

Wamweru and her step-mother

Place of origin : Siakago (Mbeere)
Narrator : Njege wa Gutu (Male; 80 yrs)

Sometime ago, there was a man who had married two wives. The second wife was proud, mean and extremely jealous.

Now, the first wife died leaving her daughter, Wamweru. That second wife also had a daughter named Wamweru. The two girls had the same name because both of them were named after their father's mother.

Now because of her jealousy, the second wife plotted to kill the daughter of her co-wife. The father of the girls had gone on a journey. The woman dug a very big hole. Then she sent her daughter somewhere so that she would not see her throwing her step-sister into the hole. After that, the woman buried Wamweru and went back home.

When the other Wamweru came back and asked where her sister was, her mother told her that she had gone to their grandmother's house. After some days Wamweru started worrying and went to look for her sister. She went to the garden singing:

Wamweru my sister
Why did you leave me?
Now, when our father brings honey
With whom shall I eat it?
Wamweru oh! Wamweru oh!
Wamweru my sister!

The child who was in the hole replied in a very weak voice singing like this:

Wamweru my sister,
My younger mother
Dug a hole for me
And buried me alive
Wamweru oh! Wamweru oh!
Wamweru, my sister!

The man returned from his journey. On arrival, Wamweru told him how her mother buried the other Wamweru alive. There and then, the man and his daughter went and removed the buried

92

child from the hole. They gave her sheep-fat and she vomitted all the soil which she had eaten while buried in the hole.

In the end, the man killed that second wife because of doing such a bad thing: burying a child alive. That man lived happily thereafter with his two children who loved each other dearly.

* * *

Muthini na giconi gitana

Tene tene muno kwari mundu umwe wari muthini muno. Ndaari na aciari kana kamugunda. Aaricaga nyama cia nyamu iria arathaga.

Muthenya umwe muthini ucio niwathiire kugwima nwati aari na mutino muno. Wa nyamu iria ageria kuratha ikaura. Nyamu ya mbere yaari mbuku. Mugwi wake niwarathire kuguru kwa mbuku nwati ikiura ta kuvucia kwa metho. Nyamu ya kairi yaari nthia na twana twayo. Mundu ucio nuungiavotire kuraga twana twa nthia, indi ona uria twonjete agituiguira ntha. Riu riria endire kuraga ng'ina akiremwa ona twana twethitha kwiwe. Kwoguo wana munyaka ucio ukimurira.

Niwegwire nai muno. Ai vakuvi kurira tiga arume matetikiritue kurira miikarireri yao. Riu nvuta yake niyagarurukire igituika nyonda. Kwoguo akiuga athii karunjiri akanyue manji.

Ai vau karunjiri, niwonire giconi atari ona ringi. Kiari kiaro muno kiina mbui cia marangi mengi. Na gitiari na guoya tondu kiambiririe kumukuviviria wana ageria gukingata. Muthiari giconi kiu giaukire gikimwikarira ciau gikimwira, "Nimbici utwire uthinikaga. Ningugutethia, nawe nwa nginya tugie na kiriko kimwe. Wanvivinya, irio ikanyumaga. Irio cia gukwigana, we, mukaguo na ciana cienyu. Nwati nawe, ndukae gukavivinya irio nyingi gukira iria ikwendekana. Niwetikira ndukae kuvivinya irio nyingi gukira iria ikwendekana?"

Mundu ucio niwetikire ati akavivinyaga wa irio ciakumwigana mai na muka na ciana ciao. Akira giconi kiu ati ndaari muguranu tondu wa thina wake. Giconi kiamwirire makinya mucii nigikumutethia kuvivinya indo cia kwigana kuriva rurayio agurane.

Makinya mucii giconi gikiina:

Nvivinya! Nvivinya!

Nvivinya! Nvivinya!"

Mundu ucio avivinya giconi, gikiuma ng'ombe na mburi. Riu giconi gikira mundu ucio nwa agurane na ng'ombe na mburi icio. Giconi gigicoka gikimuririkania enda maundu make mavue, ndakae gukavivinya irio nyingi gukira iria ciendekanite. Gikimwira ere muka na ciana matikae gukavivinya irio nyingi gukira iria ciendekanite.

Niwaguranire na akigia ciana. Na magitura na gikeno mavivinyaga irio kuma gwi giconi wariria menda.

Muthenya umwe, mundu ucio niwarakarire. Vandu va kugeria kuthiria uvoro ucio wamurakaritie na njira ingi, athiire wa gwi giconi kiria. Giconi gikiina woria kiamenyerete:

93

Nvivinya! Nvivinya!
Nvivinya! Nvivinya!

Mundu ucio akivivinya giconi na irio ikiuma woria ciamenyerete. Nwati riu, riria irio ciengivire ikigana cia andu ake onthe, mundu ndatiga kuvivinya giconi. Athiire wana mbere kuvivinya wana giconi kiaina na kamugambo kanini:

Nvivi..... Nvivi......nya
Nvivi......Nvivi........a

Mundu ucio akivivinya kirima kia irio na woria avivinyaga nwaguo nakio giconi kiathiire na mbere kuthira vinya. Vuvari, riria tuirio tunini twa muthia twaumaga, giconi kiainagaga wa:

Nv..............Nv..........
Nv.....Nv.......Nv.......

Mundu uria atigire kuvivinya wa giconi giatiga kugamba wanai vavini tondu kiai gikuu. Mundu ona giconi giakua, akiambiriria gukivurutira nwati maundu mai makuthira.
Atigirwe na kirima giake kia irio kiria giacokire gikiora tondu ndangiathiririe. Riu niundu wa maruru make, muka na ciana ciao makimutiga. Acokire kuthina muno gukira uria ekarii mbere agicoka agikua na thina na kieva.

The poor man and the benevolent bird

Place of origin : Gitituri (Embu)
Narrator : Sarah Geteria (Female; 70 yrs)

Long, long ago, there was a poor man who did not have parents or even a piece of land. He lived on the meat of the wild animals he used to hunt.

One day, the poor man went hunting as usual but he was unlucky with every animal he tried to catch. First, it was a rabbit. His arrow hit the leg but the animal fled fast like the blinking of an eye lid. Next it was an antelope and her children. It would have been easy for the hunter to kill one of the kids, but seeing how weak they were, he had mercy on them. Then he wanted to kill the mother, but seeing that the children ran to her for protection, he could not kill her. So even this chance escaped him.

He was very downcast. He almost cried, but it was against his people's custom for men to cry. The hunger had now turned into thirst and so he decided to go down to the stream to drink water.

While at the stream he saw a bird he had never seen in his life. It was beautiful, with feathers of all colours. It did not seem to be afraid of him, for it kept coming closer to him even when he waved it away. Eventually, the bird came and sat on his lap and began to talk to him.

"I know you have been suffering". The bird said. I am going to help you, but you must promise me one thing. If you squeeze me, food will come out of me. Enough for you, your wife and

94

children. However, you must never squeeze out more food than you need. Do you promise not to squeeze out more food than you need?"

The man promised that he would squeeze out only enough for himself. He told the bird that he did not yet have a wife and children because he was too poor to marry. The bird told him that as soon as they got to his house, it would help him squeeze out enough property to enable him pay dowry for a wife.

When they got to the house, the bird started singing:

Squeeze me, Squeeze me
Squeeze me, Squeeze me.

The man squeezed, and out came cows and goats. Now the bird told him he could use these animals to pay dowry for a wife. The bird reminded him that if he wanted to prosper, he was to keep the promise of not squeezing out more food than he needed. He was also to warn his wife and children not to squeeze out more food than they needed.

He married and got children. And he lived happily with his family, always squeezing out food from the bird whenever it was needed.

One day the man was angry. Instead of seeking a solution to what had angered him, he went for the bird. The bird sang as usual:

Squeeze me, squeeze me
Squeeze me, squeeze me

The man squeezed the bird and as usual food came out. However, when the food was enough for the family, the man did not stop squeezing the bird. He continued squeezing as the bird, now weak, sang:

Squee........ Sque......eze me
Sque....... Sque.....eze me.

The man squeezed out a mountain of food and as he squeezed, the bird grew weaker and weaker. Eventually, as the last morsels were coming out, the bird could only say:

Sq........Sq.......sq
Sq........Sq.......sq.

The man only stopped squeezing when the bird could not make a sound as it was dead. Seeing the bird was dead, the man tried to fan it to bring it back to life but it was too late.

He was left with his mountain of food which eventually rotted away as he could not finish it. Owing to his angry mood, his wife and children also left him. He ended up poorer than before and eventually died in misery.

Trickster stories

Uria mbuku yatuikire muthamaki wa nyamu

Tene tene muno kwai na yura bururi wa nyamu. Indi iyo munene wa nyamu aai munyambu. Kwoguo agita mucemanio munene muno wa nyamu cionthe wa kwaririria thina iyo kwonwe uria maundu mangithondekwa.

Mucemaniori ucio, wa mundu niwaverwe kamweke ga kwaria. Amwe makiuga niwaro kwenjwe manji. Amwe makiuga mathamire bururi wingi. Nwati aria maai engi, niaria maugire muthamaki niwe waregete kuruta wira wake. Kwoguo nyamu cionthe igitikaniria ithure muthamaki wingi. Nyamu cionthe cietikanirie ati uguo niguo waro.

Minthi iyo athamaki mathuragwa kuringana na vinya yao. Munyambu athuritwe niundu wa vinya yake. Riu nyamu ingi ikithurwa nwa nginya ingionanirie ati yaai vinya kwi munyambu. Nyamu iria cierutire icindane vinya na munyambu ciai ithatu. Nyamu icio ciai Njogu, Mbaka na Mbuku.

Njogu na Munyambu makirua, Munyambu ugicinda. Wa kairi aai Mbaka. Ucio nake makirua, Munyambu ugicinda ringi. Mundu wa muthia aai Mbuku.

Riria Mbuku aukire vau mbere, nyamu cionthe ikigwa na matheka. Kanyamu kanini ta kau kangiavotire atia kurua na Munyambu?

Riu Mbuku yevariritie vuru niundu wa mbaara ino. Aretete njuki na mbooro imwe, na nthakame mboorori iria ingi.

Matheka ma nyamu iria ciingi makira, Mbuku akirekereria njuki nacio ikiambiriria kuratha Munyambu. Agicoka agitiriria nthakame kiongori kia munyambu.

Munyambu amakire kimako kinene akiona nthakame ikiuma kiongori giake. Eciririe gwa kiongo giake giatumuka kwoguo akiura.

Nyamu iria ciingi ciamakire kwi Munyambu. Niciarigirwe muno uria kanyamu kanini ta Mbuku kavotire gucinda muthamaki wao munene uguo. Ciamakire muno ati gutii undu ingiekire tiga kuroria Munyambu akiura.

Kuuma indi iyo Mbuku agituika muthamaki wa nyamu.

How Hare became chief of animals

Place of origin :   Nthagaiya (Embu)
Narrator   :   Ciumwari wa Kagoce (Female; 65 yrs)

Once upon a time, there was a famine in the animal world. The chief of the animals at that time was Lion. So he organised a meeting of all the animals to discuss the problem and see how to rectify the situation.

At the meeting, everyone got the opportunity to say something. Some said they should dig for water. Others said they should move to another land. Many, however, said that the chief had been irresponsible and, therefore, they should choose another leader. All the animals agreed that this would be a good idea.

In those days, leaders were chosen according to strength. Lion had been chosen because he was strong. Now, for another animal to be chief, he had to defeat Lion in a physical contest. The animals which came forward fo the contest were three. These were Elephant, Cat and Hare.

Elephant and Lion started the fight and Lion won. Next was the Cat's turn and Lion won again. Lastly, it was the Hare's turn. When Hare came forward, many animals fell down with laughter. How could such a small animal challenge the mighty Lion in battle?

Now, Hare had done a great deal of preparation for this battle. He had brought bees in one bag and blood in another. After the other animals' laughter had died down, Hare unleashed the bees which immediately started stinging Lion. He then poured blood on Lion's head.

Lion was greatly shocked to see blood oozing from his head. He thought his head had burst and so he ran away. The other animals were more shocked than Lion. They did not see how an animal as tiny as a Hare could defeat their mighty chief. They were so shocked that they could do nothing but watch Lion run away.

From that time, Hare became chief of the animals.

* * *

King'ang'i na Iguna

Rimwe tene King'ang'i na Iguna maai urata munene muno. King'ang'i giatuire runjiri nario Iguna rigekara Mutiri wai vau rutere rwa runji.

Muthenya umwe King'ang'i nigietire Iguna iruga gwakio. Nwati Iguna rikiuria King'ang'i uria ringivota gukinya gwakio runjiri na ritiaici kuvutia.

"Aaa! Ucio ti murigo!" King'ang'i gikira Iguna. "Nwa gugukua na murukuthu ngagukua wa ngivutia nawe!"

Iguna rigitikira. Kiathi giakinya Iguna rigitwa murukuthuri wa King'ang'i woria meranite. King'ang'i nakio kigiambiriria kuvutia.

King'ang'i gikithambira gikithambira. Makithii makithii. Waindi makinya gatagatiri ka runji kuraca muno na rutere, King'ang'i gigikorora vanini gikiira Iguna, "Eee! Niwici? Muthamaki wetu nimuruaru muno na eritwe angivora wa arire ngoro ya Iguna. Riu kwa nguvirite ukarutwe ngoro muthamaki wetu arie avore."

Iguna rikivavuka vakuvi rigwe kuuma murukuthuri wa King'ang'i.

"Aaa! Munyanyawa! Ndwanamenya Maguna matigaga ngoro ciamo mitiri iguru? Riu nwa tucokire ngakugirire ngoro yakwa ethirwa niyo ukwendaga!"

Kwoguo King'ang'i gikigaruruka kierekere rutere rwa runji varia Iguna riatwire. Iguna riaigwa nthi rigitwa muti waaro wata mundu uthiite gwoca ngoro macoke mathii runjiri ringi.

Riu Iguna, riatuire yage riririthi. Rikira King'ang'i, "Munyanywa, athamia kanua nguikirie ngoro itanagwa nthi ithuka."

King'ang'i gikiathamia kanua. Nario Iguna rikinyuguta riage kabakabakaba! Puku puku puku! Wa rikithiria magego ma King'ang'i maraeterere. Magego ma King'ang'i monthe magitika nthi.

Iguna riathekire muno rikiuria King'ang'i, "Ithio riri! Wanegua mundu ugendaga atai na ngoro yake?"

Monkey and Crocodile

Place of origin : Ishiara (Mbeere)
Narrator : Paul Njuki (Male; 40)

Some time long ago, Crocodile and Monkey were very great friends. Crocodile lived in the river and Monkey lived on a tree which was there at the bank of the river.

One day, Crocodile invited Monkey to his home for a feast. However, Monkey asked Crocodile how he could reach his home and yet he did not know how to swim.

"Aaa! That is no problem!" Crocodile told Monkey. "I'll just carry you on my back and swim with you!"

Monkey agreed. On the appointed day, Monkey lay on Crocodile's back as they had agreed. Crocodile started swimming.

Crocodile swam and swam. They went, they went. Just as they reached the middle of the river, very far from the bank of the river, Crocodile coughed a little and said to Monkey: "Eee! Do you know? Our king is very sick and he has been told that he would only get well if he ate the heart of Monkey. Now I am just taking you for your heart to be removed so that our king can eat it and get cured."

Monkey was so shocked that he nearly fell off Crocodile's back. But Monkey was not a fool the way Crocodile thought. When he had swallowed the words Crocodile had told him, he said "Aaa! My good friend! Have you never known that monkeys leave their hearts on top of the tree? Now the only thing we can do is to go back so that I can get you my heart if that is what you wanted!"

So Crocodile turned and started swimming back to the river banks where Monkey lived. When Monkey was put down, he climbed up the tree very nicely just like a person who was going to take his heart and then go back for them to continue with their journey.

Now Monkey picked a raw *yage** fruit. He told Crocodile, "My good friend, open your mouth I throw my heart so that it doesn't drop on the ground and get spoilt!"

Crocodile opened his mouth. Monkey threw the *yage* fruit, *kabakabakabakaba! Puku puku puku*! The *yage* fruit found Crocodile's teeth waiting for it. In the end the *yage* fruit broke Crocodile's teeth until all of them scattered on the ground.

Monkey laughed very hard and asked Crocodile, "You big fool! Have you ever heard of a person who moves around without his heart?"

* * *

---

*Yage — a wild fruit that grows in Embu and Mbeere.

98

Uthu wa Nviti na Mbuku

Mbuku na Nviti ciendanite muno nginya ikirana iture vandu vamwe. Niciatumire wa mundu Kyaga giyake na kia ng'ina. Igicoka igituma ciaga cia ng'ombe wa mundu ruake.

Marikia gwika uguo makirana uria makarithagia ng'ombe ciao. Makirikanira wa mundu arithage mithenya itano, ucio wingi agacoka akarithia wa mithenya itano.

Nyamu ino igiri ciekarire ciendanite nati mbuku ndakenaga tondu mburi cia Nviti ciaciaraga mathaha. Niundu ucio ng'ombe na mburi cia Nviti niciengivite muno gucinda cia Mbuku. Mbuku niweguire wiru mwingi muno niundu wa indo cia Nviti.

Mbuku akivanga uria akuvenereria Nviti niguo oce indo ciake. Mbuku akira Nviti ati aa ng'ina mao ti aro niundu matimakandagia kurithia. Makivanga menuka kivwai marive aa ng'ina mao nginya riria magakua.

Riria makinyire mucii, Mbuku atumiire ugi wake. Ithenya ria kuriva ng'ina ambiririe kuriva ndarwa agitetaga akiugaga.

"We nyanya ni mucuku muno niundu ndundethagia kurithia. Uricaga irio cia mana. Umunthi nikwa ngukuraga."

Mbuku agicoka akiuga mbu na kamugambo ta ka ng'ina, "Uui! Tiga kumburaga! Uui Tiga kumburaga!"

Nviti egua mbu iria eciragia ni ya ng'ina wa Mbuku kwoguo akiamata ng'ina agitwa kumuriva. Akimuriva, akimuriva nginya agikua. Riria Mbuku amenyire ng'ina wa Nviti ni wakua acokire kumuthekerera akimwiraga, "Uui kithao giteci ugi nindui. Nindui urauragire nyukwe? Nie nyanya ai wavo, timukuu."

Nviti egwire nai muno nginya akivanga kuthama. Niundu wa marakara, Nviti ndatinda agioca indo ciake. Athamire arungii atai wanai gatui. Akira Mbuku ndakanae gugakinya gwake.

Mbuku niwakenire muno atigirwa indo cia Nviti cionthe. Mbuku athiire akira ng'ina macoke marithagie indo ciake wana cia Nviti vamwe.

Kuma muthenya ucio, Nviti na Mbuku itiendaga kuonana. Uthu wa Nviti na Mbuku waumire indori cia Nviti.

The enmity between Hyena and Hare

Place of origin :   Ivurori (Mbeere)
Narrator   :   Mwitugi Nyaga (Female; 80 yrs)

Hare and Hyena were such good friends that they agreed to live together. They built each person a hut for himself and one for his mother. They then built enclosures for their cattle, each person his own enclosure.

After doing that, they made arrangements on how to share the work of grazing their animals. They agreed that one person grazes for five days and the other one for five days.

These two animals lived together as friends for sometime, but Hare was not happy because Hyena's goats were delivering twins. As a result, Hyena's cattle and goats increased and became more than those of Hare. Hare felt very jealous of Hyena's property.

Hare planned how he would trick Hyena so that he could take his livestock. Now Hare told Hyena that their mothers were bad because they did not help them in the work of herding their livestock They agreed that when they got home in the evening they would beat their mothers until they died.

When they got home, Hare used his brains. Instead of beating his mother, he started beating a hide while at the same time complaining saying, "You, mother, you are very bad because you don't help me graze the animals. You eat food which you haven't worked for. Today I'll kill you."

Hare then screamed loudly in a voice like his mother's saying, "Uui! Don't kill me! Uui! Don't kill me!"

When Hyena heard the screams he imagined they were coming from Hare's mother. He got hold of his mother and started beating her. He beat her, he beat her, until she died.

When Hare knew that Hyena's mother had died, he started laughing telling him, "Oh! Oh! A fool who doesn't know what brains are for! What did you kill your mother for? As for me, my mother is alive; she is not dead."

Hyena felt very bad until he planned to migrate. Owing to his bitter anger, Hyena did not bother to take his property. He moved empty-handed. He told Hare never to set foot in his new home.

Hare was extremely happy to get all of Hyena's property. Hare went and told his mother they should now be herding their livestock together with Hyena's.

From that day, Hyena and Hare never want to set eyes on each other. The enmity between Hyena and Hare originated from Hyena's livestock.

* * *

Uria Muriu wavotire Mbuku

Tene tene i, Mbuku na Muriu nimaceragira mwana mwari umwe wai mwaro muno.

Muthenya umwe Muriu niwathiire gucerera mwari uyu nake akimwira, "Nie ndingivota gutua ciira uria ukangura tondu niguo muranduira. Riu nimenda kenda mutige kunduira mugauka munthi umwe tene muoiri. Uria ugakinya mbere ya uria wingi niwe ngathii nake."

Mbuku nake auka gucera mwana mwari akimwira wa uguo.

Mwana mwari niwatuirire Mbuku na Muriu muthenya wa kiathi riria akagurua.

Muthenya wakinya, Mbuku na Muriu magitungana varia maari mambiririe ivenya macindanire mwana mwari.

Riu Muriu niwaici ndangicinda Mbuku na ivenya kwoguo niweciririe uria angika niguo athii na mwana mwari. Niweciririe njira iria mbaro nwa gutua mukiari wa Mbuku. Riria ivenya riambiririe Muriu waagitwa mukiari uria wa Mbuku. Mbuku nake akivinyura akuite Muriu.

100

Mbuku niweci Muriu ndangimucinda na ivenya. Kwoguo akiuria Muriu atiri mai ivenyari, "Uru wa vuva ria ivenya?" Nake Muriu agicokia na kamugambo kanini, "Ii niruakuo." Mbuku egua Muriu acokia ai vakuvi uguo akimenya avota gukinyirwa. Kwoguo akiongerera ivenya riake.

Riria Mbuku akinyire kwaa mwana mwari agarurukire akiroria vuva. Arega kwona Muriu agikena muno akimenya niwe wacinda.

Riu mwana mwari niwaigite giti vau nja kia mundu uria ugakinya mbere. Waindi Mbuku athii gwikarira giti egwire Muriu auga, "Tenya gukambikarira munyanyawa!"

Mbuku niwamakire muno ona ati Muriu niakinyire mbere yake.

Mwana mwari atuikire niathii na Muriu tondu niwacindanire. Mwana Mwari ucio ndendete Muriu muno ta uria endete Mbuku nwati aari eke wata uria augite.

Muthiari Muriu enukire na mwiritu nake Mbuku ivenya riake rigituika ria mana.

How Chameleon defeated Hare

Place of origin : Gitituri (Embu)
Narrator : Sarah Geteira (Female; 70 yrs)

Long long ago, Chameleon and Hare were wooing the same girl who was very beautiful.

One day, Chameleon went to visit the girl and the girl told him, "I can't choose between the two of you who is to marry me, although you are fighting so much for me. Now I want both of you to come early one day so that you can stop competing for me. Whoever will arrive first is the one who will marry me." When Hare came, the girl told him the same thing.

The girl set for Hare and Chameleon the day for the race when she would get married. On the appointed day, Hare and Chameleon met where the race was to start so that they could compete for the girl.

Now Chameleon knew that he could not defeat Hare in running. So he thought of what to do in order to win the girl. He decided that the best thing to do was to climb on Hare's tail. When the race started, Chameleon climbed on Hare's tail. Hare now set off, carrying Chameleon.

Hare knew that Chameleon could not defeat him in running. So while they were racing, Hare asked Chameleon, "Are you still bringing the rear?" Chameleon replied in a soft voice, "Yes, I am still trying."

When Hare heard Chameleon reply from so close by, he feared Chameleon might catch up with him. So he increased his pace.

When Hare arrived at the girl's home, he turned and looked behind. When he didn't see Chameleon he was very happy thinking that he was the winner.

Now the girl had kept a seat outside in the yard for the person who would arrive first. Just as Hare was about to sit, he heard Chameleon say, "Take care not to sit on me, my friend!"

Hare was very shocked to see that Chameleon had arrived before him.

The girl had to be married to Chameleon because he was the one who had won the race. The girl did not love Chameleon as much as she loved Hare but she had to do as she had promised.

In the end, Chameleon took the girl to his home while Hare reaped nothing from his good performance in the race.

* * *

Ogre stories

Nthaka ya miromo iiri

Indi imwe tene kwai rwimbo rwa aari na nthaka runene muno. Rwainagwa ni andu a migongo yonthe ya Embu na Mbeere. Andu amwe a kuuma Miiru wana Ikamba aria meguite ndeto cia ruimbo ruu wanao nimevaririe kuruthii.

Riu kwai nthaka imwe irimarimu yeguire uvoro wa ruimbo ruu na ikimenya wanayo nwethii gwikenia ta nthaka iria ciingi.

Nthaka iyo yekire uguo ikithamba waaro ikineguika nguo mbaro ma. Yeroria uguo ikiona gutii mundu ungimenya ati we ni irimarimu. Riu wegioca maguru ikithii rwimbori.

Aari aria maai rwimbori ruu, gutiri we utenda kwinua ni nthaka iyo. Rwimbo nirwainirwe ma, na andu onthe magicanjamuka.

Indi ya kwinuka yakinya, aari onthe nimarumirire nthaka iyo irimarimu. Mathiicanga nthaka ikimera macoke. Ikimainira:

> Aari aya cokai
> Uyu ti mundu
> Ni nyamu ya runji
> Mucingiri!
> Mucingiri!
> Iyovete ngucu na ciuma
> Mucingiri!
> Mucingiri!

Aari megua uguo, amwe magicoka aria engi makithii na mbere na kurumirira irimarimu riria. Makithii, makithii. Nthaka iria irimarimu ikina wa ringi:

> Aari aya cokai
> Uyu ti mundu
> Ni nyamu ya runji
> Mucingiri!
> Mucingiri!
> Iyovete ngucu na ciuma
> Mucingiri!
> Mucingiri!

Riu waringi aari amwe magicoka magitigara athatu tu. Makithii, makithii. Makithii nginya magikinya runjiri. Makinya runjiri, nthaka iria ikiruga ikiringa runji.

"Ayia!" Mwari umwe akiuga. "Nimwona njuiri cia nthaka ciainaina na ava vuva cionania muromo wingi? Ayia! Tucokeni. Waguo ino ni nyamu ya miromo iiri ti mundu!

Mwari umwe wa acio engi akiuga, "Aaai! Namue mwi guoya muno! Ndukwona uria atherete: Ni mundu nikwa wavenua ni metho."

Aari airi magicoka. Makithii ucio wa kathatu akimera, "Irimu ino iguoya ino. Nie ninthii wanake buru!"

Riu nthaka igitigwa na mwari umwe. Makithii, makithii nthaka i mbere nake mwari amirumirire.

Nthaka ikimwinira karwimbo karia:

Mwari uyu cioka
Uyu ti mundu
Ni nyamu ya runji
Mucingiri!
Mucingiri!
Iyovete ngucu na ciuma
Mucingiri!
Mucingiri!

Mwana mwari ndegua nwakwa athiire na mbere na kurumirira nthaka. Makithii, makithii.

Makinya kwa nthaka mwana mwari akivewa manji, akinyua. Agicioka akivewa irio, akiria: Agicioka akionua varia akumama.

Riu irauko aramuka ethire nthaka niithiire nwa irimarimu mai nario akiambiriria kurira. Irimarimu rikimwinira na kimugambo kinene:

Nakwirire ucioke
Ukirega!
Nakuirire ucioke
Ukirega!

Mwana mwari maturire na irimarimu riu ai muka wario. Wa irauko, irimarimu rikithii kugwima rigatiga muka nyomba. Wana angiageririe kwinuka ndangiamenyire njira ya mucii tondu kundu kuu kwai mutituri mugitu muno.

Riu mundu mukoria niwakinyirie vandu akigia ivu, agicioka agiciara kavici. Kavici kau gekarii ta ithe buru. Nwati vandu va tunua twiri ta ithe, kavici kaai na metho mwiri wonthe, kwoguo kavici kaverwe ritwa "Metho".

Metho aneneva nimatuire kuthiicaga na ithe kugwima. Wa muthenya, maindagira mundu muka nyama cia andu amarugire. We ndaricaga icio aari na irio ciake mwanya.

Muthenya umwe mwana na ithe mauma ugwimiri, Metho aukire kwi ng'ina akenete muno. Aking'aria kwiwe akuite kindu athithite.

"Nyanya, ndugira tukindu tutu!"

Mundu muka akiroria, ni tukenge tuvici twa mathatha.

Atwocire, agitugumbania tondu nitwainainaga ni nvevo agicioka agituthitha. Atuthithire nyunguri vandu tutangionwa. Agicioka akirugira Metho tukindu twiri. Metho tondu karitite wa ta ithe, gakiria tukindu kaugaga, "Aayia! Kamurio. Tuvuite i!"

Nake ng'ina agaciokia, "Terire mwana wakwa. Niturugire woria mbici wendaga tunyama twaku!"

Riu tuvici turia twakurire, tugikura. Tugikura nginya tukiambiriria kuthiicaga vau nja riria Metho na ithe mai ugwimiri wao. Muthenya umwe Metho akiona tumakinyo twa tuvici tuu vau nja. Akiuria ng'ina aria maukaga kumucerera muthenya. Ng'ina aringirwe ni maruru akimugukira akimwira, "Tenya kundirikania maruru ma mwaruaiya uria mwauragire mukindetera nimurugire!"

Tondu Metho aritite wa ta ithe ndamenya uguo'ng'ina auga niatia. Nwa kuthii athiire agioca mavindi make varia aigagirwa akiambiriria kumakanda.

Tuvici turia twiri nitwakurire nginya tugituika nthaka nene. Riu muka ucio niwamavere macuma makithondekera mengere. Muthenya, riria Metho na ithe mai ugwimiri, nthaka icio nicierutaga kugwima vau nja. Ikiruta, ikiruta nginya ikimenya uria ingiuraga nyamu na mengere icio ciao.

Kivwai kimwe mundu muka ucio waguritwe ni irimarimu niwaciirire, "Muthenya ni uyu"

Nthaka nacio igiciokia wa uguo. "Muthenya ni uyu"

Nthaka ciarire waro mbere ya metho na ithe makinye. Nao Metho na ithe makinya nimethiire marugiritwe nyama nyingi muno na mavindi mengi muno. Riu indi ino mararia, Metho akeraga ithe, "Na niregua munungo wa andu."

Ithe nake akamwira na mung'oroto wake, "Tiga kunegenera ngiria."

Makiria, makiria ninya makimama wa vau maricagira makiambiriria kugona.

Indi ino niundu nthaka ciethithite itara iguru, ikigua mugono igikorora. Nake ng'ina ai ava vakuvi na marimarimu akimagariura one kana niamamu toro nene uria endaga. Akiona mamamite ta nyamu nguu. Aciokire akina ngemi iria ciainagirwa mbutu cia mbaara. Nthaka ciegua uguo ikiuma itara na ivenya ikiuraga marimarimu, ikimatemanga magikara wa ta nyamu nthinje.

Vuvari mundu muka atongoririe nthaka iria akithii akiinaga akiinaga ngemi nginya magikinya kwao mucii. Akinya mucii gikeno kiria kiari kuu kiari kinene muno! Mathinjirwa! Mundu muka agitumirwa nyomba, nacio nthaka ciake ikivewa wa mundu vandu vake va gutura. Nthaka icio niciaguranire na igitura kuu na ng'ina ucio wamarerire magituura na gikeno kinene muno.

A young man with two mouths

Place of origin : Gitituri (Embu)
Narrator : Sarah Geteria (Female; 70 yrs)

Some time long ago, there was a very big traditional dance for young men. That dance was to be attended by people from all ridges of Embu and Mbeere. Some people from Meru and even

104

Ukambani who had heard about this dance had also prepared to participate in it.

Now, there was a young ogre who heard about this dance and decided that he too could go along to enjoy himself like other young men. This young ogre did like this: he washed himself nicely and dressed in his best garments. When he examined himself he found that he was so smart that nobody would have guessed that he was an ogre. Then he set off for the dance.

Among the girls who were at the dance, there was no one who did not wish to dance with this young man. People danced and everyone had a very good time. When it was time to go home, all the girls followed the young ogre. When they had covered quite some distance, the ogre told them in a song:

Young ladies go back
This is not a man
It is a river animal
Mucingiri!
Mucingiri!

Which has adorned itself
With the best ornaments,
Mucingiri!
Mucingiri!

When the girls heard that, some of them went back but others continued to follow the ogre. They travelled, they travelled. The young man sang again:

Young ladies go back
This is not a man
It is a river animal,
Mucingiri!
Mucingiri!

Which has adorned itself
With the best ornaments,
Mucingiri!
Mucingiri!

Now again, some girls went back until only three were left. They went, they went. They travelled until they reached the river. When they reached the river, the young man jumped in and crossed it.

"Ayia!" one girl said. "Did you see that when his hair shook it revealed another mouth at the back of the head? Ayia! Let us go back! It is true this is a two-mouthed animal and not a man!"

One of the other two girls said, "Aaai! You people fear too much; you are too cowardly! Can't you see how clean he is? He is a man, only that your eyes deceived you."

Two girls went back. As they were going, the third girl told them, "Fools! Cowards! I'll go with him up to his home!"

Now the young man was left with only one girl. They went, they went. They travelled with the man leading, the girl following.

The man sang her his song:

Oh! Girl go back
This is not a man
It is a river animal,
Mucingiri!
Mucingiri!
Which has adorned itself
With the best ornaments,
Mucingiri!
Mucingiri!

The girl ignored and continued following the young man. They went, they went.

When they arrived at the young man's house, the girl was given water and she drank. Then she was given food, and she ate. Then she was shown where to sleep. Now when she woke up in the morning, she found that the young man had disappeared and she was face to face with an ogre. She started crying. The ogre sang for her in a deep frightening voice:

I told you to go back
You refused!
I told you to go back
You refused!

The girl lived with the ogre as his wife. Every morning, the ogre would go hunting and leave the woman in the house. Even if she tried to go home she could not tell the way home because the ogre's house was in the middle of a thick forest.

Now the girl got pregnant and delivered a boy. That boy looked very much like his father the ogre. But instead of having two mouths like his father, he had eyes all over his body. So the boy was named Metho, which means "eyes".

When Metho grew up, he started accompanying his father, on his hunting trips. Everyday, they would bring the woman human flesh to cook for them. She never ate that food. She had her own separate food.

One day, father and son arrived from the hunt and Metho ran excitedly to his mother. He was hiding something and when he revealed it, he told her, "Mother, cook for me these rats!"

When the woman saw them, she noticed they were twin boys.

She took them, wrapped them up as they were shaking from cold. She then hid them far away. She hid them in a pot where they could not be discovered. She then cooked two rats for Metho. Now since Metho was as stupid as his father, while he was eating the rats he was saying, "Aayia! Sweet! Very delicious rats!"

"Eat, my child. I prepared them just the way I know you like your choice of meat," his mother responded.

Now the two boys grew up, and grew up. They grew up and started going outside while Metho and his father were out hunting. One day, Metho saw the boys' footprints outside. He asked his mother to tell him which people visit her during the day. The mother was struck by bitter memories and exclaimed, "Stop reminding me of the bitter memories of my sister whom you people killed and brought for me to cook for you!"

Since Metho was as stupid as his father, he did not realise what the mother had said. He just went and took his bones from where they used to be kept and started eating them.

The two boys grew up until they became young men. Now, the woman gave them some metal with which to make themselves swords. During the day, while Metho and his father were out hunting, the young men would practise how to stalk and hunt animals just outside the house. They practised, they practised, until they knew how they could kill animals with their swords.

One evening the ogre's wife told them, "Today is the day!" The young men responded, "Today is the day."

The young men ate well before Metho and his father returned. Metho and his father came back to find a lot of meat and bones prepared for them. Now while they were eating, Metho was telling his father, "And I can smell human beings!" But the father would grunt, "Stop bothering me while I am eating!"

They ate and ate until they fell asleep just there where they were eating. They started snoring.

Now, since the young men were hiding on the rack next to the ceiling, they heard the loud snores. So they coughed. The mother for her part, turned the ogres' limbs to see if they were fast asleep just as she had hoped. She found that they had slept like dead animals. She then uttered a war cry.

When the young men heard that, they came down from the rack and killed the ogres and cut them up until they looked like slaughtered animals.

In the end, the woman led the young men out and they travelled with her ululating until they reached her home. When she got home, the joy that filled the whole neighbourhood was great. They really feasted! A house was built for the woman and then each of the young men was shown where to build and set up his homestead. The young men married and lived happily thereafter with that mother who had brought them up.

* * *

Mwaria uria waririrwe twana ni irimurimu

Tene tene muno kwari na mwana mwari iturari ria Kanthuku. Mwari ucio niwagire ivu atari mugure. Iturari riu aari matietikiritue guciarira kwao matari agure. Mwari ucio niwathithire ivu riu riake. Ekagira ruo rwarii nginya agiciara.

Riu athiire rutereri rwa muvuro agiciarira vo. Aciarire twana twa mathatha agituthitha mithanjeri. Athiicaga kwongia twana tuu wa kavwai rionthe.

Wa akinya vau muvurori akauga, "Makonde nyuma mwiri nithambe!"

Ruo rukauma, agacoka ageta twana twake akaina:

> *Twana twa mburi imii imii!*
> *Ukai mwonge ii imii imii!*
> *Nyukwe ni waca ii imii imii!*

Twana twegua mugambo ucio tukamenya ni ng'ina. Tukauma tuvinyurite tukathii tukonga tugacoka ithanjeri riria.

Mwari arikia kwongia ciana akauga, "Makonde njoka nthingatie ng'ombe cia awa." Auga uguo ruo ruria rugacoka mwiri wake akenuka.

Andu nimarikire kurania kuria mwari ucio athiicaga wa kavvai. Niwathingatirwe ni muruang'ina nginya akiona ni twana ethagirwa akiongia. Muruang'ina akithii akira aciari mao. Nwati mwana mwari aurua uvoro ucio agikana. Akithaithwa arete twana mucii akirega akiuga we ndari ciana.

Muthenya umwe mwana mwari niwathingatirwe ni irimurimu na rikithitha vandu. Rikigua auga, "Makonde nyuma mwiri nithambe!"

Makonde makiuma Agicoka akiina:

> Twana twa mburi imii imii!
> Ukai mwonge ii imii imii!
> Nyukwe ni waca ii imii imii!

Twana tugiuka, tukionga na tugicoka. Ng'ina akiuga, "Makonde njoka!' Namo makonde magicoka.

Irimurimu riona uguo rikivanga uria ringiuka kuvenereria twana niguo riturie. Riaukire rikinaina wata ng'ina wa twana:

> Twana twa mburi imii imii!
> Ukai mwonge ii imii imii!
> Nyukwe ni waca ii imii imii!

Twana tugiciria nwa ng'ina wauka gutuongia. Kwoguo tukiuma tukinamerua ni irimurimu.

Mwana mwari auka akina:

> Twana wa mburi imii imii!
> Ukai mwonge ii imii imii!
> Nyukwe ni waca ii imii imii!

Twana twake tutiauma. Agitucutha ithanjeri tugitura. Akimenya niturirwe ni irimurimu. Akinuka mucii akiriraga. Marira make wana uthani wake ndwanamucokeria twana. Mwari ucio aurirwe ni mugwi na gaconi.

The girl whose children were eaten by the ogre

Place of origin : Kiritiri (Mbeere)
Narrator : Ciamburi wa Ngari (Female; 60 years)

Long long ago, there lived a girl in the village of Kanthuku. That girl got pregnant before marriage. In that village it was taboo for a girl to give birth in her own home before marriage. That girl hid the pregnancy by weaving a very wide goatskin garment. She hid the pregnancy this way until she delivered.

Now she went and delivered on the river bank. She delivered twins and hid them in the reeds. So she would go every evening to suckle her twins. Whenever she reached the river bank she would say, "Stupid goatskin come off my body I bathe!"

The goatskin garment would come off, then she would call her children singing:

Goat's kids *ii imii imii!*
Come and suck the breast *ii imii imii!*
Your mother has come *ii imii imii!*

Whenever the children heard that, they knew that it was their mother. They would come out from the reeds and rush to feed. Then they would go back to their hiding place among the reeds.

After suckling them, the girl would now say, "Goatskin come back on my body! I follow my father's cattle!"

The goatskin would get back on her body and she would go home.

Eventually, people started wondering where the girl went every evening. Her brother followed her until he discovered that it was babies she went to feed by the river bank. The brother went and reported the matter to their parents.

However, when the girl was asked about this matter, she said there was nothing like that. The parents persuaded her to bring the children home but she refused the brother's claim that she had children by the river bank.

One day, the girl was followed by an ogre which hid itself somewhere. The ogre heard the girl say:

Goat's kids *ii imii imii!*
Come and suck the breast *ii imii imii!*
Your mother has come *ii imii imii!*

The babies came, fed and returned to their hiding place. The mother said, "Goatskin get back onto my body."

When the ogre saw that, he planned on how to come and trick these babies so that he could eat them. The ogre came and sang just the way he had heard the mother sing:

Goat's kids *ii imii imii!*
Come and suck the breast *ii imii imii!*
Your mother has come *ii imii imii!*

109

The babies thought it was the mother who had come to suckle them. So they came out and were swallowed by the ogre immediately.

When the girl came, she sang:

Goat's kids *ii imii imii*!
Come and suck the breast *ii imii imii*!
Your mother has come *ii imii imii*!

Her babies did not come out. She looked for them among the reeds and failed to see them. She knew now that they had been eaten by the ogre. She went back home crying. Her tears and her lies did not give her back her babies. That girl lost her arrow as well as her bird.

* * *

Kanya ka vava

Tene ri, mwari umwe niwocire kanya ka ithe akithii gutava manji nako. Riria avutavutagiria kanya muvurori ri, nigatwarirwe ni manji nake mwana mwari akiuga nwanginya agakinyire nginyagia riria agagakinyira.

Mwari ucio niweikirie muvurori akiambiriria kurumirira kanya ka ithe. Mwari ucio athiicaga akinaga atiri:

> *Kanya ka vava ii*
> *Vingiri vingiri*
> *Wakuria ukathii*
> *Vingiri vingiri*
> *Nwakuo ngaca ii*
> *Vingiri vingiri.*

Kanya kau kavingiritire na muvuro nginya gagitiramira gitinari kia mukuu wari munene muno. Vau gitinari kia mukuu ucio vaari na nthi nyumu.

Riria mwari ucio akinyire vau mutiri ucio niwatiramire gwoca kanya karia ka ithe. Riu ai vau, agitikirwa ni matata; matata ma nthakame, matata ma iria na matata ma uuki Agicuna matata mau monthe. Arikia gucuna matata mau, irimurimu rikiumira rikimuria, "Nindui wicirite guku mwari uyu?"

Nake mwari agicokia atiri, "Ni kanya ka vava nirathingatite."

Mwana mwari aavenererue ni irimurimu na irio mbaro na ndeto nyingi nginya gutituka gwatuka nwakwa irimurimu rieririre mwana mwari.

Kanya karia mwari athingatite gatianonwa ni andu mao. Mwana mwari akuire uthingatiri wa kanya ka ithe.

My father's gourd

Place of origin : Kiritiri (Mbeere)
Narrator   : Ciatama Njoka (Female; 80 yrs)

Once upon a time, a certain girl took her father's gourd to go and fetch water in it. As she was drawing some water in the river, it was carried away by the water. The girl decided she was going to swim and follow the gourd until she recovered it.

So she jumped into the river and started following the gourd. She swam singing like this:

My father's gourd
Roll and roll
Wherever you go
Roll roll
I shall follow you
Roll roll.

The gourd rolled in the river until it was taken under a huge fig tree. Now, at the bottom of the fig tree, there was dry land all around.

When the girl reached that place, she stopped to pick up her father's gourd. Now, while she was there, some drops fell on her; drops of blood, drops of milk and drops of honey. The girl licked all those drops. After she had licked these drops, an ogre appeared and asked her, "What have you come to do here young girl?"

"I just followed my father's gourd," the girl replied.

The girls was tricked by the ogre through delicious food and many stories until it was night. When darkness fell, the ogre ate up the girl.

The gourd the girl followed was never seen by her people. The girl lost her life just because of following her father's gourd.

* * *

Mwana mwari na irimarimu rietagwa Kibugi

Indi imwe mwana mwari niwariganirwe ni ngoi ya mwana mugundari. Riu agitigira kurumwa ni ng'ina kwoguo akiuga athii amicokere. Akithii wana akithira ngoi wa varia yatigitwe.

Riu agicoka, niwatunganirwe na marimarimu matano. Akinya kwi irimarimu ria mbere rikimuria, "Mwana mwari wauma ku kana ngurie?"

Mwana mwari akinira irimarimu karuimbo gaka:

111

Nauma na guku kianda
Kugira ngoi ya mwana
ngoi ya mwana wetu
Iriganire wa kianda
Gucia irenge na muthethu
Uthegute njira nithiire.

Irimarimu ria mbere rikitheguta mwari akivituka.
Akithii akithii. Agikinyira ria kairi. Rikimuria, "Mwana mwari wauma ku kana
ngurie?".

Mwana mwari akinira irimarimu karuimbo karia:

Nauma na guku kianda
Kugira ngoi ya mwana
Ngoi ya mwana wetu
Iriganire wa kianda
Gucia irenge na muthetu
Uthegute njira nithiire.

Irimarimu riu ria kairi rikithenguta mwana mwari akivituka.
Akithii, akithii. Agikinyira irimarimu ria kathatu. Rikimuria, "Mwana Mwari wauma
ku kana ngurie?"

Mwana mwari akinira irimarimu karuimbo gake:

Nauma na guku kianda
Kugira ngoi ya mwana
Ngoi ya mwana wetu
Iriganire wa kianda
Gucia irenge na muthetu
Uthengute njira nithiire.

Irimarimu riu rikithenguta. Nwati rikira mwana mwari emenyerere Kibugi uria wi
vuva.
Iriamurimu riu ria kana ritari riravituka buru mwana mwari akigua nwa inegene
ringi riukite:

Kubu! Kubu!
Cengere! Cengere!
Kobo! Kubu!
Cuaaa! Cha!

112

Kibugi agikinyia ai na ivanga na macembe na macuma ma mithenba mingi muno. Akiuria mwana mwari na kimugambo kinene gia kumwikira guoya, "Mwaaari, Mwaaari wauma ku kana ngurie?"

Mwana mwari ai ava riu egwire guoa-i! Agicokia na kamugambo kanini akiriraga:

> *Nauma na guku kianda*
> *Kugira ngoi ya mwana*
> *Ngoi ya mwana wetu*
> *Iriganire wa kianda*
> *Gucia irenge na muthetu*
> *Uthengute njira nithiire.*

Mwana mwari akirikia kwina uguo aari mumerie ni irimarimu riu rietagwa Kibugi. Riu andu mucii meterere mwana mwari makinoga. Ithe wa akinora ithanwa na mengere. Agioca maguru erekere njirari iyo ya mugundari. We niwamenyire tu na ngoro yake ni irimarimu riameretie mwari.

Akithii, akithii. Agitungana na irimarimu ria mbere. Akirinira:

> *Ucio warire mwivua*
> *Nanie niauke akindia!*

Irimarimu riu rigicokia:

> *Tinie narire mwivua*
> *Ni Kibugi uri vuva.*

Akithii agitungana na irimarimu ria kairi. Akirinira wa karuimbo kau.

> *Ucio warire mwivua*
> *Nanie niauke akindia!*

Irimarimu riu rigicokia:

> *Tinie narire mwivua*
> *Ni Kibugi uri vuva*

Akithii agitungana na irimarimu ria kathatu. Akirinira wa karuimbo waguo:

> *Ucio warire Mwivwa*
> *Nanie niauke akindia!*

Irimarimu ria kathatu rigicokia wana karuimbo kau kainagwa ni marimarimu mau mengi:

Tinie narire Mwivua
Ni Kibugi uri vuva

Muthuri ucio akiroria irimarimu riu muno one kana nirio riameretie mwari. Ai vau akiriroria, irimarimu ria kana rigikinya muthuri akireka riu ria kathatu rivituke, akinira ria kana:

Ucio warire Mwivwa
Nanie niauke akindia!

Nario rigicokia:

Tinie narire Mwivwa
Ni Kibugi uri vuva

Muthuri ari wa vau akigua:

Kubu! Kobo!
Cengere! Cucunguru!
Kobo! Kubu!
Cuaa! Chaa!

Egua uguo muthuri akivariria na ithanwa riake na mengere iria yake aanorete. Akivanda eterere irimarimu riu rigerie kumutema na macembe make. Irimarimu riu ria gatano riakinya vau, riona uria muthuri ucio evandite na ururu na urume mwingi, rikiambiriria kwinaina ni guoya. Wa rikinainaga uguo, muthuri akirinira na mugambo munene:

Ucio warire Mwivua
Nanie niauke akindia!

Rikithii kwina uria marimarimu maria mengi mainaga:

Tinie na.....

Muthuri agiukiririra ithanwa aritemange nwati mbere ya aritemange rikiuga, "Ika ndukamburage, avai. Ndinia kaara gaka kanini, urute mwariguo".

114

Riu muthuri atinia irimarimu riu kaara, andu aria maumire vau matongoretue ni Mwivua! Mwana mwari uria wariganiritwe ni ngoi ya mwana aumire arumiriritwe ni ciana ciingi na andu onthe a itura aria irimarimu riu riarite. Andu acio marika kuuma nimaugire nwa nginya irimarimu riu rietagwa Kibugi riuragwe ritige kuthinia andu a itura. Ithe wa Mwivua wana ndakoma Kibugi tiga kaara karia atinitie. Irimarimu riauragirwe ni andu acio riameretie.

A girl and an ogre called Kibugi

Place of origin :   Gitituri (Embu)
Narrator   :   Sarah Geteria (Female; 70 yrs)

Once upon a time, a girl forgot the baby sling at the farm. Now, she feared being scolded by her mother so she decided to go back and get it. She went and found the sling just where it had been.

While on the way back, she met five ogres following one another. When she reached the first one, he asked her, "You girl, you girl, where are you coming from? Shall I eat you?"

The girl sang for the ogre the following song:

I am coming from down the valley
To get the baby's sling;
The sling for carrying our baby,
We had forgotten it down the valley
Take a piece of pumpkin and some soil
Then move away from the path
And let me pass.

The first ogre moved aside and the girl passed. She went and went. She reached the second ogre and it asked her, "You girl, you girl, where are you coming from? Shall I eat you?" The girl sang for the ogre:

I am coming from down the valley
To get the baby's sling
The sling for carrying our baby
We had forgotten it down the valley
Take a piece of pumpkin and some soil
Then move away from the path
And let me pass.

The second ogre moved aside and the girl passed. She went, and went. She came to the third ogre and it asked her, "You girl, you girl, where are you coming from? Shall I eat you?" In response, the girl sang her song:

I am coming from down the valley
To get the baby's sling
The sling for carrying our baby
We had forgotten it down the valley
Take a piece of pumpkin and some soil
Then move away from the path
And let me pass.

The third ogre moved aside and the girl passed. She went, and went. She came to the fourth ogre and it asked her, "You girl, you girl, where are you coming from? Shall I eat you?" The girl sang for that ogre the same song:

I am coming from down the valley
To get the baby's sling
The sling for carrying our baby
We had forgotten it down the valley
Take a piece of pumpkin and some soil
Then move away from the path
And let me pass.

The fourth ogre moved aside but it told the girl to beware of Kibugi who was bringing up the rear. Before that fourth ogre had moved away completely, the girl heard a lot of noise approaching, "*Kubu! Kobo! Cengere! Cunguru! Kobo! Kubu! Cuaaa! Cha!*"

Kibugi presented himself carrying machetes, knives, hoes and all types of metallic objects. He asked the girl in a loud voice, "You giiiirl, you giirl, where are you coming from? Shall I eat you!!!" Now the girl was struck with deep fear. She responded in a weak tearful voice:

I am coming from down the valley
To get the baby's sling
The sling for carrying our baby
We had forgotten it down the valley
Take a piece of pumpkin and some soil
Then move away from the path
And let me pass.

As soon as the girl finished singing, she was swallowed up by that ogre named Kibugi.

Now the people at home waited for the girl until they got tired. The father of the girl sharpened an axe and a sword. He set off on that road leading to the farm. In his heart, he knew that his daughter had been swallowed by an ogre.

He went and went. He met the first ogre. He sang for it:

Whoever ate Mwivua
Let him come and eat me as well!

The ogre replied:

I am not the one who ate Mwivua
It was Kibugi bringing up the rear.

He went on and met the second ogre. He sang for it the same song:

Whoever ate Mwivua
Let him come and eat me as well!
The ogre replied:

I am not the one who ate Mwivua
It was Kibugi bringing up the rear.

He went and met the third ogre. He sang for it the same song:

Whoever ate Mwivua
Let him come and eat me as well!

The third ogre replied by the same song that was sung by the other ogres:

I am not the one who ate Mwivua
It was Kibugi bringing up the rear.

The old man gazed intently at that ogre to see if it was the one which had swallowed his daughter. While he was examining it, the fourth ogre arrived. The man let the third ogre pass and sang to the fourth:

Whoever ate Mwivua
Let him come and eat me as well!

The fourth ogre replied:

I am not the one who ate Mwivua
It was Kibugi bringing up the rear

Just at that moment, the man heard, "*Kubu! Kobo! Cengere! Cunguru! Kobo! Kubu! Chaa! Cha!*"

When he heard that, the man got ready with his axe and the sword he had sharpened. Then he stood upright waiting for that ogre to try and cut him with his weapons. When that fifth ogre reached there and saw how serious the man was and how ferocious he looked, he started shaking with fear. While the ogre was shaking thus, the man sang for him in a loud voice:

117

Whoever ate Mwivua
Let him come and eat me as well!

When he started singing like the other ogres:

"I am not...," The man raised his axe high up to cut him to pieces, but before he had brought it down, the ogre said, "Please, don't kill me, my age mate. Cut my small finger and get out your daughter."

When the man cut the ogre's small finger, the people who came out led by Mwivua were uncountable! The girl who had forgotten the baby's sling came out followed by many children and many people from that village who had been eaten by that ogre. When these people came out they said the ogre named Kibugi must be killed for molesting the villagers. Mwivua's father did not need to touch Kibugi except for the finger he had cut. The ogre was killed by the people he had swallowed.

* * *

Iria ria irimurimu

Indi imwe nikwari na yura riari inene muno. Riu iturari rimwe kwai na eritu airi. Eritu mau nimathiire gucaria gwa kurimia nai mone giakuria.

Eritu makithii, makithii. Wa varia makinya makerwa gutiri wira niundu yura riai kundu kuonthe. Makithii, makithii. Makiurangiriria, makiurangiriria. Makithii magikinya iturari rimwe riari na kanyomba kamwe tu. Kuu kwari kwa marimurimu, nwati matiamenya.

Magitonya kanyombari karia na makigwatwa ugeni waro muno. Riu mwene nyomba akiuma navau nja. Akimatiga onga. Eritu matigwa onga makiroraroria mone kiria mangiria. Mwiritu umwe akiona iria na kinya wa akirioca akinyua.

Magicaracaria ringi mone kiria mangiria. Maroria kuria iguru itara, makiona andu mathinjitwe macuritue kuo. Wa makirana, "Ayia! Guku nikwa marimurimu: tuure!"

Eritu makiuma mang'aritie. Riu mang'aritie uguo irimurimu riria rigicoka. Riamatura nyomba rikiambiriria gwitana, "Karia gagwa! Wiku?"

Iria riri ivuri ria mwiritu uria warinyuite rigicokia, "Ni guku ivuri ria mwiritu!"

Eritu making'aria muno. Irimurimu rikiuria ringi na mugambo munene, "Iria riakwa! Wiku."

Iria rigicokia, "Ikwa tung'aritie naava! Nguuitwe na ivu ni mwiritu!" Irimurimu riang'aririe nginya rigikinyira eritu.

Riamakinyira rikimauraga wa oiri.

Andu ma itura riu mamenya aari acio ao nimauragwa ni irimurimu makirira muno matarania ni yura riatumite mathii kwa marimurimu. Riu andu onthe makiungana vamwe makiuraga marimurimu monthe maari bururi. Ciana igicoka ikigirwa kuthiicaga maturari wa kuraca.

118

The ogre's milk

Place of origin :　Kiritiri (Mbeere)
Narrator　　　:　Mbothere wa Kienge (Male; 95 yrs)

Some time long ago, there was a big famine. Now in a certain village, there were two girls. These two girls went to look for somewhere to work and get food in exchange.

The girls travelled and travelled. Wherever they went, they were told there was no work because the famine was all over the land. They went and went. They asked everywhere and checked everywhere. They went and reached one isolated village which had only one lonely hut. It was the land of ogres, but the girls were not aware.

They entered that lonely hut and they were welcomed warmly. Now the owner of the hut went outside. He left them alone. When the girls were left alone they looked around to see what they could eat. One of the girls saw milk in a calabash. She took it and drunk it.

They checked again whether there was something else they could eat. When they looked up, they saw bodies of people slaughtered and left on the rack. They said to each other, "Oh! This is an ogre's place; let us run away!"

The girls came out and ran. Now while they were running, the ogre came back. On finding that the girls had disappeared from the hut, it started calling out, "My little milk! Where are you?" The milk in the girl's stomach answered, "I am here in a girl's stomach!"

The girls ran faster. The ogre asked again in a loud voice, "My milk! Where are you?" The milk answered, "Oh! You know we are here running!" The ogre ran and caught up with the girls. When he caught up with them, he killed them both.

When the people of that village realised that their daughters had been killed by the ogre, they mourned bitterly for them because they were aware that it was the famine that had led them into the land of ogres. Now all people met and co-operated in killing all the ogres in the land. They then warned their children to avoid visiting deserted villages.

* * *

Kiondondoe na irimarimu

Tene tene muuno, kwai kaana getagwa Kiondondoe. Getagwa Kiondondoe niundu kaai kaana kamwana mwari karitu muno. Kaana gaka gatuire na ucuwe tondu aa ng'ina na ithe maai akuu.

Kiondondoe kaai karitu tondu kangiatigiirwe nyenyi ni ucuwe gakerwa gatikarumie andu gateci nikathii gucaria andu wa njirari. Gakamava nyenyi cionthe, gagatinda kavutii. Kangierirwe gatikavingurire andu gataici riigi, Kiondondoe gatiegucaga. Munthi umwe ucuwe wa Kiondondoe niwatigire akavingira nyomba. Agikera gatikavingurire mundu. Agikera getwa ni mundu, gakire getue gutii mundu. Riu ucuwe athii woguo, irimarimu rigiuka rikiuria, "Nu wi mucii uyu?"

119

Kiondondoe agicokia, "Ninie Kiondondoe. Ndigire navingirwa nyomba ni cucu ambira ndikavingurire wanai u. Acoka ambira netwa ndigetike."

"Aaa! Niguo?"

Kiondondoe gagicokia, "Ii! Wana nyenyi atigaga ambira ndikarumanie."

Irimarimu rikimwira, "Nvingurira tuthake". Karimu karia ti Kiondondoe gakiviungura.

Riu irimarimu riocire Kiondondoe, rikimwikia mborori yake. Irimarimu rigicoka rikiria nyenyi cia Kiondondoe cionthe buru.

Irimarimu riacaragia kaana ga kuvoya irio nako. Riu wa varia mathii gakera Kiondondoe, "Kiondondeo gamba turumue kana twimwe".

Kiondondoe gakagamba, gakavoya irio kai mborori ya irimarimu. Mavewa ndigu, irimarimu rikera Kiondondoe, "Kiondondoe ruma ndigu!"

Kiondondoe gakithii kuruma. irimarimu rikameria ndigu.

Irimarimu rikiurura na Kiondondoe mithenya mingi. Makinya vandu vai ucuru, rikera Kiondondoe, "Kiondondoe gamba tukundue kana twimwe."

Magekirirwa ucuru. Irimarimu rikera Kiondondoe, "Kiondondoe kuunda ucuru".

Kiondondoe gakithii gukunda irimarimu rikanyua ucuru wonthe, "Metu"

Riu Kiondondoe nikaginjire muno tondu gationaga kindu gia kuria. Munthi umwe irimarimu niriethiririe mundu muka umwe kwao. Rikiamba rikira Kiondondoe, "Kiondondoe, gamba turumue kana twimwe."

Kiondondoe akigamba. Mundu muka akimava nyenyi ma ucuru. Irimarimu rikiria nyenyi cionthe na rikinyua ucuru wonthe. Riu tondu wa kuvaa muno, irimarimu rikigua rikienda kuthii kioro. Wa rikira mundu muka atigwe na mbooro iyo yario riambe rithii navau kathakari.

Irimarimu riathii kathakari, mundu muka akiruta Kiondondoe mboorori narua akimuthitha akinaikia ithiga kuu mboorori iyo. Irimarimu riacoka arinengera mbooro rikiuria, "Kwa yarituva atia?"

Mundu muka akiriira, "Aai nawe irimarimu kwoteci murigo waigwa nthi nuurituvaga?"

Irimarimu rigioca mbooro rikiugaga, "Ii waguo, murigo waigwa nthi nurituvaga. Nwaguo waro tondu umunthi nirio nyama ino yakwa ikuriwa".

Riu irimarimu riavangite uria rikaria Kiondondoe na marimarimu arata ake munthi ucio, Kwoguo riakinya mucii, irimarimu rikira maria mengi niwainde nyama maune ngu. Ngu ciaunirwe ni marimarimu manene na manini. Mwaki ugiakua munene muno!

Riria marimarimu mathiire kuruta Kiondondoe mboorori ya murata wamo, methire ithiga. Nimwici uria mekire methira ithiga? Mocire irimarimu riu riene mbooro riathinitie. Kiondondoe muno uguo. Mocire irimarimu riu riendaga marie iruga ria Kiondondoe. Makirikia mwakiri. Irimariumu riu nirio riokirue rigituika nyama cia marimarimu maria mengi.

120

Kiondondoe and the ogre

Place of origin :   Gaciari (Embu)
Narrator   :   Ndekere Muruambeti (Female; 90 yrs)

Long, long ago, there was a child called Kiondondoe. She was named Kiondondoe because she was a very stupid girl. This child lived with her grandmother because her mother and father were dead.

Kiondondoe was stupid because if her grandmother left food for her and told her not to give any to strangers, she would actually go to look for people up to the path. She would give them all the food and stay hungry the whole day. If she was told not to open the door for people she did not know, Kiondondoe never listened.

One day, Kiondondoe's grandmother locked her up in the hut. She told her not to open for anybody. Now, immediately her grandmother left, the ogre came and asked, "Who is in this home?"

Kiondondoe replied, "It is me, Kiondondoe. My grandmother locked me up in the hut and told me not to open for anybody whoever it might be. She also told me if I'm called I should not answer."

The ogre told her, "Aaaa! Is that so?"

"Oh yes! Even food, she leaves some for me and tells me not to give to anyone!" Kiondondoe replied.

The ogre told her, "Open the door we play."

The little fool named Kiondondoe opened the door. Now, the ogre took Kiondondoe and put her in his bag. The ogre then ate Kiondondoe's food and finished it. The ogre's intention was to get a child who could beg for food for him. So wherever he went, he used to tell Kiondondoe, "Kiondondoe, make a little noise we either be given or denied."

Kiondondoe would make noise, begging for food while she was in the ogre's bag. If they were given a banana, the ogre would tell Kiondondoe, "Kiondondoe have a bite of a banana!"

Just as Kiondondoe was going to have a bite, the ogre would swallow the whole banana.

The ogre roamed with Kiondondoe in his bag for many days. If they reached a home where there was gruel, the ogre would tell Kiondondoe, "Kiondondoe make some noise, either we are given a sip or we are denied."

They would be given some gruel. The ogre would then tell Kiondondoe, "Kiondondoe have a sip of gruel."

Whenever Kiondondoe was about to have a sip, the ogre would drink the gruel in one gulp, *Metu!*"

Now Kiondondoe grew very thin because she had nothing to eat. One day, the ogre found a certain woman in her home. He first told Kiondondoe, "Kiondondoe make a little noise we either be given or denied."

Kiondondoe made some noise. The woman gave them food and gruel. The ogre ate all the food and drank all the gruel. Now, because of having eaten so much, the ogre felt he wanted to go to the toilet. So he told the woman to keep his bag for him while he visited the bush for a little while.

When the ogre had gone to the bush, the woman took Kiondondoe out of the bag quickly and hid her. She then put a stone in that bag. When the ogre came back and she gave him his bag, he asked, "How come it has become so heavy?"

The woman told the ogre, "Ah! You ogre! Don't you know that when a load is put down it always becomes heavier?"

The ogre took his bag, saying, "Oh! Yes! When a load is put down it becomes heavier. That is good because today is when this meat of mine will be eaten."

Now the ogre had planned how he and his ogre friends would feast on Kiondondoe that day. So when he arrived at his home, the ogre told his friends that he had brought meat so they should collect firewood. The firewood was collected by all the ogres, big and small. The fire that was lit was huge!

When the ogres went to remove Kiondondoe from their friend's bag, they found a stone. Do you know what they did when they found a stone? They took the ogre who owned the bag and who had troubled Kiondondoe so much. They took that ogre who had planned that they feast on Kiondondoe. They threw him into the fire. That ogre is the one who was roasted and became meat for his fellow ogres.

Chapter 6

NYIMBO — ORAL POETRY/SONGS

Lullabies and children's songs

Mwana-i kirai   **Baby stop crying****

Mwanai-i kirai   Oh! baby, stop crying
Ngagukurira nduuma   I shall dig out arrow roots for you
Iria nyukwe arimire   The ones your mother cultivated
Na karo ka muvuti**   With the *muvuti* weeding stick
I kirai   Oh! stop crying
I kirai   Oh! stop crying
Wa kaningu!   Child of big mouth!

---

*Muvuti is an indigenous Embu tree.
**A lullaby.

Ucia wathiota   **Whoever has farted***

Ucia wathiota-i   Whoever has farted
Arogirirwa   Let him be brought
Njagi murengi   Njagi the cutter
Wa kumurenga   To trim him
Varia vatune   That red part
Ta ruririmbi   Red like the flame
Rwa mwangi.   Of fire.

---

*A teasing song

123

Mwiigananio Watere ciura matina

Mwiigananio watere
Ciura matina.

Mwiigananio watere
Ciura matina.

Mwiigananio watere
Ciura matina.

Blind competition cost frogs their buttocks

Blind competition
Cost frogs their buttocks.

Blind competition
Made frogs lose bottoms.

Blind Competition
Cost frogs their buttocks.

Guku guku guku

Guku guku guku
Ndunve migwi itano
Ya kuratha rwigi
Rwanthiriria ciana
Ciana miro-ngwena
Guku guku twine
Guku guku twine.

Coo coo coo*

Coo coo coo
Give me five arrows
To shoot the hawk
It has finished my children
My forty children
Coo coo coo let us sing
Coo coo coo let us sing.

*Imitating doves.

Mbura uura turange maria

Mbura uura
Turange maria
Mbura uura
Turange maria
Mbura uura
Turange maria

Rain pour we play in the puddles*

Rain pour down
We play in the puddles
Rain pour down
We play in the puddles
Rain pour down
We play in the puddles.

124

Mbura uura	Rain pour down
Ciana ciina mutondo	The children are muddy.
Mbura uura	Rain pour down
Ciana ciina mutondo.	The children are muddy
Nathiire Tharaka	I went to Tharaka
Gwa Ciambau Tharaka	To Ciambau's home in Tharaka
Kwendia ing'ang'i	To sell crocodiles
Gwa ciambau Tharaka	To Ciambu's home in Tharaka.
Ningwamba	I'll start
Kondo gakwa i	Weaving my basket, Oh!
Ningwamba	I'll start
Kondo gakwa i	Weaving my basket, Oh!
Nyambaga	I usually start
Kondo gakwa i	Weaving my basket, Oh!
Nyambaga	I usually start
Kondo gakwa i	Weaving my basket, Oh!
Wone ngiambai	See how I start it
Wone ngiambai	See how I start it
Wone ngiamburai	See how I undo it
Wone ngiamburai	See how I undo it.
Nacaga gutigwa	I was about to be left
Tukinuka i	When we were going home
Nacaga gutigwa	I was about to be left
Tukinuka i	When we were going home.
Tone ngiamba i	Look and see how I start it
Tone ngiamba i	Look and see how I start it
Tone ngiambura	Look and see how I undo it
Tone ngiambura.	Look and see how I undo

---

*Children's musical game.

Njogu mwarire mungu

Elephants you licked salt *(A children's game)*

Njogu mwarire munyu	Elephants you licked salt
Murokua murothira	May you die may you get finished
Njogu mwarire munyu	Elephants you licked salt
Murokua murothira.	May you die may you get finished.

Mwatiganirie ciana	You abandoned the children
Marimari ma nviti	In hyenas' dens
Ii murothira	May you get finished
Ii murothira.	May you get finished.

Mwana niarira akerwa	Whenever a child cries he is told
Kira	Keep quiet
Na arira ringi akerwa	And if he cries again he is told
Onga.	Suck the teat.

Njogu mwarire munyu	Elephants you licked salt
Murokua murothira	May you die may you get finished
Njogu mwarire munyu	Elephants you licked salt
Murokua murothira.	May you die may you get finished

Mwatiganirie ciana	You abandoned the children
Marimari ma nviti	In hyenas' dens
Ii murothira	May you get finished
Ii murothira.	May you get finished.

Muko u ugukia

You woman grinding millet*

Muko u ugukia	You woman grinding millet
Ndunumie kamere.	Give me some dough for eating

Mere ti ya kuria	The dough is not for eating
Ni ya gutenderia ithiga	It is for smoothening the grinding stone

Munyanyaguo ari va?	Where is your co-wife?
Ari na varia nyunjuri.	She is behind the house

126

Agika atia navo?	What is she doing there?
Agikanda ndaa	She is crushing lice with her teeth
Iria twakanirue	The lice we were forbidden to crash
Ni aka a aturi	By the blacksmith's wives
Waminainia we	If you shake me
Ningukwinainia	I'll also shake you
Waninga-i we	If you hit me
Niringire nanie.	I'll also hit back.

*Children's song for teasing women.

Nitukumatongoria

We shall lead them*

Thikiririai-i	Oh! Listen
Thikiririai-i andu aya	Oh! Listen you people
Tukamatongoria	We shall lead them
Tukamatongoria	We shall lead them
Tukamatongoreria gacirari	We shall lead them on the path
Cianjue agatigwa agiokothaga ndigi	We shall leave Cianjue weaving fibers
Muthanje wi nthunu uregere	The reed skirts on waists will loosen
Kaviu kai mnthunu karegere	The knives tied on the waists will loosen
Njamba nene irire	The brave warrior will cry
Njamba nene irire nerire	The brave warrior will cry and cry
Methori mengi mengi	Many many tears
Methori ma nthaka	Tears of a young man
Methori ma mwita	Overflowing tears
Manginyondokia ngwaci	Which can quench the thirst of sweet potatoes

Wana wamona na njira	Even if you see them walking along the road
Twa onthe makagurwa na mburi	Not all of them will have goats paid for them
Amwe makagurwa na mbaki yeniuru	Some of them will have nose snuff as dowry
Naengi magurwe na runi	And some will be married on loan
Nthu ingiuka ni vakuvi	If any enemy attacked while I was near
Ningiumbuthuka nduru	I would rush out naked
Ningiurara nthu iri thome	I would kill any enemy in the homestead
Aka na arume magege	Till men and women wonder
Mundu muka ndendetwe	A woman is not loved
Ta gacau ka ng'ombe	Like a cow's calf
Nwakwa aciaraga ariu	It is only that she bears sons
Nyombetai arume ikona giagwitiira	So that a house without men gets a source of pride
Ningikatia avai	What can I do my friend?
Ningikatia avai muruaiya akanora?	What can I do my friend to grow fat?
Ningikatia avai twone ngeci ya ndundu	What can I do to find the time for consultation
Twitiage na ngombe cietu?	Boasting about out cattle?

*A grazing song sung by boys.

Mundu niakuraga

A person grows old*

Ndathiire ugeni kwa	I went for a visit
Ndaragutu	At Ndaragutu
Ndathirie ugeni kwa	I went for a visit
Ndaragutu	At Ndaragutu
Ngithira marimu makienjana	I found ogres shaving each other
Ngithira marimu makienjana	I met ogres shaving one another
Makimboca makimbikia kienji	They took me and set their knife on my head
Kienji kiu mwa gutema ithiga	That knife was sharp enough to cut a stone
Ngu! Ngu! Ngu! Ngu!	Ngu! Ngu! Ngu! Ngu!

Mwari kanguve ndeto mwariro	Young girl let me tell you frankly
Mwari kanguve ndeto mwariro	Young girl let me tell you frankly
Mundu niakuraga akagondoka	A person grows old and brightens
Mundu niakuraga akauviga	A person grows old and grows wiser
Agekirwa muthiori ni ngoma	And gets dressed by devils
Agekirwa muthiori ni ngoma	And gets dressed by devils
Cii! Cii! Cii! Cii!	*Cii! Cii! Cii! Cii!*

*Small boys' song.

Njogu na miguongo

The elephant and its tusks**

Iai njogu iguca-ii	*Iai* the elephants have come
Iai njogu iguca-ii	*Iai* the elephants have come
Iai njogu iguca-ii	*Iai* the elephants have come
Iai njogu niirigia miguongo ndigiyio	The elephants are swinging their tusks
Iturite muti wa kuvira njara ii!	They have missed a tree to lay their hands
Iai njogu iguca-ii.	*Iai* the elephants have come

Njogu nyamu nene	The elephant a big animal
Njogu nyamu nene iri vinya	The elephant a strong animal
Njogu nyamu nene ii yai!	The elephant a big animal *ii yai!*

Iai na mwari ndujengecie mbugi	*Iai* young girl swing my bells
Iai na mwari ndunjegecie mbugi	*Iai* young girl swing my bells
Nyukwe akona ng'ombe ya gukama	So that your mother can get milk cows
Ango akona njovi ya kunyua	And your father can get enough beer to drink
Iai mwari ndujengecie mbugi	*Iai* young girl swing my bells

Njogu nyamu nene	The elephant a big animal
Njogu nyamu nene iri vinya	The elephant a strong animal
Njogu nyamu nene ii yai.	The elephant a big animal *ii yai.*

Work Songs

Njara nicio wira

Ajiai wira nwa njara
Njara nicio wira
Muveria mundu ni
Uria umunaga njara

Ukai ii tukure nyaki
Cucu atige kurara
Akiurirwa-ii

Turaugire nituthii
Wana eritu
Niguo nyaki igane
Ya kwimbira cucu nyomba

Nyaki ya kwimbira cucu nyomba ii
Ikuragwa ni ari
Na aka ma ciana ciake
Wira nwa njara

Wira ndumenagà njara
Kira wa kibi
Nirukwona uria njara ingika
Cucu ndakaurirwa ringi.

Hands make work

Iai work is hands
Hands make work
The only way to destroy a person
Is to break her hands

Come let us cut grass
So that our grandmother
Stops being rained on at night

We decided to go
Even with girls
So that we can get enough grass
To thatch our grandmother's hut

The grass for thatching grandmother's hut -*ii*
Is cut by girls
And their sons' wives
Hands make work

Work does not hate hands
Keep mum
You will see the power of hands
Our grandmother will never be rained on
again.

Gutiri kiumaga varo

Wira ni uri ururu
Nati gutiri kiega kiumaga vega
Gutiri thina ituraga
Urimi wana ucimbi
Nicio ikaruta Mumbeere kieva!

Nothing good comes easily

Work is painful
But thee's nothing good that comes easily
No poverty is permanent
Cultivating and digging
Are the only things which will rescue
Mbeere people from sadness!

130

Niturime wa kurima	Let us weed thoroughly
Nitutherie migunda-i	Let us clean up our farms
Niturime wa kurima-i	Let us weed thoroughly
Gutiri kiega kiumaga vega!	Nothing good comes easily
Ciana rimai	Children cultivate
Athuri cimba migunda	Men dig the farms
Ongia ni matherie migunda	Women weed the farms
Turime wa kurima-i	Nothing comes easily.
Gutiri kiega kiumaga vega.	

Vinya yonthe ikarika ni muthua — All strength will be eaten by ants

Kava kurima	It is better to cultivate
Kava kurima	It is better to cultivate
Kava kurimira ciana	It is better to cultivate for the children
Ciana itige kuthii ivutii	So that children do not go hungry
Ciana itikae kwiya	So that children may never steal
Vinya yonthe ikarika ni muthua	All the strength will be eaten by ants
Wana ivuno vinya yocio	Even the lazy ones their strength
Ikarika nwa muthua	Will be eaten by ants
Muka muvuno	The lazy woman
Nworia muthunu	And also the mean woman
Agetikwa nu mambura make makinya?	Who will answer her call
Kava uria witikaga aria engi mbu	when she has a work occasion?
Kava uria urimaga	During her ceremony?
	It is better the one who answers others' call
	It is better the one who cultivates
Wira uyu ni werima	This is the work of cultivation
Wa mundu arime	Everybody should assist
Tucara twingi tumenanagira urii-ri	Some people's hands breed hatred at the eating time
Nati vinya yonthe ikarika ni muthua.	And yet all strength will be eaten by ants.

Ndumitwe wira ni Karwenji na Kanoro	**I have been asked to assist in work by Karwenji* and Kanoro***

Ndumitwe wira ni Karwenji
Na murume ni Kanoro
Ndumitwe wira ni Karwenji
Na murume ni Kanoro
Mwene mwere mukunwona?
Nari ndinamwona muthokoro!

Karwenji asked me to assist in work
And her husband is Kanoro
Karwenji asked me to assist in work
And her husband is Kanoro
Have you seen the millet owner?
Oh no! Strange, I haven't seen her.

Ndumitwe wira ni Karwenji
Na murume ni Kanoro
Ndumitwe wira wokori wa mwere
Nguo ucuru wovuri ukuwona?
Nari ndinawona muthokoro!
Na mivuro ni-ikuvura
Ihi muthokoro!

Karwenji asked me to assist in work
And her husband is Kanoro
I have been asked to thresh millet
And have you seen the gruel for the threshers?
Oh no! Strange I haven't seen it
And the threshing sticks are still threshing
Oh! How strange!

Ndumitwe wira ni karwenji
Na murume ni Kanoro
Numitwe wira wetiri ria mwere
Ngwinuka na wa kauga
Nati mwene mwere mukumwona?
Nari ndinamwona muthokoro!

Karwenji asked me to assist in work
And her husband is Kanoro
I have been sent to the millet threshing ground
I shall take half a calabash of millet home
But have you seen the owner of the millet?
Oh! no! I haven't seen her, how strange!

Ndumitwe wira ni karwenji
Na murume ni kanoro
Nkumitwe wira ni karwenji
Na murume ni kanoro
Naamo augiri wira mukumengua?
Nari ndinamona muthokoro.

Karwenji asked me to assist in work
And her husband is Kanoro
Karwenji asked me to assist in work
And her husband is Kanoro
And have you seen the cooks or the threshers?
Oh! No! I haven't seen them, how strange!

---

*Karwenji is a sharp knife and *Kanoro* is a stone for sharpening knives.

Wira ni wetu

Iai wa mundu
Wa mundu na muru wa ng'ina
Ii niguo kurathii mainda, aya!
Umunthi yauga ndaka
Ni icimbirwe ndaka
Aka ni matavire manji
Wira ni wetu!

Iai wa mundu
Wa mundu na muru wa ng'ina
Nyomba ya muka muviki
Umunthi ni ithingwa
Mwongia narara kuo umunthi
Nituthinge twarikia
Tunyue uki wigane!

The work is ours

Iai every person
Everybody for his own brother
That is how it is these days, *ayia!*
Today the house decided to be mudded*
Let mud be dug for it
Let the women bring water for it
The work is ours!

Iai every person
Everybody for his brother
A bride's house
Today it will be mudded
And the woman will sleep in it today
Let us mud it and when we finish
We drink our fill!

*The walls of traditional houses were made of mud.

Twakinya gukinya

Twakinya gukinya
Ana enyu maguca
Twakinya wa thuonthe
Tukite wa thuonthe
Tukite wa thuonthe
Tutitiganaga
manji nimatavwa
Megane nyanya
Na matigare
Nwanga arume magatucambithia!

Tugite nitwicovera buru
Tugite tutingiveria
Tugite nwathue tukwirete
Tukite guka
Tukitè wathue thuonthe!
Nwaŋga arume magatucambithia!

We have arrived indeed

We have arrived indeed
Your people have come
All of us have arrived
We have all come
We have all come
We never leave any of us behind
Water will be fetched
It will be enough
Enough and to spare
Unless the men let us down!

We have decided to show off our wealth
We have decided to put away all callousness
We have decided to present ourselves
Of our own accord
We have come indeed
We have come all of us
Unless men decide to let us down!

133

Njovi ni ya mundu murume wi kio

Iai nyomba iri nja
Iai nyomba iri nja
Nyomba niyambwa
Nyomba itai njovo
Wana itugi ndiri ii!

Njovi irugitwe mucii uyu
Ti ya mwana ni ya wira
Wira wa mwana ni ya wira
Wana nyovo ii
Wana nyovo ii!
Arume a rika ni tugutema
Nyovo wana itugi!

Iai njovi ni ya arume
Mundu murume ute kio
Mundu murume kivuno
Ndarugagirwa njovi ii!

Beer is for a hardworking man

Iai the house is already standing
We have already set it
We have started building it
But it is a house without rafters
And it has no poles either!

The beer brewed,
It is not child;
It is for workers
The workers who are cutting poles
And rafters as well, ii!
My agemates let us cut
Rafters as well as poles!

Iai beer is for men
A man who is not hardworking
A man who is lazy
Nobody prepares beer for him ii

Wira ni muku

Iai wira ni muku-i
Iai wira ugukinya-ii
Wamundu akuite giceri
Mugunda niurimwa ndute!

Andu marauragia wira
Ni wari?
Nimerwe ari a Ngithi
Marimaga ngurukio!

The workers have come

Iai the workers have come ii
Iai the workers have arrived
Each person is carrying her own Panga
The shamba will be cleared of weeds

People have been asking
When will the workers come?
Tell them the daughters of Ngithi clan
Cultivate without joking!

134

Wira utumanitwe	When workers have been sent for
Ndutigaragua-ii!	They never fail to turn up!
Andu etu ndweke mwone	Our people just stop and watch
Kurima na kwivecana	We cultivate with all dedication
Nurimwa uthire	This shamba will be cleared completely
Ari a Kathi	The daughters of Kathi clan
Matii mathe-ii	Are no joke
Iai wira ni muku!	The workers have come!

Njara imwe ndikandii wira

One hand cannot manage work

Njara imwe ndikandii wira	One hand cannot manage work
Muvuri ndungivura mwere na njara imwe	A threshing stick cannot thresh millet with one hand
Tucara twingi tumenanagira urii-ri	Some hands breed hatred at the eating time
Gutii uthwire gukandua	Nobody hates being assisted

Mwere niuvurwe	Let millet be threshed
Niuvurwe niuvurwe	Let it be threshed, let it be threshed

Ndemera muvuro	Cut a threshing stick for me
Muka kivuno	A lazy wife
Nikwa enukagua	Is taken back to her parents
Mbura yarega kuura	When the rain fails
Igwatagia rukungi	It blames the wind
Nake muka kivuno	And a lazy woman
Egwatagia muvuro	Blames the threshing stick

Ndemera muvuro ii	Cut a threshing stick for me — *ii*
Mwirua ndemera muvuro	My co-wife cut me a threshing stick

Mwongia mwene mambura	You woman, owner of this occasion
Ririkana wira ni nda	Remember that work is the stomach
Menyerera ndukae gutuvutithia	Take care not to starve us
Mivuro ni ikuruma	The threshing sticks are sounding
Mwere ume itiriri.	Let the millet leave the threshing ground

Mwongia ocagwa ni ari make	**A woman is helped by her daughter**
Mwongia wanaciara ii	A woman who has ever given birth *ii*
Mwongia ari andu make	A woman has her own people
Ndeganene notari ciana	She is not like a childless person
Mwongia etikagwa mbu	The screams of a woman
Ni andu make	Are answered by her own offspring
Mwongia ocagwa	A woman is helped
Ni ari make	By her own daughters
Mwongia uri keritu	A woman who has a daughter
Tiwe uthinaga	Is not the one who suffers
Utari keritu	Whoever has no daughter
Niwe witavagira manji ii	Fetches water for herself
Nyanya nitwauka	Mummy we have come
Nitwauka gugwitika mbu	We have come to answer your screams
Ii tukumigua ii	*Ii* we have heard it *ii*
Tumana mivuro	Send for the threshing sticks
Mwere nitweta itiri	We've spread the millet on the threshing ground
Ni uvurwa buru	We shall thresh all of it
Nituvurire nyanya mwere	Let us thresh mummy's millet
Mwongia ocagwa ni ciana ciake	A woman is helped by her own children
Nyanya niwaciarire ari	Mummy you gave birth to daughters
Ciakunda manji.	Let the whole world know.

Utari mwana akue ithiga!	**Whoever has no child, carry a stone**
Iai urimi uri mucii	*Iai* the workers are at home
Iai urimi ni ari ma mwene mucii	*Iai* the workers are her daughters
Mundu nwa mwana wake	A person's strength is her daughters
Wira uyu utumanitwe	This work has been organised
Ni Irumbi	By Irumbi clan

Mwari wa mucii uyu ii	The daughter's of this home
Utari mwana akue ithiga!	Whoever has no child should carry a stone
Iai mami ndangirirara mugundari	*Iai* mummy should sleep in the shamba
Mundu uri andu make	Whoever has her own people
Mdarikaga ni nyamu	Should never be eaten by wild animals
Akiugaga mbu	While she screams
Uyu wira ii	We workers for this occasion
Niturima mugunda nthirio	We shall clear this shamba completely
Titutigaria wana vanini	We shall not leave even a tiny space
Wira ni wa mwari!	Workers are daughters!

Ongia ni matindikwe

Let women be supported

Wira wa ongia niguo utatiragwa iiai ui	Workers never fail to turn up to a woman's work
Mwendwa niaka ma rika riake	The one loved by her agemates
Cierume wetu twaruire nake	Cierume* our girl, we were circumcised together
Twaria wiritu nake	We enjoyed our maidenhood together
Twagurua Ikandire nake	We got married in Ikandi clan together
Riu ni mbu naca kumwitika	Now I have come to answer her scream
Ya ukuri wa nyaki ya kwimba.	For assistance in cutting thatch grass
Ayai uu ongia ni matindikwe	*Iyai* uu let women be supported
Ongia a rika riakwa matindikagwa ndindiko	The women of my age-set are supported diligently
Na ucuru wa mwere	With millet gruel
Na ugicokererua iria ria kinya	Seconded by fermented milk from a gourd
Mwongia utari ng'ombe	A woman with no cows in her shed
Na wingi utari mburi	And the one without goats
Matici gutindikana na ongia	Don't know of women's support for each other
Kwa muka kivuno kuthiicagwa nu?	Who goes to a lazy woman's house?
Mbu ya muka kirimu itikagwa nu?	Who responds to the call of a foolish wife?

137

Iyai ni ongia ni matindkwe	Iyai ni let women be supported
Ongia a rika riakwa matindikagwa ndindiko	The women of my age-set are supported diligently
Nimatindikwe na ucuru wa mwere	With millet gruel
Na iria ria kinya ithethuku	Seconded by fermented milk from a gourd
Iyai uu ongia ni matindikwe	Iyai uu let women be supported
Wira mutute tiga weterere	The work which has already been completed
Iyai ui ni matindikwe	Is not like the one which is still waiting to be done
Mundu etikagwa mbu ni andu mao	A person's cry is answered by her kin
Mbu ya muka kivuno itikagwa nu?	Who responds to the call of a lazy wife?
Iyai uu ongia ni matindikwe	Iyai uu let the women be supported
Ongia a rika riakwa matindikagwa ndindiko	The women of my age-set are supported diligently
Ni matindikwe na ucuru wa mwere	Let them be supported with millet gruel
Na ugicokererua iria ria kinya	Second with fermented milk from a gourd
Iyai uu ongia ni matindikwe!	Iyai ui let women be supported!

---

*Cierume is a renowned Mbeere woman who was so brave that she fought alongside men. Cierume implies a woman who has character traits regarded as masculine.

Wedding songs

Niivingurirwe

Open for them

Niivingurirwe ii uui	Open for them ii uui
Niivingurirwe ii uui	Let someone open for them ii uui
Na guku kwa andu a Kina	In this clan of Kina
Ni ciingire kigwanja	Let them enter the pen
Tucite na mburi ii	We have brought goats ii!
Tucite kurayia ii	We have brought goats!
Niciingire kigwanja.	Let them enter the pen!

Wana ng'ombe iguca	Even the cattle have come
Wana ng'onbe igukinya	Even the cattle have arrived
Niciingire kigwanja	Let them enter the shed
Ni itugwe gutungwa	Let someone come and meet them
Niciingire kigwanja	Let someone enter the shed
Turi andu a vata	We are important people
Twi na mwari wenyu	We have your daughter
Mumenye niwakinyire	So that you may know she arrived
Nituguituniviria	We shall slaughter one for blessing
Kaguo mwamukire	So that you can appreciate them
Wana rwaga tutume	We shall even build the shed
Niivingurirwe!	Let someone open for them!

Gwa kanyanya gutiumbagua	**Never get angry with the in-laws**
Mundu mugurire mati vanene	A person whose daughter
Na wingi utai mugurire	Has been taken in marriage
Kanyanya thira irigi	Is different from
Igua uri mwiganiru	The one whose daughter is not married
Mwana ndugurikaga	My in-law stop sulking
Na uthoni nduthiraraga	Feel satisfied
	A child can never be bought
	And marriage links have no end!
Narete ndurume	If I bring a ram
Woce wana ngatho	Take it with gratitude
Wa kiria ninakio	Whatever I have
Ndukanae gukivuthia	Do not belittle it
Wirumire ii	Just taste it
Iai uthoni nduthiraga!	Because marriage links
	Have no end!
Uthoniri gutirumanagwa	At the marriage negotiations
Mwana ndagurikaga	People do not abuse one another
	A child can never be bought
Athoni nitwendane	Our in-laws let us love one another
Tumatie urata	Let us beef up our friendship
Kanyanya igania!	My in-law feel satisfied!

Nitwendaga gutwarwa

Nitwendaga gutwarwa
Nitwendaga gutwarwa ii
Nii muvuro wa Thura ii
Tukiringia ng'ombe wana mburi
Tukite uthoni
Turetete ruraiyo

Nayo njovi ya mwana ii
Nitungitwarirwe ni muvuro
Andu a rungo
Tukite uthoni Nthagicu

Nitutungwe muvirigari
Ni mburi na ng'ombe ii
Niivingurirwe rwaga
Andu a uthoni nimakinya
Athuri njovi ya mwana niyakinya

We were about to drown

We were about to drown
We were about to drown ii
In Thura river ii
Driving cattle and goats across the river
On our way to marriage negotiations
Bringing bride-price

And a child's beer ii
Should not spend the night on the way
We almost drowned
We people from far away
Coming for marriage negotiations in Nthagicu!

Meet us at the gate and welcome us
It is cattle and goats ii
Which are making so much noise at the gate
Let someone open the shed for them
The in-laws have arrived
Oh! You men!
The child's beer has arrived!

Kanyanya wa mwana

Kanyanya wa mwana ii
Nagamba wa tiru! tiru!
Wagikinya muvirigari
Niatungwe waro
Ni kanyanya wake

Akuite uki wa mwana
Akuite nvuva iria mbarii
Akinya muvirigari

Kanyanya*, mother of the groom

Kanyanya, mother of the groom
As she walks she sounds tiru! tiru!
Just as she reaches the gate
Let her be met and welcomed
By her kanyanya, mother of the bride

She is carrying the beer of the child
She is carrying the biggest gourd
When she reaches the gate
Let her be welcomed

Kanyanya wa mwana ai gitio	Kanyanya, mother of the groom
Atonye ai mwamukire	is greatly respected
Guku kwa athoni	Let her be escorted as she enters
Muka mwene nthaka	This home of her in-laws
Iria ina mwari wa mucii uyu	The mother of the young man
	Who has the daughter of this home
Kanyanya wa mwana	Kanyanya, mother of the groom
Niagamba tiru! tiru!	As she walks she sounds *tiru! tiru!*
Akuite uki wa gutuniviria	She carries the honey for blessings
Mwana ii niagamba tiru! tiru!	Oh! My friend!
	As she walks the ground sounds, *tiru! tiru!*

---

*Kanyanya is the name used by the bridegroom's mother and the bride's
mother to address each other.

Uuki uyu ni wau?

Whose honey is this?

Uuki uyu ni wau ii?	Whose honey is this?
Uuki uyu ni wau ii?	Oh! Whose honey is this?
Ni wa Mukwegoki	It belongs to Mukwegoki
Uramukagia murume mari toro	Who wakes her husband from sleep
"Nduramuke!	"Wake up!"
Tucaririe andu enyu kia makaria	Let us look for something
Etu nimarire	To feed your family in future
Enyu makagunwa niki?"	My family has already reaped benefits
	On what will your family benefit?"
Ningundue ikivituka	Let me be given as it passes along along
Ningundue ikivituka	Let me be given some as it passes along
Yakinya kwi arume yathii magambori	Once it reaches the men it is for disputes
Ii ningundue ikivituka!	Let me be given some as it passes along

Uuki uyu ni wau ii?	Whose honey is this?
Uuki uyu ni wau ii?	Whose honey is this?
Ni wa muka uria	It belongs to the woman
Utararaga thome yene	Who never sleeps in other people's homesteads
Nwa ararire thome iri kithici	Who only sleeps in a home
Agaturirwa njura agaturirwa thiaka	Which has a love-making gadget
Uuki nyu ni wau ii?	Then she is make a sword and its sheath
	Oh! Whose honey is this?

Ii undu ukunyua	Now, while you drink
Undu ukunyua ugecuna nomo	While you drink until you lick your lips
Murimu uria uri ururu niu?	Which labour is more painful?
I wa kavici ungirikagia ngirikio	Oh! That of a boy makes me faint
Uuki uyu ni wau ii?	and come back to life
	But that of a girl makes me faint completely
	Oh! Whose honey is this?

Ningundue ikivituka	Let me be given some as it passes along
Njovi ino ni ya mwana twaciarire	This brew belongs to a child we delivered
Arume nwatwici nimwethithite tugiciara	You men! We know you were hiding while
Ningundue ino ya mwana	were delivering
Ningundue ikivituka	Let me be given this beer of a child
	Let me be given some as it passes along

Ya mwana ndiimanangwa	People should never be mean with a child's beer
Mwana ti wa mundu umwe	A child does not belong to one person
Twi ene mwana ucio	We are the owners of the child
Nitukundue ikivituka!	Let us be given some as it passes along.

Kanyanya ngutindike

Kanyanya let me push you along

Kanyanya ngutindike	Kanyanya let me push you along
Kanyanya ngutindike	Kanyanya let me push you along
Umbirire muthoni	So that you can deliver a message for me
Niandetere nthenge iri maguenje	To my son-in-law
Ya kuuma muguta	Tell him to bring me a hairy he-goat
Nginevaka ciero	A hairy he-goat which can produce fat
Ni igutura!	To rub on my thighs
	They are painful

142

Ngiciara mwana uyu	While I was delivering this child
Arume nimwethithite	You men were hiding
Mutakegua ngicacika	To avoid hearing my groaning
Hmn! Hmn! Hmn! Hmn!	Hmn! Hmn! Hmn! Hmn!
Kanyanya ngutindike	*Kanyanya* let me push you along
Kanyanya ngutindike	*Kanyanya* let me push you along
Umbirire muthoni	So that you can deliver a message for me
Niandetere nthenge iri maguenje	To my son-in-law
Ya kuuma maguta	Tell him to bring me a hairy he-goat
Nginevaka ciero	A hairy he-goat which can produce fat
Ni igutura!	To rub on my thighs
	They are painful!
Ngiciara mwana uyu	While I was delivering this child
Arume nimwethithite	You men were hiding
Mutakegua ngicacika	To avoid hearing my groaning
Hmn! Hmn! Hmn! Hmn!	Hmn! Hmn! Hmn! Hmn!

Kuria twarutire murimi	**Where we got a farmer from**
Tukite wa kavora	We are coming slowly
Tukite wa kavora	We are coming slowly
Tukite kwona ii	We are coming to see, oh!
Kuria nthaka yetu yarutire	Where our son got an industrious farmer
Murimi munene	
Murugi mwaro	And a good cook
Wana mukii mwaro	And even a good grinding woman
Tukite wa kavora ii	We are coming slowly
Nitukite waro	We are coming peacefully
Ni gwa kanyanya ii	And Kanyanya, deserves respect
Na kanyanya ai gitio	We are very happy
Nikuvewa mwongia	To have been given a wife
Mukii mwaro	A good grinding woman
Acite gwetu nja	Has come right to our home

Wana nthoki	We have brought gifts
Niya kanyanya ii	They are for Kanyanya
Mburi cia ngatho	The goats are for gratitude
Ngo'ombe cia gikeno	The cows are for joy
Njovi ni ya athuri	The beer is for the men
Tukite wa kavora.	We are travelling, coming slowly.

Kanyanya mwaganu — Bad in-laws

We Kanyanya tigana nanie	*Kanyanya*, my in-law, leave me alone
Tiga kungunya riria ngumenire	Stop pinching me, I hate you
Wandutire mwana mucii	You chased my child away
Ukiremwa ni kumumenyerera	You were unable to look after her
Ukimuthiithia na weru	You made her travel through the whole wide land
Utanginjokeria we mucii	You refused to bring her home
We Kanyaya tigana nanie	You *Kanyanya*, my in-law, leave me alone
Ndici nindui tugucirira	I don't know why we have a dispute
Ciira ya mwari ni ya athuri	A brides dispute is settled by men
Athuri matua ciira ino	The men have ruled
Athoni ni marete uki	That the in-law should bring beer
Macoke marete ndegwa	And then they bring a bull
Ya kuvorovia magambo	To crate peace
Mwari weru acoke	So that our daughter can return
Uthoni nduri magambo	Marriage affairs are not for legal cases
Uthoni uri gitio.	Marriage affairs are maintained by respect.

Kundia monthe — Serve it to everybody

Njovi ni ikinyire	The beer has finally arrived
Njovi ni yaretwe	The beer has been brought
Njovi ni yakinya mucii	The beer has finally arrived at home
Ya mwana ndiimanagwa	The brew of a child is never denied anyone

144

Athoni maguca	The in-laws have come
Athuri mutiukire	The elders in this home rise
Munyue ino ya mwana ii	So that you may drink this one of a child
Ndimanagwa	It is never denied anyone
Kundia monthe	Serve it to everybody
Ndugatigarie wana umwe ii	Do not leave our a single person
Ni inyuwe ni andu monthe	Let it be drunk by everybody
Njovi ino ya mwana	This beer is for a child
Yumite kwa athoni	It has come from the in-laws
Ni inyuwe ni andu monthe.	Let it be drunk by everybody.

Songs on childbirth and child-naming

Mwana aguka waro	**The baby has arrived safely**
Iai turaurangia ndeto	Iai we have been asking this
Iai turauragia ndeto	Iai we have been asking this
Mwiegu ndeto cia mucii uyu?	Have you heard any news about this home?
Kana kwi mumigua	Has anybody heard
Ya gukinya kwa mwana?	Whether a baby has arrived?
Mwana aguka waro	The baby has arrived safely
Turamweterere na ngatho	We have been eagerly waiting for him
Ni Ngai nayo ni mbaro	We are grateful to our ancestors
Iratukinyirie mwana waro	Our God is good
	He brought our baby safely
Ng'ina wa mwana	Mother of the baby
Uri murathime muno	You are indeed blessed
Ukira unyue ucuru	Wake up and drink gruel
Na iria unyue	And drink milk as well
Uvote kurera mwana	So that you can suckle
Mwana uyu ni wetu.	Our baby well
	This is our baby

Mwana uyu niarugua nu?

Mwana uyu niarugua nu?
Iai mwana uyu niarugua nu ii?
Tondu ni muciare
Aciaritwe guku kwa andu a Njiru

Niarugue
Niavewe iveo na ngatho
Tondu ni kirathimo kia Ngai
Kia mwana muciare

Ni gukena tugukena umunthi
Mwana uyu ni wau?
Mwana niarugue kurugua
Amenye ena ene.

Who will make this baby dance?

Who will make this baby jump up?
Iai who will make this baby dance ii?
Because he is born
He has been born
In Njiru's family.

Let him be made to jump up
Let him be make to dance
Let him be given gifts with gratitude
Because he is God's blessing
To have a baby born

We are very happy today
We shall be full of joy today
Whose baby is this?
Let the baby jump up
Make the baby dance
So that he can know
He has a home.

Muciari wa mwana ti umwe

Muciari wa mwana ti umwe
Muciara wa mwana ti umwe
Munini inde nguo
Tata inde manji
Nwa Ngai nguthathaiya
Tukina kira Kathi
Kaana getu

Tukite thuonthe
Kugwata mwana uyu muciare
Tukite thuonthe
Tukite mucii
Kugwata mwana uyu muciare
Twegua ni muciare

The mother of a child is not one

The mother of a child is not one
The mother of a child is not one
Co-wife bring clothes
Aunt bring water
It is God's own blessing
As we say keep quiet Kathi
Our little baby

We have all come
To hold the new-born baby
We have all come
We have come home
To hold the new-born baby
We have heard the news!

Kathi ni arugue kurugua	Make Kathi jump up
Kathi ni ainue kwinua	Make Kathi dance
Iai Kathi ni muciare	Iai Kathi is born
Muciari wa mwana ti umwe	The mother of a child is not one
Kathi ni muciare.	The baby Kathi is born!

Twauka kwona mwana	**We have come to see the baby**
Mwatwigua ii ui	If you hear us ii ui
Twathii ugwatiri wa mwana	We have gone to see our baby
Mwana muciare	A new-born baby
Ni kirathimo kwi thue	Is a blessing to us
Twathii wa thuonthe	We have come all of us
Kugwata mwana wetu	To hold our baby
Nitutungwe wa nevenya	Welcome us quickly
Nitutungwe muvirigari	Meet us at the gate
Tunengerwe mwana turugie	Let us be given the baby
Nitwigua ni Cierimba	So we can make her jump
Uria wetu muciare	We hear it is Cierimba
	Our Cierimba is born
Mwatwigua ii ui	If you hear us *ii ui*
Twathii ugwatiri wa mwana	We have gone to see our baby
Mwana wetu ni muciare	Our Cierimba has come back
Cierimba uria wetu agucoka	We thought she has gone
Twaugaga niwathii	God has bought her back *ii*
Ngai niwamucokia ii	Make the baby jump up
Mwana niarugue kurugua	make the baby dance!
Mwana niainue wa kwinua!	

147

Male initiation songs

Nimbugaga ugutira	**I thought it had been postponed**
Nimbugaga ugutira	I thought it had been postphoned
Njokie mbui kiigori	I put my feather back in its place
Nimbugaga ugutira	I thought it had been postponed
Njokie mbui kiigori	I return my feather in its place
Uui gara nicienuka!	*Uui* the battalions have returned
Nimbugaga ugutira	I thought it had been postphoned
Njokie mbui kiigori	I return my feather in its place
Murui ti mutiru avai!	My fellow initiate
Nimbugaga ugutira	It has not been postponed *avai**
Njokie mbui kiigori	I thought it had been postphoned
	I put my feather back in its place
Uu garu cia thiri monja** *ii*	*Uu* young warriors linked by the same secret
Nimbugaga ugutira	I thought it had been postphoned
Njokie mbui kiigori	I return my feather in its place
Nyanya munini aguca	My step-mother has arrived
Wuuuui!	*Wuuuui!*
Wuu! Gakai ka mbu!	I will scream!
Nimbugaga gutira	I thought it had been postponed
Njokie mbui kiigori	I put my feather in its place
Nimbugaga ugutira	I thought it had been postponed
Njokie mbui kiigori.	I put my feather back into its place.

*avai — a form a address used by men of the same for each other
**thiri monja — corruption of Swahili "siri moja", which literally means "the same secret".

148

Njererwe	I got late*
Njererwe ii njererwe	O got late *ii* I got late
Weru gati	In the middle of the land
Ngigiga nyambo	While sharpening my weapons
Na ruciu gwakia	And tomorrow morning
Namukirue muruiithia	I shall be taken to the circumciser
Na guku kwa andu a Mburi	That side of Mburi clan
Ngarauka ruciu	I shall go there at dawn
Ruciu gwakia	I will not leave my weapons
Ndigutiga nyambo	I will not leave my weapons
Ndigutiga nyambo	The weapons belong to the initiator
Nyambo ni cia muruithia	
Namo atiri mari va?	Where are the advisers
Migua na ndigi	Thorns and strings
Ngarauka ruciu	I will not leave the weapons
Ndigutiga nyambo.	The circumciser with a knife
	I shall go there at dawn
	I will not leave the weapons.

---

*Sung a few days before initiation by the initiates and their older escorts
while wandering in the bush as a form of exercise.

Muruithia agirirwe ku?	Where did they go for the initiator?
Muruithia agirirwe ku?	Where did they go for the initiator?
Ku hiyia?	Where *hiyia*?
Muruithia agirirwe ku?	Where did they go for the initiator?
Ku hiyia?	Where *hiyia*?
Atiri magirirwe ku?	Where did they go for the advisers*?
Ku? Ku hiyia?	Where? Where *hiyia*?
Atiri mari naku?	Where are the advisers?
Ku? ku hiyia?	Where? Where *hiyia*?
Na nigukere?	And the day has dawned?

Narume magakinya ri?	When will the uncles arrive?
Uiya!	Uiya!
Narume magakinya ri?	When will the parents arrive?
Uiya!	Uiya!
Na nigukere!	And the day has already dawned!
Nyanya magakinya ri?	When will the mothers **arrive**?
Uiya?	Uiya!
Aciari magakinya ri?	When will the parents **arrive**?
Uiya!	Uiya!
Na nigukere!	And the day has already dawned!
Mwana agekarua nthi ri arue?	When will the child be circumcised?

---

*Each initiate has an adviser known as *mutiri* as the original. The term literally means "the one who supports". He supports the initiate physically, psychologically and socially during initiation and after.

Ngekuruka nake

I shall go down with him

Ngekuruka nake ii ai	I shall go down with him ii ai
Ngekuruka nake na rwarai	I shall go down with him to the deep valley
Ngekuruka nake iiai na rwarari	I shall go down with him to the deep valley
Ngina na murume ndige	I shall leave his mother and her husband
Mukauragia mwana athiire naku?	They will be left asking where did our child go?
Mukauragia mwana athiire naku?	They will be left asking where did our child go?
Muruithia auka	When the circumciser comes
Ngekuruka nake narwarari	I shall take him down to the deep valley
Akarengwa auvige	To be cut as that he can become wiser
Akarengwa aume nthakame	To be cut so that he can bleed
Ngekuruka nake na rwarari.	I shall go down with him to the deep valley.

Maugaga ndari narume	**They thought he had no uncle**
Maugaga atia ii?	What were they saying ii ?
Maugaga mwana ndari narume	They thought the child had no uncle
Maugaga mwana ndari narume	They were saying the child had no uncle
Umunthi nirio makumenya	Today is when they will know
Makumenya narume ari muoyo ii	They will know that his uncle is alive
Maugaga atia ii ?	What were they saying?
Mauagaga muthenya ndagakinya	They thought the day would never come
Umunthi nirio makurua	Today is when they will be circumcised
Umunthi nthakame ni igwitika	Today is when the blood will be split
Manganga atia ii ?	What were they saying ii ?
Manganga muruithia ndugakinya	They were saying the circumciser would never come
Umunthi muruithia agukinya	Today the circumciser has arrived
Umunthi nthakame ni igwitwa.	Today the blood will be split.

Iui gugukia	**Oh! It has dawned***
Iui gugukia	Oh! It has dawned
Niuria njiniki uvira ku?	You asking for a loin-cloth to take where?
Ii ii gugukia	*Ii ii* it has dawned
Niuria njiniki uvira ku?	You asking for a loin-cloth to take where?
Mwici wa Ngiro gugukia	Uncircumcised man of Ngiro It has dawned
Niuria njiniki uvira ku?	What do you need a loin-cloth for?
Nwangana nyukwe ugukuguna	Now only your mother can help you
Mwici wa Ngiro	Uncircumcised man of Ngiro
Niuria njiniki uvira ku	What do you need a loin-cloth for?

Nuite nyukwe akwonganire	Won't you call your mother to plead for you
Iai gugukia	Oh! it has dawned
Niwitia njiniki uvuira ku?	What do you need a loin-cloth for?

*Sung while escorting the initiates to the river on the morning of initiation.

Mwana agwikara woria ng'ina akarii	**The child is just the way his mother is**
Mwana agwikara	The child has become
Mwana agwikara	The child has become
Mwana agwikara	The child has become
Mwana agwikara	The child has become
Woria ng'ina akarii	Just the way his mother was
Mwana agwikara	The child has become
Mwana agwikara	The child has become
Mwana agwikara	The child has become
Mwana agwikara	The child has become
Woria ng'ina akarii	Just the way his mother was
Mwana agwikara	The child has become
Mwana agwikara	The child has become
Mwana agwikara	The child has become
Mwana agwikara	The child has become
Mwana agwikara	The child has become
Mwana agwikara	The child has become
Woria ng'ina akarii	Just the way his mother was
Mwana agwikara	The child has become
Woria ng'ina akarii	Just the way his mother was
Mwana agwikara	The child has become
Woria ng'ina akarii	Just the way his mother was

*Sung after circumcision.

152

Kivici kingikanuma	**If ever an uncircumcised boy dares abuse me***
Kivici kingikanuma ii	If ever an uncircumcised boy dares abuse me
Kiri kia muthoni	Even if he is the son of my father in-law I would rather break
Uthoni ugukua	The relationship between me and my in-law
Arume ii kingikanginya ii _Kiri kia muthoni_	My fellow men, listen! If ever an uncircumcised boy dares step on me _ii_
Uthoni ugukua	I would rather break the relationship between me and my in-laws
Ka tukethanie _Ka kukethanie_ _Ii kwi mwago tugikethania_	Let us greet each other Let us greet one another Greeting one another Brings great joy
Avai! Ngiuma karimari _Nari muviki niukinyukaga_ _Arumei ngiuma karimari_ _Nari muviki niukinyukaga i hii!_	_Avai!_ My fellow men! When I was coming from the hill A bride is better she takes a step My fellow men when I was coming from the hill A bride is better she takes a step! hii!
Iui! Ngiuma karimari _Ndiaici mirigo nirituvaga_	_Iui_ when I was coming from the hill I did not know the goods could be this heavy
Noguo ii ngiuma karimari _Ndiaici mirigo nirituvaga_	Oh yes! When I was coming from the hill I was not aware the goods could be this heavy
Kivici kingikanuma _Kiri kia muthoni_ _Uthoni ugukua_	If ever an uncircumcised boy dares abuse me Even if he is the son of my father-in-law I would rather break the relationship
Murua mwaitu _Kingikanginya_ _Kiri kia muthoni_ _Uthoni ugukua_	My brother If ever he dares step on me Even if he is my father-in-law's son let the relationship break

153

Ndurutire arume rwiga	Give men food to eat
Cianaria	May the uncircumcised boys
Irogirwa niruo ii	Who have been eating the food
	Be cursed!

Ina mwaitu rutira arume rwiga	Oh! Mother!
	Won't you give me food to eat?
Cianaria	May the uncircumcised boys
Irogirwa niruo	Who have been stuffing themselves
Ihii!	Be cursed!

---

*Sung the day after circumcision while initiates are taken for a walk.
This day was known as "the day of ugali".

Female initiation songs

Vacavucia ituike   **Shake your body until beads break***

Vucavucia ituike	Move your body with abandon
Ciakamwitha oyio ho!	Move your body with abandon, oh!
Vucavucia ituike	Move your body with abandon
Vucavucia ituike	Move your body with abandon, oh!
	And let the beads break
Nyukwe arimagira u ?	For whom does your mother cultivate?

Vucavucia ituike	Shake your head with abandon
Vucavucia ituike	Shake your head with abandon, oh!
Ciukamwitha oyio ho!	And let the beads break
Vacavucia ituike	Shake your head with abandon
Vucavucia ituike	Shake your head with abandon, oh!
Ciukamwitha oyio ho!	And let the beads break
Ni nyukwe urukuvakire	It is your mother who fixed them for you!

154

Thiga mbui ikigwa	Trample on the feathers as they drop
Uthige mburi ikigwa	Trample on the feathers as they drop, oh
Ciukamwitha oyio ho!	Ciukamwitha oyio ho!
Thiga mbui ikigwa	Trample on the feathers as they drop
Uthige mbri ikigwa	Trample on the feathers as they drop, oh
Nyukwe arimagira u?	For whom does your mother cultivate?

*Sung a few days before initiation in a dance known as Njai.

Ninjunga nau?   With whom shall I dance?[22]

Ninjunga nau?	With whom shall I dance?
Ninjunga naki?	With whom shall I dance ?
Ninjunga na kinja kia ndigu i	I shall dance with a banana stem, oh!
Ii ayia ninjuga naki?	Oh! Yes, with what shall I dance?
Na muruaiya ndai muka	Since my brother has on wife
Ii ayia ninjunga naki?	Oh! Yes, with what shall I dance?

Mburi itiaukire ikiriraga i	The goats did not come crying
Ayia mburi itiaukire ikiriraga	The goats did not come crying, oh!
Mburi caukire ikithekaga i	The goats came laughing
Ii ayia mburi ciaukire ikithekaga	The goats came laughing, oh!

Ninjunga nau ?	Which whom ʼce?
Ninjunga naki?	With what sʰ
Ninjunga na kinja kia ndigu i	I shall danc
Ii ayia ninjunga naki?	Oh! Yes, v
Ii ayia ninjunga naki?	

Muka wa vava ?	My fatʹ
Muka wa vava i ?	My fa
Ii ayia muka wa vava	Oh! ʹ
Ni uria mwiru muteme ngoroce i	Is tʰ
Ii ayia muka wa vava	Oh

Ninjunga nau?	Which whom shall I dance?
Ninjunga naki?	With what shall I dance ?
Ninjunga na kinja kia ndigu i	I shall dance with a banana stem, oh!
Ii ayia ninjunga naki?	Oh! Yes, with what shall I dance?
Na ndii cucu	And I have no grandmother
Na ndii cucu i	And I have no grandmother oh!
Ii ayia na ndii cucu	Oh! Yes, I have no grandmother
Ninjunga nake i?	With what shall I dance ?
	Oh! Yes, with what shall I dance?
Ninjunga nau?	Which whom shall I dance?
Ninjunga naki?	With what shall I dance ?
Ninjunga naki	I shall dance with a banana stem, oh!
Ii ayia ninjunga naki?	Oh! Yes, with what shall I dance?

---

*Performed on the morning of initiation in a dance known as *mugeco wa aari*.

Nyanya maguka?	**Have my mothers come?**
Nyanya aguca?	Has my mother come?
Nyanya maguca?	Have my mothers come?
Marevitaga	They were swearing
Marevitaga	They were swearing
Ningikarira	If at all I cry
Ningikarira	If at all I cry
Ndigakinya mucii	I should not go back home
Ndigakinya mucii	I should not go back home
Tata maguca?	Have my aunts come ?
Tata macuca?	Have my aunts come ?
Marevitaga	They were swearing
Marevitaga	They were swearing
Ningikarira	If at all I cry
Ningikarira	If at all I cry
Ndigakinya micii	I shall not go back home
Ndigakinya mucii	I shall not go back home

Cucu maraugaga	My grandmothers were saying
Cucu maraugaga	My grandmothers were saying
Nimeci ningaumiriria	They knew I would persevere
Muruithia anenga	When the initiator cuts me
Ndingikarira	I would not cry
Ndingikarira	If at all I cry
Ndigakinya mucii.	I would not go back home.

Ningucacika

Oh! I am feeling anxious*

Ii ningucacika	I am feeling anxious
Ningucacika i	I am feeling anxious
Ii ayia! Ningucacika	Oh! Yes I am feeling anxious
Ngakiria muriki gucacika i	My anxiety surpasses
	The anxiety of a bride
Ii ayia! Ningucacika!	Oh! Yes, I feel anxious!

Ii ninthiira naku?	Oh! Which way shall I go ?
Ninthiira naku i ?	Oh! which way shall I follow ?
Ii ayia ninthiira naku ?	Oh! Yes, which way shall I follow?
Ya varavara	The wide road that thorny bushes
Iri kithigia njogu i	Oh! Yes, which way shall I follow?
Ii ui ninthiira naku?	

Ayia ii tutiriraga	We don't cry
Tutiriraga i	We don't cry, oh
Ii ayia tutiriraga	Oh! Yes we don't cry
Nwanga mwana	The only person who would cry
Wacire na ng'ina	Is a child who came with his mother
Ii ayia tutiriraga	Oh! Yes we don't cry!

Ii ningucacika	I am feeling anxious
Ningucacika i	I am feeling anxious
Ii ayia ningucacika	Oh! Yes, I am feeling anxious
Ngakiria muviki gucacika i	My anxiety surpasses
Ii ayia! Ningucacika!	The anxiety of a bride
	Oh! Yes, I feel anxious!

*Sung by the initiates and their escorts on the morning of initiation.

Muka Mutemi	**You woman cutter***
Njuri njuri	*Njuri njuri*
Ya Ndiririri	Oh! the Ndiririri lineage
Irothiga mbui ikithii	Let it trample on a feather
	As it passes along
Muka mutemi	You woman cutter
Nduici gutema	You don't know how to cut
Cioka ringi	Come once again
I njuri!	*Njuri!*
Na mwari waririre	And any girl who cried
Ndakambikie ciuma ciake	Should never put her beads on me
Njuri njuri	*Njuri njuri*
Ya Ndiririri	Oh! the Ndiririri lineage
Irothiga mbui ikithii	Let it trample on a feather
	As it passes along
Muka mutemi	You woman cutter
Ndwici gutema	You don't know how to cut
Cioka ringi	Come once again
I njuri!	Oh! *Njuri*

*Sung by initiates and escorts during the initiation.

Satirical songs

Nikwinwa ni mundu na muruang'ina

It is the brothers dancing

Mugoiyo ii mugoiyo ii	The dance, the dance
Niwinua ni mundu na muruang'ina	It is being performed
Na nyomba itikurimanira	By a person and his brother
Iiai mugoiyo ii mugoiyo ii	The problem is that
Niwinua ni mundu na muru ang'ina	The houses cannot weed together
Na nyomba itikurimanira iai	*Iiai* the dance, the dance
	is being performed by brothers
	And the houses cannot weed together

Mururi uyu wa manji
Mukonge Njoka wa Mweti
Na kithao kiria ti Gitende
Nirio rikumuringira iioe
Mutige kuvavia ongia

Arume nimavavia ongia
Makiugaga nimo maramendia
Nati ithao iria
Ti Gitende na Njoka wa Mweti
Nimo maramendia
Nimburia atiri
Nituvavua uu nginya ri?

The clan of water
Go and bribe Njoka son of Mweti
And the fool called Gitende
They are the ones betraying you
Stop blaming women

Men are blaming women
Claiming that they are betraying them
And it is those fools
Gitende and Njoka son of Mweti
They are the ones betraying them
My question is this
For how long shall we be blamed like this?

Mwari mucambu

Iai mwari mucambu
Iai Wamathiga agucamba
Iai Wamathiga aracambire
Vamwe wana ng'ina
Iai Wamathiga na ng'ina
Nimararire gaturu
Magigetaga nyama

Ni nthaka iriku
Ikagura Wamathiga?
Nuriku ungigura mundu mucambu?
Muka wanaria nduru
Mwana na ng'ina nimacambu
Andu maricaga nduru

Wagura Wamathiga
Ukarugagirwa nduru utuku

A girl who has disgraced herself

Oh! dear! A girl who has disgraced herself
Iai Wamathiga should be shamed
Iai Wamathiga has disgraced herself
Together with her mother
Iai Wamathiga and her mother
They ate a little squirrel
Calling it good meat

Which young man
Will marry Wamathiga?
A person who has disgraced herself
A woman who has eaten a squirrel?
A girl and her mother have disgraced
themselves
People who eat squirrels
If you marry Wamathiga

You will have a squirrel
Prepared for you at night

159

Wamathiga mwari mwitii
Aitiaga na ndeci nimucambu
Wanegua muka ukuria nduru?

Wamathiga is a proud girl
She boasts yet she does not know
That she has ruined her reputation
Have you ever heard of a woman
Who eats squirrels?

She picks men indiscriminately

Athuraga nthaka nthuro
Na ndeci ni mucambu
Ii Wamathiga na ng'ina
Ni macambu ii!

Iai Wamathiga and her mother
They have ruined their reputation
They have disgraced themselves.

Oh! this girl!

Iai mwari uyu!

Oh! This girl!

Iai mwari uyu!
Athiite kiathi Kirimari
Iai mwari uyu!
Athiite kiathi Kirimari

Oh! This girl!
On her way to the market at Kirimari*
Oh! This girl!
On her way to the market at Kirimari

Niauga ndinirue mutanda
Iai ndinirue mutanda
Urari mwithi
Iai mwari uyu!

She says a chunk be cut for me
Oh! cut a chunk for me
Even though it is raw
Oh! This girl!

Iai mwari uyu!
Athiite kiathi Kirimari
Iai mwari uyu!
Niatigwe gwa Kivaravara
Iai mwari uyu!

Oh! This girl!
On her way to the market at Kirimari
Oh! This girl!
Let her be left
At Kivaravara's home
Oh! This girl!

Kirimari, literally "at the hill". It is used for Embu Town.

Nyaga wa Gituro naumba aka monthe	**Nyaga son of Gituro woos all women**

Nyaga uyu mukwona	This Nyaga you see
Nyaga uyu mukwona wa Gituro	This Nyaga you see son of Gituro
Nyaga uyu mukwona wa Gituro	This Nyaga you see son of Gituro
Ndari undu ateci	There is nothing he does not know
Wana kumba aka	Even wooing women
Wana kumba ari	Even wooing girls
Naumba onthe	He woos all of them
Nienuka namo	He takes them home
Amagweie njara!	holding their hands!

Nyaga uyu mukwona	This Nyaga you see
Nyaga uyu mukwona wa Gituro	This Nyaga you see son of Gituro
Niamakitie athuri	Has shocked elders
Na akamarakaria	And has also angered them
Niaumba ari wana aka	He is wooing women and even girls
Naumba monthe	He woos all of them

Ni enukia wa Kindaruma	He takes them home
	All the way to Kindaruma
Niaumba monthe	He woos all of them
Akivira Kindaruma	And takes them to Kindaruma!

Kavici kung'enda	**A disobedient boy**

Uka kana mbuke ii	Come or I come oh!
Uka kana mbuke ii	Come or I come oh!
Kari ngurumo ya Thitha	He is in the valley of Thiba River
Uka kana mbuke ii	Come or I come oh!
Kari ngurumo ya Thitha	He is in the valley of Thiba River
Karingagia ng'ombe na itaru	He ferries the cows across
Kari ngurumo ya Thitha	In a makeshift boat
Ngurumo ya Thitha	Indeed he is in the valley of Thiba River
Na karingagia ng'ombe na itaru!	And he ferries the cows across
	In a makeshift boat

Kavici kung'enda
Kavici kiongo kiumu
Mundu uteragwa
Mwana atari murungi
Ni waki?

This boy is very stubborn
This boy is a hard core
A person who never listens to advice
A child who can never be corrected
Of what use is he?

Ndu etu mwana aura wa biu!

Oh! Our people!
The child is completely lost!

Nocera ng'ina na ithe migwi
Kararingia ng'ombe na itaru
Wa thitha
Uka kana mbuke!

He confronts his mother and father with arrows
And he ferries the cows across
In a makeshift boat
Come or I come!

Niauririrua mburiririo

They are asking for her all over

Nauririrua ii mburiririo
Ukwona mwari wetu?
Kwi mundu mwonu Ciagitune?
Aciari na andu merika
Wana athuri a muviriga
Mimauria uu
Mwari wetu akwonwa?

They are asking for her all over
Have you seen our girl?
Has anyone seen Ciagitune ?
The parents and the agemates
And even the clan elders
Are searching for her all over
Has anyone seen our girl?

Amwe nimauga
Arathiire wana njira ya Mwambatha
Arathimirwe irinda Cogoria
Nakio gicieko Arathimirwe Kagoco
Mwari mwoce

Some are saying
She took the path to Mombasa
She was fitted a dress at Chogoria
And the petticoat was measured at Kagoco
A girl has been taken away

Ari a mbeere
Mukwaga varara
Mwanegua mundu ukwiendia?

Daughters of Mbeere land
You have no behaviour
Have you even heard of someone selling
herself?

Mwari ukwivira
Guocwa na mata ta nthua?
Mundu munene na ni kirugamo!
Mwari mugima na nwa kirugamo!

A girl taking herself
To be licked with saliva like a flea?
A big person yet not mature in deed!
Big for nothing girl!

Mwari ukwendua kiru	A girl being sold in kilogrammes
Iai ningwaria mbario	Iai I shall talk frankly
Ni mbaria cia mwariwa ii	I am talking about my daughter
Ta njanji ari kiamari	Like a judge in a court
Nimbaria cia mwari	I shall talk about a girl
Mwari uri mucii uyu ii	The girl in the home
Ta njanji ari kiamari	Like a judge in a court
Mwari wakwa akendagua	Any daughter of mine
	Will be sold in kilogrammes
Na kiro iria ikwendia mboco	The kilogrammes in which beans are sold
Iai ningwaria	Oh! I will talk
Ta njanji ii ari kiamari	Like a judge in a court, oh!
Mwari wakwa ti wa raici	My daughter is not cheap
Yura ni ra goro	Famine is expensive
Mwendi mwari uyu	He who wants my daughter
Ni wa kira ii	She is worth kilogrammes!
Mwari uyu wakwa	This daughter of mine
Nimurerete na thina	I have brought her up with difficulties
Nginya akengana uguo	Until she has grown up
Ningumwedia na kiro	I will sell her in kilogrammes
Iria ikwendia mboco ii!	The ones in which beans are sold!

Mwaka uyu tinima	This year I shall not dig
Ii ai raruyiu! Nimbuga uu	Ii ai raruyiui! I will say this
Nie mwari wa Ngithi	I daughter of the clan of Ngithi
Ni na mugambo wa kuuga	I have a voice to speak
Mwaka uyu tinima	This year I will not dig
Na ti na ngwa	And I will not starve
Na ti nvota kuria ukia ukiriwa	I will not live in poverty
Iai mwaka uyu tinima	Iai this year i will not dig
Na ti na ngwa ii!	And I will not starve!

163

Nie mwari wa Ngithi	I daughter of the clan of Ngithi
Nanarima miaka mingi	I have dug for many years
Nanaithaika urimiri	I have tied myself to cultivating
Miaka mingi	For many years!
Na yura riauka	But when famine comes
Ndigatigwa ni andu	I am never left behind
Makithii Gikuu	By people going to Gikuyuland
Makithii uthuguriri Gikuu	In search of food in Gikuyuland
Tinima mwaka uyu	I will not dig this year
Na ti na ngwa!	But I will not starve!
Kwarimwa ngaria	When people dig I will eat
Ciakethwa ngavaa	When food is harvested
Nati nie mwaka uyu	i will be satisfied
Tinima!	But me this year
	I will not cultivate!

War songs and recitations

Ndikera mwanwakwa niakarime ***rwanda***	**I shall never send my child to cultivate in the valley***
Ndikera manwakwa	I shall never tell my child
Niakarime rwanda	To cultivate in the valley
Rwanda ruri maitha ii	The valley harbours enemies
Ndikera mwanwakwa	I shall never send my child
Niakarime rwanda	To cultivate in the valley
Rwanda ruri maitha ii	The valley harbours enemies
Iyu huu yu huu!	*I yu huu yu huu!*
Ndikera mwanwakwa	I shall never tell my child
Niakarime rwanda	To Cultivate in the valley
Rwanda ruri maitha ii	The valley harbours enemies

I yu huu yu huu!
Ndikera mwanwakwa
Niakarime rwanda
Rwanda ruri maitha ii!

I yu huu yu huu!
I shall never send my child
To cultivate in the valley
The valley harbours enemies, oh!

*Sung by warriors when doing exercise.

Tukaruira ngaari

We shall fight for vehicles*

Andu aria mwi Miiru
Mugwitia ng'ombe
Ciaca gutura
Tukaruira ngaari
I yu huu yu huu!

You people of Meru
You have asked for cattle
If they are not available
We shall fight for vehicles
I yu huu yu huu!

I yu huu yu huu
Kangangi uri Miiru
Ugwitia ng'ombe
Ciaca gutura
Tukaruira ngaari

I yu huu yu huu!
Kangangi in Meru
You have asked for cattle
If they are not available
We shall fight for vehicles

I yu huu yu huu!
Andu aria mwi Miiru
Mugwitia ng'ombe
Ciaca gutura
Tukaruira ngaari
I yu huu yu huu!

I yu huu yu huu!
You people of Meru
You have asked for cattle
If they are not available
We shall fight for Vehicles
I yu huu yu huu!

*Sung by warriors when doing exercises.

Taroria mundu mwanake	**Look at his hero***
Aririrüti!	*Aririrüti!*
Taroria mundu mwanake	Look at this hero
Uyu ukuitwe ni ithe	Look at this young warrior
Nake akamukua	This one carried by his father
Na kagina kari njuki	And he in turn carries him
	With a gourd full of the bees goodness!
Aririrüti!	*Aririrüti!*
Muvuvi wa coro ya Kirumbi	The horn-blower of Kirumbi
Rukiiri!	In the early morning
Ukagiria tukamakua	The one who will protect us
	So that we shall never be scared
Ni kivici kia muka Mumbeere	Of the uncircumcised son of a Mbeere woman
Kana kia muka Mugikuu!	Or the uncircumcised son of a Gikuyu woman!
Aririrüti!	*Aririrüti!*
Aririrüti!	*Aririrüti!*
Niuga ninguite kithinthiiti	Why should I call you slow-footed ?
Kwoia muviki?	Are you a bride ?
Nwa ngwitire kithandika	I would rather call you an explosive
Mbariki ya rugundu	Castar oil seeds from a plant on fallow land
Iria ikathandika	The seed that will explode
Ciaragori cia muriama	In the fields of the one
Irari cia muriama	Who stands for absolute truth
Igatuika ciaku!	In such a way
Aririrüti!	As to make you inherit these fields!
	Aririrüti!
Aririrüti!	*Aririrüti!*
Tathii unacoke	Go and come back
Vuva iri mwene	Behind there are owners
Mbere iri mwene	Ahead there are owners
Aririrüti!	*Aririrüti!*
Aririrüti!	*Aririrüti!*

---

*Recited by women at a ceremony held to send warriors off to war.

166

Ka ngutare mbaru wa nyanya	Let me count your ribs my mother's son*

Ariririiti!
Ka ngutare mbaru wa nyanya
Uria wanatarwa ni rutere
Mamira na ndami
Mathangu mathirua kithaka
Ni mugaciriai!

Ariririiti!
Let me count your ribs my mother's son
The way you were counted by the hedges
O poor thing!
You have been blowing your nose with rags
The bush having been stripped of
All its leaves by the enemy!

Ariririiti!
Taroria mundu mwanake
Uyu ukuitwe ni ithe
Nake akamukua
Na kagina kari njuki!

Ariririiti!
Look at this hero
Look at this young warrior
This one carried by the father
And he in turn carries him
With a gourd full o bees goodness!

Ariririiti!
Muvuvi wa coro ya Kirumbi
Ruukiri
Kariua gatanarunguria nthi
Kana karunguria murithi wacio
Ariririiti!
Ariririiti!

Ariririiti!
The horn-blower of Kirumbi
In the early morning
Before the little sun scorches the ground
Or burns the herdsman
Ariririiti!
Ariririiti!

Ariririiti!
Niuga ningwite kivingiiri
Niuri muviki?
Nwa ngwitire kithandika
Mbariki ya rugundu
Iria ikathandika
Ciaragori cia muriama
Irari cia muriama
Igatuika ciaku
Ariririiti!
Ariririiti!

Ariririiti!
Why should I call you slow-footed ?
Are you a bride ?
I would rather call you an explosive
Castor oil seed from a plant
On fallow land
The seed that will explode
In the fields of the one
Who stands for absolute truth
In such a way
As to make you inherit these fields!
Ariririiti!
Ariririiti!

---

*Recited by women welcoming warriors home from battle.

Political songs

Kagoce na ndia ndiku

Iai Kagoce niaukira ndia ndiku
Iai Kagoce niaukira ndia ndiku
Akithingithia engi namo magiukira
Akiurua ni Ngaro ii niugendaga ku?
Akiuga ninthii wa Thabathaba
Gukethania kuria kwa bwana Nguku

Iai Kagoce niaukira ndiari ndiku
Iai Kagoce niaukira ndiari ndiku
Akauga niatiramira wa Thabathaba
Nenda kwona aria makurimirwa
Aria managiria andu mao
Marere ciana ciao na ukiriiru
Niauga bwana wa Thabathaba
Niwe avatere ii

Iai Kogoce niaukira ndiari ndiku
Iai Kagoce niaukira ndiari ndiku
Akainaina ageta bwana
Naguo urume nwata wa Kathigira
Mwana muciare ni ng'ina na urume.

Kagoce and the deep waters*

Iai Kagoce is in deep waters
Oh! Kagoce is in deep waters
He engineers others and they stand up
He is asked by Ngaro, oh where are you going?
He says I am going as far as Saba Saba
To visit and take my greetings
To Mister Nguku's home

Iai Kagoce is in deep waters
Oh! Kagoce is in deep waters
He says his destination is Saba Saba
He wants to see those
Whose farms are being cultivated for them
The ones who have always prevented
His people from bringing up their children
in peace
He says he wants to confront
The master of Saba Saba

Iai Kagoce is in deep waters
Oh! Kagoce is in deep waters
He is shaking and calling the master
His violence and bravery
Is like that of Kathigira
His mother bore him
With that violence and bravery.

*Sung against forced labour in European settler's farms during the colonial era.

Mugongo munene

Mugongo munene
Twina mugongo munene wa Mbeere
Ii ninguria kiuria
Murikanu wana Irungu Mume wana
gucokia
Mumburirie kiuria mutongoria wa Iringu
Uria Cierume athaga mugongo
Guku awatarii atia?

Kiuma arambirire
Cierume atige atewa
Muvakari wa Wmbu na Mbeere
Makithii kirimari
Kiuma, andu etu, ni wanaruona!

Nderi iria ngutuma
Iria ngurekia mugumori
Uria uri Kiambere
Kindaruma mucii wanathina
Nduthiraga kieva
Mucii wanarwera
Nduthiraga ivoru

Mugongo munene
Twina mugongo munene wa Mbeere
Ii mwanarwigua
Mucii wanathira
Nuthiraga ivoru
Kieva kithingataga uthini!

A great people

Many people, a great people!
Oh! Mbeere people are a great people
Oh! I want to ask a question
My agemates and even Iringu elders
Give me a reply
Tell Kiuma the leader of Iringu
When Cierume* was our ruler
How was our land?

Kiuma told me
Cierume was left abandoned
At the border of Embu and Mbeere
While they were going up the mountain
Kiuma, my people,
There are no wonders he has never seen!

The vulture I will send
The one I shall drop
At the *mugumo* tree on Kiambeere hill
Hmn! Wait and see!
A home that has suffered poverty
Will never cease to experience sorrow
A home that has been rejected
Will never cease to experience loneliness

Many people, a great people!
Mbeere people are a great people
Oh! Have you heard?
Oh! Have you observed?
At home that has lost people
Will never cease to experience loneliness
Poverty precedes sorrow!

---

*Cierume was a famous Mbeere woman leader during the colonial era.
Cierume means one who has masculine qualities.

169

Unene wa Ikombo*

Munene wa Mbeere nene
Ikombo wa Munyiri irari iyu! ii!
Iyai unene ucite Mbeere kwa Ikombo
Ikombo wa Munyiri niwe ugutwatha
Ikombo wa Munyiri niew ugutwatha

Iai Ikombo! Ikombo
Mutimwigue ii ayiai Ikombo
Iai Ikombo! Ikombo!

Kirima Kenya kinene
Kiandikithitue na Ikombo
Mbaka Mwea nwa Ikombo
Mwire Njenga wa Gioko
Arekie nthi ni ya Mumbeere

Iai Ikombo! Ikombo
Mutimwigue ii ayiai Ikombo
Iai Ikombo! Ikombo!

Andu a Gikuu iguai uu!
Nthi ni yandikithitue na Ikombo
Tigana na nthi ino
Nthi ino nirekue
Ni ya Mumbeere!

Iai Ikombo! Ikombo
Mutimwigue ii ayiai Ikombo
Iai Ikombo! Ikombo!

The leadership of Ikombo[34]

The leader of great Mbeere land
Ikombo son of Munyiri irai iyu! ii!
Iyiai leadership has come to Mbeere
Leadership has come to mbeere in
Ikombo's homestead
Ikombo son of Munyiri
Is the one who willrule us
Ikombo son of Munyiri
is the one who will rule us

Iai Ikombo! Ikombo!
Listen to him! Obey him!
Ii ayiai Ikombo!
Iai Ikombo! Ikombo!

The great mount Kenya
Has been registered in the name of Ikombo
Even Mwea belongs to Ikombo
Tell Njenga son of Gioko
To leave the land alone
It belongs to Ikombo

Iai Ikombo! Ikombo!
Listen to him! Obey him!
Ii ayiai Ikombo!
Iai Ikombo! Ikombo!

Gikuyu people listen to this!
The land has been registered in the name
of Ikombo
Leave this land alone
This land should be left alone
It belongs to Mbeere people!

Iai Ikombo! Ikombo!
Listen to him! Obey him!
Ii ayiai Ikombo!
Iai Ikombo! Ikombo!

---

*Ikombo was a famous Mbeere chief during the colonial era.

Niathimwa racima*	**They are being weighed by force**
Ioe! niathimwa racima	Oh! He is being weighed by force
Ioe! niathimwa racima	Joe! He is being weighed by force
Nayo racima ni wira wa mundu	Their work is being weighed by force
Nimaririkana icamba ria Ikora	They are remembering Ikora's farm
Ioe kuria mathimagwa racima	Where their work was being weighed by force
Wira utari kiguni	Work that was of no benefit to them
Kunyarira ciana cia Mbeere ii!	It was sheere exploitation of Mbeere children!
Nimaririkana vakuvi ni iria ria Naivasha	They recall their experiences near lake Naivasha
Vakuvi na iria riri	Near this lake
Nivo njenda yathirire	That is where many people lost their lives
Itwaritwe kuthimwa racima	Having been taken to be weighed by force
Wira utari kiguni	Work that was of no benefit to them
Wira wananyarira mwana wa Mumbeere	Forced labour made Mbeere children suffer
Nimathimwa racima makarira	They are being weighed by force and driven to tears
Ciana na ongia manarirua ni racima	
Andu a Mbeere manatigwa mari ndigwa	Mbeere women and children wept bitter tears
Niundu wa racima	Because of forced labour
Nimburia racima	Mbeere people were orphaned
Ikathira ri?	Because of forced labour
	My question is this
	When will forced labour cease?

---

*Protest song against forced labour during the colonial era. *Racima* is a corruption of the Kiswahili word '*lazima*' which means 'by force'.

Nthaka cia Mbeere nicio ciagire thigari	**Sons of Mbeere are the soldiers****
Thigari ii! Thigari ii! Thigari	Soldiers oh! soldiers oh! soldiers
Thigari ikuthii macii* ii	Soldiers have gone marching ii!
Nimandika marua	They write letters
Igacukira ng'ina	And the letter is read
Nayo marua ikathomwa	And it says good morning
Ikauga ngundi moning'i*	I am just sending you greetings
Ningethi na ningauka	And I shall come at the end of the year
Mwico wa mwaka	White men are no joke!

Mwico wa mwaka
Ucomba.ndukwenda mathaka

Thigari ii! Thigari ii! Thigari	Soldiers oh! Soldiers oh! Soldiers
Ciana cia Mbeere nicio ikuvirwa	The songs of Mbeere are taken
Mavuti ni magamba mwea	To take these positions
Ciana cia Mbeere nicio ikuruta	Children of Mbeere are the ones
Wira utakumenyeka	Who are taken to do unknown jobs
Thigari ii! Thigari ii! Ikithii maci!	Soldiers oh! Soldiers oh!
Nthaka cia Mbeere nicio ciagire thigari ii!	Soldiers have gone marching
	Sone of Mbeere are the soldiers now!

Avici a Mbeere	The sons of Mbeere
Riu ni athigari	Are now soldiers
Ivici cia Mbeere	The uncircumcised sons of Mbeere
Riu ciikaraga kuraca na mucii	Now stay away from home
Ciana ciao na aka mao	Their children and their wives
Matimonaga ii!	They never see them oh!
	The chief is a white man

*maci is 'marching' and ngundi moning is 'good morning'.
**Protest against the conscription into the army during the colonial era.

Civu ni muthungu   **It is only his skin which is black**

Na civu ni muthungu	Oh! the chief is an Englishman
Nikwa ari gikonde kiiru	It is only his skins which is black
Na civu ni muthungu	Oh! the chief is a white man
Nikwa ari gikonde kiiru	

Ta mwaririe kithungu	Speak to him in English
Wigwe uria agugucokeria	And you will hear how he will reply
Yesi! No!	Yes! No!
Yesi! No!	Yes! No!

172

Mugucu* ni muthungu	Mugucu* is an Englishman
Nikwa ari gikonde kiiru	It is only his skin which is black
Mugucu ni Mmuthungu	Mugucu is a white man
Nikwa ari gikonde kiiru	It is only his skin which is black
Ta mwaririe kithungu	Speak to him in English
Wigue uria agugucokeria	And you will hear how he will reply
Yesi! No!	Yes! No!
Yesi! No!	Yes! No!

Mugucu (Mugushu) was a famous chief of Runyenjes in Embu during the colonial era.

Njomo akuma Ruraya

Jomo* has come from abroad

Njomo akuma Ruraya	Jomo has come from abroad
Turaugaga ndagaca	We thought he would never come back
Turaugaga tumwetẹrere	We were waiting for him anxiously
	We were asking ourselves
	When will he come back?
Njomo akuma Ruraya ii!	Jomo has come back from abroad Oh!
Agucá na uyathi	He has brought independence
Mbirirwe mucungu	Tell the white man for me
Arekerie Njomo giti	To leave the seat for Jomo
Njomo niwiganite	Jomo is capable
Wa kwatha bururi	Of ruling our country
Mbirirwe mucungu	Could someone tell the white man for me
Athamie indo ciake!	To move his belongings!
Bururi ni wetu	The country is ours
Tutikwenda mucungu ringi	We do not want the white man any longer
Njomo akuma Ruraya	Jomo has come from abroad
Aguca na uyathi	He has brought independence

173

Mucungu niaume Kenya
Atutigire nthi yetu
Njomo akuma Ruraya
Aguca na uyathi.

The white man should leave Kenya
He should leave our land to us
Jomo has come back from abroad
He has brought independence.

---

*Jomo refers to Jomo Kenyatta, the first President of Kenya.

174

Chapter 7

NTHIMO — PROVERBS

Cautionary proverbs

1. *Murata wa mundu niwe umuviraga ivu ria kumuria.*
   A person's best friend is the one who gives her the pregnancy that eventually kills her. Cautions against too much trust in one's friends. Similar to the Swahili proverb, *"Kikulacho ki nguoni mwako"*.

2. *Mucera na mukundu akundukaga taguo.*
   Whoever keeps the company of a wicked person becomes wicked just like him.

3. *Uteci wingi amwitaga gaaka.*
   Whoever does not know a person calls him this small thing.
   Avoid judging people or situations from their face value.

4. *Kai urume kenukagia ng'ina kivara.*
   The brave child returns to his mother full of wounds.
   Warns against taking risks thoughtlessly.

5. *Murega akiathwa ndaregaga akivetwa.*
   He who refuses to take advice has no choice when he is being folded.
   Once someone rejects good advice he is left to his own devices but must face the consequences of his actions.

6. *Wendo ni unyamario.*
   Love means trouble.
   Warns against infatuation or obsession.

7. *Moneka narua yuraga wa narua.*
   Easily found, easily lost.
   Warns against unplanned and thoughtless acquisition of property, including taking what does not rightly belong to one.

8. *Mukami tiwe munyiti njau.*
   The one who milks is not the one who holds the calf.
   One can manage to do only one thing at a time.

9. *Mucakwe ugwithagia njamba.*
   A maize cob can knock down a cock.
   An apparently insignificant affair can cause a great person's downfall.

10. *Nyungu ithekaga ruio.*
    A pot laughs at the potsherd.
    Today it is me tomorrow it is your turn.

11. *Muthii ndaumbikaga ndigu.*
    The traveller does not leave a banana roasting on a fire while he goes on his journey.
    Warns against embarking on new tasks before completing those at hand.

12. *Muvuro utwaragia muthambiri.*
A river drowns the best swimmer.
Warns against being over-confident.

13. *Ivenya inene riunaga gikwa ithatha.*
Too much hurry breaks a twin yam.
Hurry hurry has no blessings.

14. *Ruku ruria ruri gitarari ruthekaga ruria ruri riko.*
The firewood on the rack laughs at the one which is on the fire
(similar to No. 10 above).

15. *Mwathwa ni ivu ndagicaga indo.*
Whoever is ruled by his stomach never grows rich.
Warns against thoughtless consumption without any regard for the future.

16. *Ng'ondu irumagirira muthinji.*
A sheep follows its butcher.
Your best companion is the one who brings about your downfall (also similar to No. 15 above).

17. *Nderi yarutirwe iguru ni uri.*
The eagle was brought down from the sky by greed.
Greed is the roof of destruction.

18. *Irigu rikavuragwa ni guciara.*
Too many bananas from one stem causes the stem to break.
Avoid involving yourself in too many things.

19. *Gutii wiriraga nwa agicioka.*
Nobody regrets when going, it is only when coming back.
Think before you act.

20. *Muti ndutwicagwa kwambiriria neguru.*
One does not climb a tree from the top.
Think about the possibility of what you intend to do before you begin.

21. *Menya kuvuravuria njoka irinari riayo.*
Do not disturb a snake in its own hole.
Cautions against seeking out trouble.

22. *Nviti ndinengagirwa mwana.*
A hyena is never given a child.
Do not entrust your enemy with your most valuable things.

23. *Ngoma ithwire kuthekua.*
Devils hate jokes.
Relate to people according to their temperaments.

24. *Murimu wa kwigirira nduri ururu.*
A self-inflicted ailment does not pain.
If you get into problems through your own thoughtless actions you have only yourself to blame.

25. *Kaviu gacangacangi gatigaga kwao gukithinjwa.*
A knife which roams around leaves home while an animal is being slaughtered.
One who desires too many things loses all.

26. *Kwigita ti guoya.*
Keeping off trouble is not a sign of cowardice.

27. *Mbari ya ngeka yethirwe itekite.*
The clan of "I will do it" was found not having done.
Warns against procrastination.

28. *Mbeterera ndikinyaga.*
He who waits does not arrive.
Tomorrow tomorrow does not come.

29. *Kindu kioneku gitii muvuthia.*
What has already been found should not be taken lightly.
Utilise the opportunity that has already availed itself to you; if you wait for something better you may never get it and it may be too late to take the initial chance.

176

30. *Tenya ugacindana na njogu kumia.*
    Never compete with the elephant in defecating.
    Know your strengths and limitations and avoid comparing yourself with those who are better than you.

31. *Mwigerekanio watere ciura matina.*
    Copying others caused frogs to lose their buttocks.
    Warns against blind competition.

32. *Mwinji kithima nwawe uciokaga gukirika.*
    He who digs a well ends up falling into it.

33. *Murogi arogaga gwake mbere.*
    A wizard bewitches his kin first.
    Similar to No. 32 above; however it originates from the belief that witches and wizards try their powers and the potency of their concoctions on their own children first before practising their evil on others.

34. *Kanua karia karire mbeu nwako kauragia ngaara ndui.*
    The mouth that ate the grain is the same one which asks what shall I plant.
    Warns against the tendency to consume without thinking about tomorrow.

35. *Ngarari nyingi ciuragaga uthoni.*
    Too many arguments kill marriage negotiations.
    Warns against pointless arguments.

36. *Mwivariria niwici nukuthii rwimbori.*
    The person preparing himself knows he is going to a dance.
    Warns against lack of focus and aimlessness.

37. *Kuthekua tikuo kwendwa.*
    A smile is not love.
    Beware those who joke and rejoice with you for they may be harbouring ill motives against you.

38. *Gukira kwii ngatho.*
    Silence breeds gladness.
    Silence is golden.

39. *Matu timo mbura.*
    Clouds do not always forecast rain.
    Avoid jumping to conclusions from superficial observations.

40. *Mutuma ndugu na giton'go athokagirua mai.*
    He who befriends the beetle is brought presents of dung.
    Be vigilant when choosing friends.

41. *Ndugu ti nduguto.*
    Friendship is not a newly-cultivated *shamba*.
    Avoid investing too much in a new friendship for it is bound to break one day.

42. *Gutii murio utamiwa.*
    There is no sweetness which is not eventually defecated.
    Everything, however sweet, comes to an end.

43. *Ana mucemi nukungaga.*
    Even an expert hunter squats.
    Humility is important even from the most able.

44. *Kuga ni noru ti kuga nithinjwe.*
    Saying it is fat does not mean that it should be slaughtered.
    Do not depend on what others say; the final decision rests with you.

45. *Micingu iiri yaunire nviti maguru.*
    Two smells (from roasting meat) caused the hyena to break its legs.
    Do not serve two masters.

46. *Kwii rukuu rwa kinya rutangitumika.*
    There is a crack on a gourd which would be impossible to stitch together.
    There are some losses that are irreparable.

47. *Kiriko gitigiragia ndeto ivitane.*
A promise does not prevent disagreement.
Do not take promises on face value.

48. *Uthani ti thiiri ati nwa urandurue.*
Lies are not debts that one can demand back.
Assess the validity and the credibility of
what you are being told and then, if you
allow yourself to be fooled, you will have
only yourself to blame since you have no
right to chase the liar.

49. *Uvoro wa vata niguo uriganagira.*
Important matters are the ones which are
easily forgotten.
Take precautions on important matters for
these are easily forgotten.

50. *Kwiyonera ti kwirwa.*
Seeing for oneself is not the same as being told.
It is better to investigate for oneself than
to depend on what others say.

51. *Kwona kimera ti guketha.*
Blossom does not necessarily promise a
bumper harvest.
Avoid jumping to conclusions (on seeing)
apparently favourable signs.

52. *Manji ma Thura matigunaga mundu wa
Thagicu.*
A person living all the way in Thagicu
cannot depend on water from Thura.
In order for one to benefit from something
one has to be close by.

53. *Kii ngoro kirutagua na miario.*
What is stored in the heart comes out
through talking.
Warns against bottling up one's
frustrations.

54. *Mwiririria niwe mucuku.*
The avenger is the bad one.
Owing to anger, the person who has been
wronged may do his opponent greater

harm than what he suffered and people
are likely to notice it more than the
original injury.
For this reason the proverb cautions
people not to take revenge.

55. *Mwinji ngwaci atumagira muro mugi.*
If a person wants to dig out sweet potatoes
he uses a sharp digging stick.
Use a tool or reason that matches the task
or problem at hand.

56. *Mucaria nai nuumionaga.*
Whoever looks for trouble finds it.
Cautions against courting trouble as well
as against looking at things from the
negative angle.

57. *Mwana mwaganu ndaniaraga methori.*
The face of a mischievous child never
dries of tears.
A wicked or mischevous child always
receives punishment; the proverb
therefore warns against misdemeanour.

58. *Mwaria ciene ndeci cia gwake.*
He who talks about other people does not
know what others say about him and his
kith and kin. Warns agaisnt gossip and
loose talk.

59. *Mutongoria irua nwanginya arue.*
The leader of a circumcision ceremony
must be circumcised.
You cannot lead others through a situation
you are ignorant of.

60. *Muthuguri nwawe ukuaga.*
The one who goes to look for food is the
same one who carries it. You reap what
you sow.

61. *Ng'ombe itionagwa ni kiguta.*
A lazy person can never get a herd of cattle.
Laziness leads to poverty.

62. *Ngwaci ikumagua ciariwa.*
Sweet potatoes are praised after they have been eaten.
The proof of the pudding is in eating it.

63. *Muvuravuria ndauragagua mbarari.*
He who incites others to go to war is never killed at the battle front.
Beware of trouble-makers because when problems come, it is the innocent, not the inciters, who suffer.

64. *Muvuravurania ndaturaga ruvara.*
One who always starts a fight never misses a wound.
Cautions against the tendency to fuel conflicts.
This proverb may appear as a contrast to No. 63 above.

65. *Muthikani ndathikagwa.*
He who buries others is never burried.
People should do good turns cautiously since good turns are often repaid with evil.

66. *Mwakiriria ciiri imwe niirunguraga.*
If a person cooks two pots of food at the same time, one of them gets burnt.
Avoid handling too many things at the same time.

67. *Muthani ndathekaga.*
A liar never laughs.
Liars are deceptively innocent-looking; you have to look deeper to detect them.

68. *Muvenia mundu mugo eciragia murimu niwathira.*
He who cheats a medicineman thinks the disease is completely cured.
When a good deed is done to you, do not forget that it is not the end of problems.

69. *Murio nduthiragia yura.*
Sweet taste does not bring hunger to an end.
Cautions people to think about tomorrow even if there is abundance today.

70. *Murio uthiragia magego.*
Sweetness finishes teeth.
Beware what appears good as it can destroy you.

71. *Murio urutaga nvungu muti iguru.*
Sweetness removes the hawk from the top of a tree.
Warns against greed. Just as sweetness brings a hawk from the safety of the tree, so would it lead a person to destruction.

72. *Muvuro uringagirwa varia ukugambira.*
People usually cross a river where it sounds loudest.
Still waters run deep

73. *Ungiona ikirite niimeretie.*
If you see it silent (snake) it has swallowed (prey).
Similar to No. 72 above.

74 *Mwene mburi ndavecanaga ruo.*
The owner of the goat does not give away the skin.
Warns against too much generosity.

75. *Ndugu niitecanaga.*
Friendship ruins.
Beware of bad company.

76. *Mugeni akigirua mirigo ndaigagirua metho.*
When you store a visitor's belongings you do not store his eyes.
Be vigilant when you have visitors for they can be intrusive.

77. *Mukua mboru aminukagia wa mucii.*
He who carries rotten stuff takes it right into his own home.
When you are in public, sieve what you gather because some of it may spoil your home.

78. *Mari ndugu nimamenanaga.*
People who were once friends turn out to be enemies.

179

Be careful about trusting friends excessively, some may disappoint you.

79. *Wira wa mwitumithio ndwi murugiri.*
One is never fed by working for a person who has not requested for help.

80. *Warire athinagia waigire.*
Whoever consumed his harvest disturbs the one who stored.
Cautions against misusing resources without thinking about tomorrow.

81. *Menya ndugate inya ukinyirite inyanya.*
Take care not to lose four chasing eight.
One bird in the hand is worth more than two in the bush.

82. *Iria ngiri niyo ngunyi.*
The silent animal is the one which scratches.
You cannot judge an evil person by his looks.
Still waters run deep (similar to 73 above).

83. *Njira iria nguvi ndikinyagia muthii.*
The short-cut does not take the traveller to his destination.
The shortest route is not necessarily the safest.

84. *Kava mutura weka kwi muturania na arogi.*
It is better to live alone than to live with witches and wizards.
It is better to be a hermit than to associate with evil people.

85. *Rumirira muvuro na niukuona iria.*
Follow the river and you will find the sea.
If you examine a situation closely and patiently, you will understand it fully.

86. *Mutwii muti nevenya agwicaga nai.*
Whoever climbs a tree in a hurry falls down badly.

87. *Mutwii kirima mbere athuraga kathiga karia agwikarira.*
Whoever arrives at the mountain-top first

chooses the stone on which to sit.
First come first served.

88. *Mukovi thiri ndendete kuriva.*
He who likes borrowing does not like repaying.
Great debtors are poor at honouring their promises to pay back.

89. *Mundu ndauragaga nguku iria irekagia matumbi niundu weruga.*
A person does not slaughter the hen which lays eggs just because he has a feast.
Cautions against the tendency to utilise resources out of excitement without considering their long-term benefits.

90. *Gutii wi muoyo utari nthu.*
There is no living person who has no enemies.
Cautions against over-confidence in those with whom one interacts.

91. *Wakinya mai na kuguru kumwe kinya na moiri.*
If you step on faeces with one foot step with the other one as well.
If you make a mistake, face the reality.

92. *Kwenda muno ni guta.*
Loving too much is to destroy.
Spare the rod, spoil the child.

93. *Nyungu imwe ithiragia yura ria muthenya umwe.*
One pot (of food) satisfies one day's hunger.
Try to save for tomorrow.

94. *Ngethi ivecanagwa ciatumanua.*
Greetings are delivered once someone has been asked to deliver them.
Never involve yourself in affairs which do not concern you.

95. *Menya ciaku tiga cia Uvariri.*
Know your own (affairs) leave those of Uvariri alone.
Avoid interfering in other people's affairs.

96. *Gutii utari murimu wake.*
There is no one who does not have his own disease.
No one can boast of not having a weakness, therefore nobody should laugh at others. Examine yourself before you criticise others.

97. *Kirumi kia mundu wi muoyo gikirite kia mundu mukuu.*
The curse from a living person is worse than that from a dead person.
Do good to the living for they are capable of doing you great harm.

98. *Wana kava mburi imwe kwi mburi ikumi mbii.*
It is better to possess one goat than to have ten which steal (other people's crops).
It is better to have one reliable friend than to have many evil ones.

99. *Mainagira gwa kiguoya na makaririra gwa kaiurume.*
They dance at the coward's home and mourn at the brave person's home.
Warns against taking risks thoughtlessly.

100. *Kirima na kirima ititunganaga.*
A mountain and a mountain never meet.
Never harm a fellow human being because, unlike mountains, human beings are destined to meet.

101. *Nai ningiaici yukaga mwico wovoro.*
"I wish I knew" always comes at the end.
Consider the consequences before you take action to avoid regrets.

102. *Mundu wina manji ndakinyaga kithimari.*
One who has water does not need to go to the well.
Mind what concerns you; avoid getting involved in affairs which don't concern you.

103. *Igego rithekagia itumu.*
A tooth laughs with the spear.
It is difficult to detect trouble; it is very easy to court it without realising what is happening.

104. *Nviti kiguoya niyo ituraga.*
A cowardly hyena is the one that lives long (similar to No. 100 above).

105. *Uria ugaga mbeterera augaga mari wavamwe na aria mathiire.*
The one who says wait for me thinks he is still with those who went ahead.
Avoid postponing things otherwise you will realise it when it is too late.

106. *Nguo iria mende ni mwene niyo irikaga ni makindu.*
The garment which is loved by the owner is the one which is usually eaten by rats.
What you love most is what is often damaged or lost.

107. *Mugiri mwaki naguo ugiakana ucokaga kumuvivia.*
The person who brings the hot charcoal to start the fire is the one who eventually gets burnt when the fire is lit.
Trouble usually boomerangs on the one who started it.

108. *Uka turie nawe agakuria na miromo*
'Come we eat together' is the one who will eventually eat you with his mouth.
The person who pretends to be your best friend is the one who eventually puts you into trouble, for example by talking ill about you.

109. *Kwanika ti kwanura.*
Hanging (e.g. clothes) is not bringing down.
Learn to distinguish between building and destroying.

110. *Muthingata njuki ndaturaga uki.*
He who follows bees never misses honey.
There is a reward for positive action. The proverb is often used as a warning to make someone conscious the possible repercussions of his actions.

111. *Mari gwitika matiri mwoci.*
Once water is spilt, nobody can retrieve it.
Do not cry over spilt milk.

112. *Mutego utegukagira mwene.*
A trap traps the owner (similar to No. 107 above).

113. *Itheru ni ria murata.*
Jokes are to be shared only with close friends.
Avoid closeness with all and sundry.

114. *Urume ndurekaga mundu akire mivuro ithatu.*
A fierce person cannot cross three rivers.
Fierce people are always in trouble because of constant friction with other people.

115. *Muragani ndaugagia.*
A murderer does not announce his arrival.
Evil deeds are often accompanied by hypocrisy.

Proverbs on wisdom and advice

116. *Mwingatwa na kivoto tita mwingatwa na nthimbu.*
One who is chased away with a solid argument is not like the one who is chased away with a club.
Good sense speaks louder than physical force. When good sense is used to show someone that he is wrong, he will yield of his own accord because of the power of the argument. In this case, good sense is a better weapon than a rod.

117. *Mundu akirungwa indi iria yagirire ndegucaga.*
When a person is being advised at the right time he never listens.
Warns people to listen to advice even if they may assume it is not appropriate, one never knows when advice may come in handy.

118. *Mugi ni mutare.*
A wise person is the one who listens to advice.
The proverb stresses the importance of advice in contributing to wisdom and knowledge.

119. *Ngiariria kiri nthi wana ki itara ni gikuigua.*
When I am talking to those on the ground even the ones on the rack above can hear.
It is wise to listen to advice even when it is not directed at you since it may be useful later.

120. *Kirimu mwata nwatu.*
A fool is like a beehive.
A beehive is thought to be foolish because it is used by bees to make honey in it and all the honey is harvested with the beehive getting nothing in return. Just as the beehive cannot tell when it is being exploited, a fool cannot see when he is being cheated.

121. *Mwana mugi ndai muvere wa ndeto.*
A clever child requires no style in the way a message is communicated to him.
A clever child understands easily.

122. *Irimu ithekaga mara.*
Fools laugh at intestines.
Fools do not think ahead.

123. *Ugi ndutongoragia ta urimu.*
Wisdom is not as commonplace as foolishness.

124. *Kirimu gitii mwiri.*
A fool has no adviser.
A fool does not see sense; advising a fool is a waste of time because he always assumes he knows.

125. *Mucirirwa atai vo ni kirimu.*
Whoever has his case judged in his absence is a fool.
One should always avail himself

whenever something that concerns him is being discussed so that he can give the other side of the story. Only a fool cannot spare the time.

126. *Urimu na yura ni mundu na muruang'ina.*
Foolishness and famine are brothers.
Foolishness is extreme deprivation just like famine. Also, famine is brought about by foolishness in using available food resources.

127. *Uthuri wa miario ukirite wa miaka.*
Maturity by advice is greater than maturity by the number of years.
An elder is respected more for the quality of his advice than for his age.

128. *Mukanie ndai ngarari.*
He who respects good advice never argues.
A person who knows the value of good advice listens without arguing with his adviser. He can then interpret, adapt and adopt it at the appropriate time.

129. *Mundu mugi nuugarurukaga meciria indi mundu kithao ndagarurukaga.*
A wise person changes his mind at times but a fool never changes his mind.
A wise person appreciates different points of view.

130. *Mugi erutaga na mavitia ma andu aria engi.*
A wise person learns through other people's mistakes.
Wise people increase their knowledge to avoid mistakes they have seen others make.

131. *Gutii mukuru utangirungwa.*
There is no old person who cannot be straightened.
Nobody is too old to learn.

132. *Auke ni ya kirimu.*
The day after tomorrow belongs to a fool.
Fools are the easiest to cheat beause they are unable to see the emptiness of promises for the unspecified future.

133. *Ugi wi mbere ya urimu.*
Intelligence comes before foolishness.
An intelligent person is stronger than a foolish one because he can use his intelligence to survive.

134. *Muti wa kirimu wirugamagia na mugi.*
A fool's walking-stick supports itself against a clever person.
A foolish person always tries to cover up his foolishness by associating with clever people.

135. *Mbura matu maturaga ciano na ciau.*
Those who are hard of hearing sharpen weapons with their thighs.
Those who do not listen to advice engage in foolish self-destructive actions.

136. *Uteci ndeci ati ndeci.*
He who does not know does not know that he does not know.
Those who have limited knowledge assume they know everything because they also have limited enthusiasm to seek further knowledge.

137. *Uteci u eci u.*
He who does not know this knows that.
Nobody knows everything; knowledge cannot be monopolised.

138. *Gutii kirimu gitanonga ng'ina.*
There is no fool who never sucked from his mother's breasts.
Even a fool is a human being.

Proverbs on struggle, patience and perseverance

139. *Kavora kai indo.*
Slowness brings property.
Patience pays. If one works steadily and

patiently, then there is no reason why he should not succeed.

140. *Muthii kavora anyunyaga manji me makembu.*
A slow walker drinks clear water.
If one fetches water from a well or a river in a hurry, it is stirred and gets mixed up with the soil at the bottom. Similarly, if one attends to one's affairs in a hurry one is bound to mix up good plans with bad ones and end up in a mess.

141. *Njira nguvi nwa ya uriri*
The only short-cut is the one which leads to bed.
There is nothing in this world which is obtained easily; one has to struggle and be patient.

142. *Giconi giakaga nyomba na muthece umwe.*
A bird builds a house with only one beak.
If a bird can manage to build its house with only a beak, why should human beings not manage to do much more with two hands?

143. *Njogu ndiremagwa ni miguongo yayo.*
An elephant is never defeated by the weight of its tusks.
Carry your own burdens without complaining; the way an elephant carries its heavy tusks.

144. *Wa mundu atandikaga uriri wake.*
Each person makes his own bed (similar to No. 143 above).

145. *Murii kavora acokaga gukaameria.*
One who eats slowly eventually swallows.
To attain your goal you do not necessarily have to hurry; take your time.

146. *Mwana wi kio ndaturaga muthambia.*
A hardworking child never misses someone to wash him.
Hard work is like an investment; it yields fruits.

147. *Uthaka nducaagwa.*
One does not whine when being groomed.
To attain beauty or accomplishment in anything, one has to persevere however painful the process.

148. *Ngai atethagia witethetie.*
God helps the one who helps himself.
We cannot expect blessings from God if we do not work.

149. *Mundu utanona thina augaga weru wonthe nwa nyuee.*
Whoever has never had problems thinks that the whole landscape is level.
Problems teach people about the reality of life.

150. *Nthoki ndiucuragia ikumbi.*
You cannot fill your store with what other people bring you.
The proverb discourages dependency and encourages people to work hard and be self-reliant.

151. *Iguta anacio ni ciiriragiria mbura yure.*
Even lazy people wish for the rains to come.
Ordinarily, lazy people wish the rain to fall so that they can shelter from the rain and evade work.
Hardworking people who are serious farmers also wish for the rainy season so that they can plant their crops. The proverb has therefore got a double meaning. The implication is that there are times when life is so hard that even lazy people who do not like the rainy season demand for work in the farm wish they could get even the hardest of jobs in order to survive.

152. *Kuria wira ni kuruta.*
If you ask for a job you have to do it.
If you start on a task you have to complete it however difficult it may be.

153. *Mageria nwamo mavota.*
Attempts make success.

This proverb encourages effort; without attempting, one cannot expect any result.

154. *Mucaria ndaturaga.*
He who searches never misses.
Seek and you will find.

155. *Mutigirwa indo ndeci kuimenyerera.*
He who inherits does not know how to take care of the property.
Achieving through hardwork makes one responsible.

156. *Munyaka wii mbere ya kithaka.*
Good luck is beyond the bush.
Success comes after a hard struggle (clearing the bush) and not just a matter of good luck.

157. *Wiru ndugiragia mucaria atonge.*
Jealousy does not prevent a hardworking person from becoming rich.
Do not allow people's jelous talk to deter you from struggling.

158. *Nduruma irina tiyo ndaara kuo.*
The animal that digs the hole is not the one which sleeps in it.
Do not assume that you will be the only beneficiary of your efforts, other people can also reap fruits from your labour.

159. *Ivenya ringi rii rukungu.*
Too much hurry blows dust.
Hurry hurry has no blessings.

160. *Kuvitia gaconi na mugwi kurutaga mugwimi wara.*
Missing to shoot a bird teaches the hunter tact.
Failure teaches and improves skill.

161. *Ringiara muno nirituraga murioti.*
If it (the sun) shines too much it misses someone to bask in it.
There is a limit to hard times.

Proverbs on kinship

162. *Mwana muciare ndatecagwa.*
A child who is born is never thrown away.
However bad your child is he is a human being and you should never abandon or mistreat him.

163. *Rurira ti rurico.*
The umblical cord is not a sweet potato vine.
Kinship should not be taken for granted.
Blood is thicker than water.

164. *Nviti ndiricaga mwana wayo tiga riu ikorokete taki.*
A hyena does not eat its child regardless of its greed.
There's a natural love and tenderness for one's offspring even if one is cruel and hard.

165. *Muciari ndai ngoro ya mamira ma mwana.*
A parent is never nauseated by the mucus of her child.
A parent loves his child unconditionally.

166. *Mwana mwende aricaga aciari make.*
A child who is loved depends on his parents for his livelihood.
If a child is loved by his parents, he cannot suffer.

167. *Mwana mwende ndatangatangaga ndaka.*
A child who is loved does not trample on mud (similar to No. 166 above).

168. *Mwana ndavecanagwa.*
A child is never given away.
One's child is too precious to be given away as a gift.

169. *Muciari ari ntha.*
A parent is merciful.
A parent is sensitive to his child's needs.
Anybody who has children extends mercy to other people as well.

170. *Muviriga ti rwirigo.*
A clan is not a fence. Members of the same clan are linked by a stronger bond than the nominal lineage relationship.

171. *Nthi na iguru itimenyanaga.*
The earth and the sky do not know one another.
People do not affiliate with those with whom they have no relationship.

172. *Ng'ombe cia mundu umwe iricaga kigwanari kimwe.*
The cattle belonging to one person eat in the same shed.
Kith associates with kin.

173. *Mundu wi muruang'ina ndarivagwa ngariuriro.*
A person who has a brother is never beaten to death.
To have a brother is to be assured of security.

174. *Kithoko kingirengwa muting'oe ni kingi wingi uciokaga ukiuma.*
If a lizard gets its tail cut by another lizard another tail grows.
You cannot hate your relative to the extent of disowning him.

175. *Munyi ithwire mai mayo.*
A rhino hates its own faeces.
People are never happy about the success of their close relatives.

Proverbs on communal life and cooperation

176. *Mwana ti wa muciari umwe.*
A child does not belong to one parent.
A child belongs to the entire community and not to his biological parents alone.

177. *Kiara kimwe gitiuragaga ndaa.*
One finger cannot kill a louse.

No person is self-sufficient; he needs the help of others to survive.

178. *Ngwaci ya mwana wene niyo ivoragia mwaki.*
The sweet potato that belongs to a child from another home is the one which puts out the fire.
People have a tendency to blame other people's children unnecessarily (this proverb somewhat contradicts No. 176).

179. *Ngiti ikumaga kuria yocetwe.*
A dog barks where it has been adopted.
A person should restrict his rule within the spheres of his influence.

180. *Wa mundu arithagia mburi ciake.*
Every shepherd grazes his own flock (similar to No. 179 above).

181. *Njara nyingi imenanagira uriiri.*
Many hands develop hatred during eating.
People co-operate better when sharing work than when sharing the benefits of thier work.

182. *Riua ritukomaga twiganene nati wa mundu ai nyomba yake.*
The sun warms us equally but each person has his own house.
Although in a community everybody has an equal share in communally owned recources, individual rights should be respected.

183. *Ndongoria ingithua cionthe niciathua.*
If the leader (of livestock) limps all the others start limping.
Leaders should set a good example.

184. *Cia mucii ti como.*
The affairs of the home are not for public consumption.
This proverb advises people to have limits as to how much of the affairs of their homes they should share with the rest of the community, there are matters which

186

are too sensitive to be shared with the public.

185. *Mumbeere ndaugaga mbaura nwa augire mbaika.*
A Mbeere person never says help me put this load down; he only says help me lift this load.
People have a tendency to take advantage of communal sharing and stress receiving more than giving.

186. *Muembu ndeci marumua aici maimwa.*
An Embu person remembers only when he was denied something but he does not remember when he was given.
People easily remember the wrongs done to them and hardly remember the good turns.

187. *Murimi tiwe murii.*
The farmer is not the consumer.
Be prepared for others to benefit from your work; personal gains are not always commensurate with individual effort.

188. *Andu matai gwataniro mauragagwa na njokoma imwe.*
People who lack unity are killed with one club.
In unity there is security.

189. *Kirimu gikuaga mugongo wonthe.*
A fool carries the whole community.
One should be careful not to allow oneself to be exploited in the name of co-operation.

190. *Kuthokagirua wanathokia.*
He who gives also receives.
You should not expect people to bring you things if you never give anything in return.

191. *Mbu ya mundu umwe itumaga andu matura toro itura igima.*
One person's screams interrupt the sleep of a whole village.
One person's problems are the problems of an entire community.

192. *Gutiganwa nwakuo kuriganwa.*
Separation is disagreement.
Lack of co-operation leads to disintergration of relations.

193. *Matumbi ma njamba matithanduranaga.*
A cock's eggs do not hatch each other.
People need each other — big and small and men and women.

194. *Mutura wenga nwata murogi.*
Whoever lives alone is like a wizard or a witch.
People who live on their own or who do not co-operate with others are considered ill-intentioned.

195. *Mutura weka akucaga wa weka.*
Whoever lives alone dies alone.
If you do not cooperate with others no one will come to your aid when you need them.

196. *Niukarwara murimu nvuvaga.*
One day you will suffer from a disease I usually heal.
You can never predict when you may be in desperate need of a particular person's assistance and therefore do not act as if you are self-sufficient.

197. *Mwendia nuuguraga.*
He who sells also buys.
No one is so self-sufficient that he does not need the help of other people.

198. *Muguriri mundu wa itura nwata muvewa.*
Whoever buys from a neighbour is like a beggar.
If you buy something from a neighbour, jealous people keep on commenting.

199. *Mugwi wene niguo uturikagia thiaka.*
Another person's arrow is the one which makes a hole on the quiver.
Owing to jealousy, people usually blame others who have made it.

200. *Mundu mugo wa itura ndai ngumo.*
The medicineman has no fame in his own village.
A prophet has no honour in his hometown.

201. *Andu metura rimwe nimatigithagia mundu nviti.*
People from the same village rescue each other from the fangs of a hyena.
People from the same neighbourhood provide security for each other.

202. *Ruku rumwe rutiraragia mwaki.*
One piece of firewood cannot keep the fire burning throughout the night.
People need each other to survive.

203. *Nyungu ya mucii ndituraga muteguri.*
A cooking-pot in a homestead never misses someone to put it down (when the food is ready).
In a community, there is always someone to come to one's aid if faced with a crisis.

204. *Andu makiaga utuku ni kuthuna.*
People grind at night because of meanness.
Only mean people manage their affairs in secret.

205. *Uthoni wa vakuvi ni rumena.*
Marriage ties with neighbours create enmity.
Familiarity breeds contempt.

206. *Icigara rigwatagirira ithuriri.*
A creeper supports itself on a cactus.
Lazy people are parasites of hardworking ones. Also, the proverb emphasises interdependence in a society.

207. *Kamwingi gocaga ngimi.*
Many people can lift a mortar.
Unity is strength.

208. *Wira wa mwingi uragaga kirimu.*
Communal work kills a fool.
Participate in group work but remember you still need to survive as an individual.

209. *Mekaranagia uria mecene.*
People stay together if they know each other.
People cannot live or share things with their enemies.

210. *Menya kwina rwimbo rutai mukui.*
Avoid singing a song without a soloist.
Be careful not to do something for which you have nobody to support you.

211. *Munyambu wa kwenyu ukuricaga ndigario.*
When lion from your neighbourhood eats you, some left-overs can be traced.
Your enemies within your neighbourhood are better than strangers.

212. *Njara igiri niithambanagia.*
Two hands wash each other.
The proverb emphasises the interdependence of human beings.

Proverbs on women

213. *Kava kuvitia nguo kwi kuvitia mwongia.*
It is better to make a mistake when buying a garment than when marrying a woman.
A man who marries a woman with whom he is incompatible cannot get rid of her as easily as he would a garment.

214. *Mwongia mukuru acokagirwa ni gikuu.*
A man returns to his old wife only if the young one dies.
An old wife is considered useless as a man's companion.

215. *Uria utanona wiritu wa ng'ina atetagia ithe akimwira ni ng'ombe ateere.*
Whoever never saw his mother as a maiden querrels his father that he wasted his cattle.
Age takes its toll on beauty, and so one should not assume that some not-so-beatiful people or things were always the way they are.

216. *Ng'ina wa ndurume ndai nvia.*
The ewe that delivered the ram has no horns.
Do not disregard an old woman, she may be the mother of an important man.

217. *Ndeto cia aka ciitikagua ciarara.*
News brought by a woman is believed the following day.
Women are believed to engage in gossip and idle talk. The proverb therefore advises men to verify anything said by a woman before they take it seriously.

218. *Muciere ari ma.*
A woman who has delivered recently is an honest witness.
The pain of delivery sharpens the perspective of a woman who has just given birth. Secondly, the fact that the new mother stays at home during seclusion gives her the opportunity to observe what goes on in the home without being influenced too much by gossip.

219. *Mwana kirimu ni kiriro kia ng'ina.*
A foolish child is his mother's sorrow.
A mother is more sensitive to her child's weakness than the father. This is partly because of her maternal love for her child and partly because society always blames the mother for her children's weakness.

220. *Aka airi ni nyungu cia urogi.*
Two wives are two pots of poison.
The jealousy between women, especially co-wives is seen as venomous.

221. *Gicieko gitirimaga.*
A woman's underskirt does not cultivate.
The manner in which a woman dresses does not depict how hard she works. A good wife is the one who works hard. Men are warned to look beyond the physical appearance of a woman when they are searching for wives.

222. *Mwathwa ni ng'ina nwata mwathwa ni ivu.*
A person who is advised and controlled by his mother is like the one who is controlled by his stomach.
A person who always attends to the wishes of his stomach cannot plan because the stomach gets full one minute and the next minute it wants to eat again. A parallel is drawn here between the influence of the stomach and that of a woman since women are regarded as people who do not think beyond the nose and who do not see the importance of thinking about tomorrow.

223. *Mwathwa ni ng'ina ndai ume.*
Whoever is controlled by his mother is a fool.
Women are considered unintelligent; a man who follows his mother's advice he is bound to get lost since he is being guided by a fool.

224. *Ndundu ya mwana na ng'ina nditonyagirirwa.*
One should never intrude in a private meeting between a child and his mother.
Sons are seen to be closer to their mothers than to their fathers. Fathers then feel left out in the dealings between sons and mothers. The proverbs has negative overtones considering mother's influence on their sons is viewed negatively.

225. *Mwongia utari keritu niwe witavagira manji.*
A woman who has no daughter is the one who fetches water for herself.
Women have many tasks to perform and daughers are seen as their only help in their burdens. The proverb therefore is like a lament from women for any in their lot who does not have a daughter.

226. *Muka mucangacangi ndaturaga mwana.*
A woman who roams around does not miss a baby.

189

The proverb discourages promiscuity and marital infidelity by warning that such behaviour is bound to end in unwanted children.

227. *Mundu muka ndauragagua.*
A woman is never killed.
Women are considered weak. In time of war, women are not killed but are captured and forcefully married by the enemies.

228. *Mundu muka ndatumagwa akarandure.*
A woman is never sent to demand a debt.
Women cannot be trusted.

229. *Kugia ivu ti wonje.*
Pregnancy is not a physical handicap.
Conception is considered part and parcel of womanhood.

230. *Muremwa ni ngu augaga mukwa ni muraca.*
She who cannot manage to carry a load of firewood claims that the rope is too long.
A lazy person will always look for an excuse for his failure to do his duty.

231. *Mwana ndetemaga agitemera ng'ina.*
A child does not cut himself when cutting something for his mother.
One can go to any extent to cater for his mother.

232. *Mwongia mwaro ndanunungariria.*
A good wife never grumbles.
Women are expected to be polite, patient, understanding and tolerant.

233. *Arume makaga nyomba namo aka magaka micii.*
Men build houses but women build homes.
When a woman is married she is provided with a house by her husband but the job of making the house into a home is hers.

234. *Mwii na kivici akenaga kiarua nwati mwii na muka akenaga akua.*
One who steal with an uncircumcised boy is happy when he gets circumcised, but one who steals with his wife is relieved only when she dies.
Women cannot be trusted to keep secrets.

235. *Mwitwa ni aka nwata mwitwa ni gikuu.*
One who is called by women is like the one who is called by death.
Women are regarded as the cause of men's downfall.

236. *Ungira mwari wa nyukwe ekare waro akirega muthekerere.*
If you tell your sister to sit decently and she refuses you should laugh at her.
A woman is expected to be decent and not to provoke men. Failure to do so has its consequences.

237. *Muka aciara nyamu augaga yuragwe kavora niwamikuire mieri kenda.*
If a woman gives birth to an animal she pleads that it should be killed gently as she carried it for nine months.
Every child is a child regardless of its nature or looks.

238. *Arume makaremwa ni gwika aka matigeragia.*
If men are defeated women dare not attempt.
Women are believed to be weak and men strong.

239. *Nthenge ingiremwa ni gukinda nwa nvarika ingivota?*
If a he-goat cannot overturn would a she-goat manage? (Similar to No. 239 above).

240. *Mukii nuukundaga ucuru wa ng'ina.*
The one who grinds gets a share of her mother's gruel.
Good work is rewarded just as a girl who

190

helps her mother grind is rewarded by a token share of the gruel.

241. *Muthitha uka ndaciaraga.*
Whoever hides her womanhood never gives birth.
A woman wins recognition of her worth from her society through playing her role in procreation: giving birth. Therefore if a woman decides to prolong her maidenhood she loses face with her community.

242. *Gutura mburi nwakuo gutura mwongia.*
Missing goats is missing a wife.
When a woman is getting married, her suitor has to pay livestock as dowry to her mother. A poor man therefore finds it difficult to get a wife as nobody is willing to give away his daughter free of charge.

243. *Kirimu kiongaga ng'ina nai mukuu.*
A fool sucks his mother's breasts even when she is dead.

244. *Guciara ti kumia.*
Giving birth is not the same as defecating.
Emphasises the maternal role and love of a mother for her child.

Proverbs on men

245. *Mwana mugi ni gikeno kia ithe.*
An intelligent child is the joy of his father.
The success and strength of a child are attributed to the efforts of the father while his failure and weakness are attributed to the mother. Hence the two proverbs which refer to this belief are sometims stated as a single proverb. An intelligent child is his father's joy, a foolish child is his mother's sorrow, (see proverb No. 219 above).

246. *Kwa arume gutii gikeno.*
In men's place there is no joy.

The duties and responsibilities of a man make his life difficult.

247. *Arume mai rwamba.*
Men make one itch.
This is a warning to young girls not to succumb to the temptation to be with men.

248. *Kuthama nikuo kuvika kwa arume.*
Migration is the way men get married.
When a woman gets married she is supposed to leave her home and join the husband in his house.
A man is never expected to move from his house except in the case of migration.

249. *Mwana ndacunaga ithe irio.*
A child never snatches food from his father.
A child is expected to treat his father with great respect.

250. *Arume ni ma karugi.*
Men are swift.
Men are expected to be always alert and to be ready to defend those around them, especially women and children.

251. *Arume ni arumani.*
Men bite (similar to No. 247 above).

252. *Mucii utai muthuri ti mucii.*
A home without a man is not a home.
Men are supposed to be the heads and leaders of homes. Therefore, however successful a home may be if it is headed by a woman it is not considered a home.

253. *Mumbiria arume aumburaragwa na njokoma.*
Whoever sulks at men has his anger released with a club.
A man is supposed to be the head of a household and therefore his word is law. A wife who gets angry and sulks is asking for a beating.

254. *Mwana amenyaga ithe na ciiko.*
A child knows his father by his actions.

Fathering a child is not as important as bringing up the child.

255. *Gutii njamba ya mwera umwe.*
There is no cock that serves only one hen.
This proverb justifies polygamy.

Proverbs on the socially and physically handicapped

256. *Gacau ka ngia niko gecunaga mugongo.*
An orphan calf kicks its own back for itself.
An orphan nurses his own problems.

257. Kutii *nai ti kwenda kwa mwene.*
To lead an unhappy life is not one's wish.
This proverb advises people not to laugh at the less fortunate, indirectly warning that the same fate could befall anyone.

258. *Ndukatheke kirema gitakuvitukite na wi muoyo.*
Do not laugh at a cripple before he passes by and while you are still alive.
It is believed that if you laught at a physically handicapped person you are bound to be punished, for example, by giving birth to a cripple or becoming cripped yourself.

259. *Thina ndui waria mwana wa ngiti.*
Poverty has never killed a puppy. Puppies live on left-overs thrown away by human beings; the poor can survive even better because they are human beings living among other human beings.

260. *Ukirumia iconi mwere rumia nguku irume.*
While you are giving millet to the birds some also give the chicken to eat.
The proverb advises that while helping people who are not so close, you should also think about those who are near, e.g. kin.

261. *Kamene niko kauragire munyambu.*
The despised is the one who killed the lion.
Everybody has internal strengths that may not be apparent to everybody else. The proverb advises against underrating people.

262. *Mumenwa ndari mbaki mbaro.*
The despised one has no ripe tobacco.
When people despise someone they never see anything good in him.

263. *Ciana cia ndigwa itiri kieva.*
Orphans have no sorrow.
The sorrow of losing a parent is so great that after suffering this deprivation, nothing can cause sorrow to an orphan.

264. *Gutii mwana na irumwa ni nviti.*
There is no difference between a child and the remnant of a hyena's prey.
Do not despise children however bad-looking or poverty-stricken they may be because every child is a human being.

265. *Gutii wevu na wa murukuthu.*
There is no child who was conceived in the womb and another in the back (similar to No. 265).

266. *Muthure nuucokaga kwendwa.*
The despised person eventually gets loved.
Nothing is permanent. All siutations are bound to change. The proverb comforts the despised to take courage because one day those who despised them will change their attitude.

267. *Gaconi kanini gatiri murire.*
A small bird has no feeding style.
People who are low on the social stratum have no say.

269. *Mburi ya muthini yaciara nirio muthini agicaga vata.*

A poor man becomes important when his goat delivers.
People start noticing a poor person when he begins to show signs of coming out of his poverty.

269. *Muvoi ndai ngoro.*
A beggar is not sensitive.
A beggar's knees are supple.

270. *Uria wi kironda ainagira nja ya itiri.*
A person with a wound dances outside the dancing arena.
Beggars are not choosers.

271. *Mwiwa ni mundu tiundu umwe na mwiwa ni nviti.*
Whoever is robbed by a person is not the same as the one who is robbed by a hyena.
If a person steals from you be merciful to him as he is your fellow-human being.

272. *Thina nduturaga mwene.*
Poverty does not pain the owner.
Poverty is not a disease. Those who are poor have learnt to live with it.

273. *Thina ni kiviu gia kuvigia muro.*
Poverty is a knife for sharpening a digging stick.
Poverty makes one wise.

274. *Utari ni mwigire.*
He who does not have has his share stored somewhere.
Poverty is not a permanent condition.

275. *Muveria ngia ndagiragia gukia*
He who refuses to help an orphan does not prevent the day from dawning.
Mistreating an orphan cannot prevent them from one day coming out of their misery.

276. *Uria wi rungu rwa muti niwe wici kiria nthigiriri iricaga.*
The person under the tree is the one who knows what ants feed on.

It is difficult to understand fully the plight of the handicapped or disadvantaged person.
The proverb exhorts people to be sensitive towards the handicapped or disadvantaged.

277. *Ndivuthagirua kirugamo.*
It is never minimised because of the way it stands.
Never despise a person because of his size.

278. *Muthini ndavaraga.*
A poor person never goes bankrupt.
The proverb states the irony of the plight of the poor. The poor have so little that they have nothing to lose. They cannot be bankrupt because they already are.

279. *Mundu arakinda wingi ndamuthingatagia iteke.*
Once you have knocked someone down you do not follow him with a kick.
Never hit someone who is already down.

280. *Mwana wa muthini ndatigaga irio mbitiku nthi.*
A poor person's child never leaves food that dropped on the ground.
Those who have known poverty learn to be frugal.

281. *Rurimi rwa muthini rutithiraga kimanda.*
A poor man's tongue is always thin.
A poor person has to humble himself before others in order to survive.

282. *Ng'ombe iria ithuaga inyunyaga manji ma munju.*
The cow which limps drinks dirty water.
The proverb comments on the rule of the jungle: survival for the fittest. It also discourages sluggishness.

283. *Gukuviva ti gutinua.*
Being short is not as a result of being cut.
Congenital traits may be looked down upon by some people but should not be regarded as defects or illnesses.

Proverbs on fate, fortune and misfortune

284. *Kuria ikagua tikuo igwicaga.*
Where it is thrown is not where it lands.
What people wish for someone is not necessarily what happens to him.

285. *Mburi njeru yuraga ikionekaga.*
A white goat disappears while the owner looks on.
Some misfortunes cannot be prevented.

286. *Nyamu ya gukua ndigucaga mithega.*
An animal bound to die does not respond to medicine.
A person (thing) fated to die (person) cannot be saved.

287. *Igai ria mundu ritiocagwa ni wingi.*
A person's share is never inherited by someone else.
What one is destined to achieve cannot be thwarted by someone else's achievements.

288. *Gutandika uriri wega tikuo kumama waro.*
Spreading the bed properly does not guarantee peaceful sleep.
Sheer hardwork does not guarantee achievement; fate, fortune and misfortune have a part to play.

289. *Kinya gikucagira murangori wa nyomba.*
A gourd breaks right at the doorstep.
Things have a tendency to go wrong at the most promising moment.

290. *Riru ndici muthamaki.*
Slipperiness knows no king.
Problems do not distinguish between great and small.

291. *Mwiro wa ngoro ndukinyaga.*
The desires of the heart do not materialise.
What you desire is not what you get.

292. *Ya kuvia ivicaga na ma mbere.*
The dish that is destined to be fully cooked gets read with the first lot of water.
Success can be detected from the start.

293. *Kiria gikaria mundu nwa nginya kioneke.*
What will cause the death of a person must be detected.
Sense trouble before it comes.
The symptoms of what will cause a person's downfall can be seen well before he eventually falls.

294. *Gikuu gitii kiriko.*
Death has no promise.
You cannot foretell death.

295. *Guciarua nai ti kwenda kwa mwene.*
Being born unlucky is not the person's wish.
Nobody likes misfortunes.

296. *Kiara kiruaru gitiregaga gukomorua.*
A toe which has a sore never misses to be hit by the ground.
Misfortune follows those who are already suffering.

297. *Iciaraga nai mwene acuthiririe.*
It calves with difficulties while the owner is watching.
There is nothing you can do to prevent misfortune.

298. *Kurithia imwe ti kwenda kwa mwene.*
Tending only one animal is not the owner's wish (similar to No. 295 above).

299. *Mucangacangi agwicagira ndathe.*
He who travels a great deal ends up getting what has been hunted by others.
One has to look for fortune and good luck.

300. *Mwoni umunthi twa nginya akona ruyu.*
He who finds today is not guaranteed to find tomorrow.
One's good luck is not guaranteed to last for ever.

301. *Mutino urutaga mundu uriri.*
Bad luck takes one right from bed.
One cannot run away from fate.

302. *Mwambiriria tiwe urikagia mukwa.*
Whoever starts making a rope is not the one who finishes it.
Fortune is fickle.

303. *Ngai ndaricaga ngima.*
God does not eat *ugali*
Unlike man (who eats commonlace food), God is not slow to reward or avenge those who deserve assistance.

304. *Munyaka ndwetagirira mundu.*
Good luck does not wait for anybody.

305. *Ya muuro ndivoragia ndemwa.*
The animal which is fated to get lost does not dry its tattoos.
Though tatooed for easy identification, the animal still gets lost.
This proverb comments on the inevitability of fate.

306. *Mutino ugendaga na mwene.*
Bad luck travels with the owner.
You cannot escape misfortune.

307. *Mutino ndui njamba.*
Bad luck has no hero.
Bad luck does not depend on your status.

308. *Ni yumbukaga wana iri nvute.*
It can fly even when its feathers have been removed.
You cannot escape bad luck.

309. *Ya muuro ivaragwa thano.*
The animal fated for destruction diarrhoeas during the dry season (similar to No. 305 above).

310. *Igiciara wana ikivuna muviamire nwomwe.*
Whether it is giving birth or having a miscarriage its posture is the same.

You can never predict the outcome by the symptoms. This proverb contrasts No. 309 above.

311. *Mwana utai muciare ndatucagirwa ritwa.*
An unborn child is never given a name.
You cannot count your chicks before they hatch.

Proverbs on general reflections on life

312. *Metho ma ciura matigiragia ng'ombe inyua manji.*
Frogs' eyes do not prevent cows from drinking water.
People's comments cannot prevent a person from achieving his goal.

313. *Mwana wa njoka nwa njoka.*
The child of a snake is also a snake.
A child takes after his parents, especially their negative traits.

314. *Kenyu na kenyu ikomanagira ivuri.*
A piece and a piece meet in the stomach.
Little things always join each other to form big ones.

315. *Kumagwa nigucokagwa.*
A place that has been abandoned is usually revisited.
Something that was once found useless can prove to be useful.

316. *Kuria mbere ti gukoroka.*
He who eats first is not greedy.
The proverb commends those who achieve due to their alertness and swiftness.

317. *Muti ukonjagwa wi mwigu, wauma niuthinagia mukonji.*
A stick is shaped while it is still moist because when it dries up it becomes a problem shaping it.
A child's behaviour is moulded at an early

age otherwise it is difficult to correct it when he is an adult.

318. *Mukuru nuutumagwa nwakurumwa atarumagwa.*
An elder can be sent, it is only insulting him that is not allowed.
Tradition demands that one respects one's elders. The proverb is said by a person sending someone who is older than himself as a way of indicating that the request is not a sign of disrespect.

319. *Mumeneri wingi kuria amwitaga gikoroku.*
A person who hates another due to his eating habits says that he is greedy.
A person who hates a trait will always look for another way of making that trait seem odious.

320. *Mundu ndamiaga kirarori.*
A person does not defecate where he sleeps.
A person should respect where he gets his livelihood.

321. *Mbura yarega kuura igwatagia rukungi.*
If the rain fails, it blames the wind.
People have a tendency of blaming others for their mistakes.

322. *Nyonda ya gikuu ndinyondokagwa.*
Death's thirst is never quenched.
Death is a continuous reaper of the living.

323. *Ururu ndwigucanagirwa.*
A person does not feel another's pain.
Nobody can esperience another person's suffering.

324. *Mugeni ni muvuro.*
A visitor is a river.
Treat a visitor well because he is not going to stay permanently in your house.

325. *Mugeni amiaga mbirirari.*
A visitor defecates at the cemetery.
A visitor cannot know the affairs of the place he is visiting.

326. *Rurigi rwi nja rutituraga gia kwova.*
A rope that is outside can never miss something to tie.
There is nothing that is completely useless.

327. *Ukuru ndugagia ugiuka.*
Old age does not announce its arrival.
Everybody grows old as time goes on.

328. *Muumbi wa nyungu arugaga na rugio.*
A potter cooks with a potsherd.
It is ironical that people may take good care of others and not be able to care for themselves.

329. *Mundu ndavecanaga wira wa uriri wene.*
A person cannot testify about someone else's bed.
It is difficult for someone to know the inner secrets of another.

330. *Mwathwa na muragi ndavitagia njira.*
A person who is brought up with a whip does not miss his way.
Spare the rod and spoil the child.

331. *Mariko matireranaga.*
Cooking stones cannot bring up one another.
Little children cannot bring up each other.

332. *Ngethi ti kivako kia ndigu.*
Greetings are not a bunch of bananas.
Denying someone greetings cannot make him suffer.

333. *Ukuru ti uruaru.*
Old age is not a disease.
One should not worry or be embarrassed about old age as it is a natural state and not a disease.

334. *Gukura ni gucuku gutumaga mundu acae.*
Old age is bad for it makes one whimper.
Old age forces people to lose control of themselves and sometimes makes them behave abnormally.
This proverb contrasts No. 333 above.

335. *Kiria gikenagian guku tikio gikenagia nvungu.*
What pleases a chicken is not the same as what pleases a hawk.
One man's meat is another man's poison.

336. *Murumua ndakathimaga.*
One does not get fat from the piece of meat he is given by someone else.
Be contented with whatever you are given. What you receive from people cannot be as good for you as what you get for yourself.

337. *Mundu mukure igego ndaturaga mung'ethu.*
A person whose tooth has been extracted does not miss a gap.
A bad deed always leaves a mark on the victim.

338. *Gutethia gutiiriragwa.*
One does not regret having helped another.
You lose nothing by helping others.

339. *Kiguoya kimenyekaga na nthimbu.*
A coward is known by the type of weapon he carries.
It is difficult for one to hide one's character.

340. *Kanua kari mata gutii undu gatangiuga.*
A mouth with saliva has no limits as to what it can utter.
People's comments can go to wild extents.

341. *Gikaro kimwe kii ndaa.*
Staying in one place can give someone lice.
Travelling gives people experience and opens up opportunities for them.

342. *Mitugo ikirite gutonga.*
Good behaviour is better than wealth.
Property is superficial when compared with one's reputation.

343. *Njokoma mbaro yumaga ikuirori.*
A good club comes from the original tree from which it is made.
A well-behaved person comes from a good background. A socially integrated child is the one who has been taught good behaviour right from infancy.

344. *Rurigi rwetagirira mukanda.*
A string awaits a rope.
Achievements which appear insignificant may lead to great things.

345. *Gukira ni kumenana.*
Silence means hatred.
People who hate each other have nothing to share with one another. If you care for each other you need to open up to each other.

346. *Gutiri ukinyaga ta wingi.*
Nobody walks like another.
Everybody has his own way of doing things.

347. *Gutiri ucuku uturaga.*
There is no evil which lasts.
Inhumanity and its effect on the victims is doomed to end.

348. *Kumenya muno ni kumenyura.*
Knowing too much is to spoil.
Knowledge sometimes brings pain rather than pleasure.

349. *Kwambiriria mucii ni kwambiriiria thina.*
Starting a home is to start problems.
Building a home is not an easy thing.

350. *Ndurume irivagwa na ingi.*
A ram is paid for with another.
Tit for tat.

351. *Ng'ombe ti ndigu.*
Cattle are not bananas.
Cattle are not given away without a very good reason.

352. *Mwana wagitang'a akunyaga wata gitang'a.*
A leopard's child scratches like the leopard (similar to No. 314 above).

353. *Gitang'a gitieci gukunya nikwonua kionirue.*
The leopard did not know how to scratch but it was taught.
The environment determines a child's behaviour.

354. *Ngoro ni muruang'ina na mundu.*
The heart is the brother to a person.
The heart determines a person's behaviour.

355. *Murimu wa mundu wingi ndungigiria umame.*
Another person's pain cannot prevent you from enjoying your sleep.
Every man for himself.

356. *Mucii ndwathagwa ni muvituki.*
A home is not ruled by a passerby.
Keep off the affairs of other people's homes.

357. *Mugunda munoru umenyagwa na maciaro.*
A fertile farm is known by the harvest it yields.
A good person is known by his deeds.

358. *Iria ina mwithua niyo itwaraga mutiri.*
The animal whose body is iching is the one who goes in search of help and not the other way round.
The person who has a problem is the one who goes in search of help and not the other way round.
The patient goes to the doctor, the doctor does not look for the patient.

359. *Muvarwa niwe uthingataga kithaka.*
The person suffering from diarrhoea is the one who goes to the bush (similar to No. 360 above).

360. *Murogi tiwe murogori.*
A wizard or a witch is not the same as a medicineman.
A person cannot be good and evil at the same time.

361. *Kivayii gitici mieri.*
A satisfied animal does not know the months.
In the days of plenty people tend to forget the passage of time and they do not think about the future.

362. *Kari nthongo ni muthamaki gatagati ka ndumumu.*
A one-eyed person is a king among blind people.
Ability or skill, however insignificant, can make a great deal of difference.

363. *Nthirika nicio ciakagia mwaki.*
Small pieces of wood are the one which are used to start the fire.
Small things build big ones.

364. *Kathiga kanini niko gaikagua mwereri.*
The small stone is the one which is thrown into the millet field.
When a person is chasing birds away from a millet field, one uses small stones because big stones are not as swift and are more likely to break the millet plants in the process. In the same vein, people usually send younger people and children to deliver messages or undertake menial errands,

365. *Kuria kuri ngu gutii mbokua.*
Where there is firewood there is no meat to roast.
One cannot possess everything.

366. *Menya ukeganania nvaa na nvuna.*
Never equate satisfaction with constipation.
Things are never the same.

367. *Nvayii iraraga muromori wa irina.*
The satisfied animal sleeps at the entrance to the hole.

When people are satisfied they become careless and forget even their own safety.

368. *Kauga gatume ni nyamukano.*
A stitched half-calabash is separation.
Conflicts which cause social disintegration, even when bridged, have the effect of permanently affecting future relations.

369. *Gutii kiathi gitue gitakinyaga.*
There is no date which is made that fails to materialise.
Everything that has a beginning has an end.

370. *Rwigi ruciaraga icia.*
The eagle gives birth to a dove.
A very bright person can give birth to a foolish person.

373. *Gutii ungikundura ikundo ateci uria rikundikitwe.*
Nobody can untie a knot if he does not know how it is tied.
In order to solve a problem it is important to understand the cause.

372. *Ng'ombe ndici murithi ta mukami.*
A cow does not know the herdsman as much as it knows the milkman.
A person is closest to those with whom he interacts closely.

373. *Makuvenerie kiathiri ugitetagia njira.*
They cheated you at the market but you blamed the path as you walked along it.
People have a tendency to vent their frustrations on the innocent who cannot hit back.

374. *Utethio uvecagwa uria muruaru ti uria muvutu.*
It is better to help the sick than the hungry.

The sick will be grateful when he is healed but the hungry will forget as soon as he is satisfied.

375. *Nthia ituire mumianiriri kwi mumirathi.*
A gazelle hates the one who shouts and reveals its hiding-place more than the one who eventually shoots it.
The person who incites others to cause trouble is worse than those who actually do the harm.

376. *Ciakuraca iricaga nvurio.*
Those from far eat left-overs.
You cannot benefit when you are far from the source.

377. *Wa gukuithia mbaka na wa gukuithia ng'ombe gutii utai mukuire.*
He whose cat has died and he whose cow has died, neither has not experienced death.
Every problem has its unique effect on the victim.

378. *Mundu aithuaga varia agwikinyira.*
A person scratches himself where he can reach.
One attends to one's needs according to one's ability.

379. *Kironda gii itina gitumaga mundu amenya itina rii vata.*
A wound in the buttocks makes one realise that buttocks are important.
Experience is the best teacher.

380. *Ka mwana munyi kauragira njarari.*
A young person's belongings disappear while he is holding them in the hand.
Young people do not know how to take care of property.

Chapter 8

RIDDLES AND PUZZLES

RIDDLES

Riddles on the human body

1. *Naikia ndongu mugongo uuria.*
   I have thrown a seed in a far away land.

2. *Nairiga rugiri rwa kariaria.*
   I have fenced with creepers.

3. *Turima twiri tuvanene.*
   Two identical hills.

4. *Mwana wakwa aturaga gatagati ka micumeno na ndatinagua.*
   My child lives between two saws and he is never cut.

5. *Amwirire nguua ningagukua.*
   He told him carry me and I shall carry you one day.

6. *Uturaga umeragia na nduri wavaa.*
   You always swallow it but you never get satisfied.

7. *Ruveni njuguri.*
   Lightning in a pigeon peas plantation.

8. *Ndumire nyomba yakwa kirima iguru.*
   I have built my house on a hill.

9. *Kinii giteta.*
   An inverted container that never spills.

10. *Mbembe kanua mwita.*
    Maize grains full in the mouth.

11. *Nathinja mbogo na ndineicuria ngundi.*
    I have slaughtered a buffalo but I have not filled one hand.

12. *Ngamaga ng'ombe yakwa na kaara kamwe.*
    I milk my cow with one finger.

13. *Ikuitwe ikinainaga.*
    They shake as they are carried.

14. *Kithanje cwaa!*
    Reeds cwaa!

15. *Whooo!*
    Whooo!

16. *Karuki mukunduku.*
    A restless straight person.

17. *Ya nyukwe inyinginyaga.*
    That which belongs to your mother and it shakes.

200

18. *Gia cuguo kinene.*
    That which belongs to your grandmother
    and is big.

19. *Kwa mama ni gukuvi na ndingikinya.*
    My uncle's home is near but I can't reach.

Riddles on animals

20. *Nauma mutituri na tuthanju twiri.*
    I have come from the forest holding two
    sticks.

21. *Eitieitie!*
    Eitieitie!

22. *Kivici muti iguru.*
    An uncircumcised boy up on a tree.

23. *Na guku nwa tutu na kuu nwa tutu.*
    This way you hear tutu, that way you hear
    tutu.

24. *Na kuu wa viu na guku nwa viu.*
    This way you hear viu, that way you hear viu.

25. *Wetikira?*
    Would you agree?

26. *Kuru kuru ndumari.*
    Kuru kuru in the arrow-roots garden.

27. *Ndacaga naca.*
    I was about to carve.

28. *Ciaroria iguru ta igukua.*
    They are looking up like soloists.

29. *Kagego mwenyenyo.*
    A shaking tooth.

30. *Ng'endaga na mwaburi ana ngithii
    mugundari.*
    I travel with an umbrella even when I am
    going to the garden.

Riddles on insects and small creatures

31. *Muviki munini ukiritie nyukwe ukii.*
    A small bride who grinds better than your
    mother.

32. *Nthiite muvuro ngicaria ikinyo ria ng'ina
    wa Kinyua.*
    I am walking down the river looking for
    the footsteps of Kinyua's mother.

33. *Uyu wavitukira ava na cuti mbiru nu?*
    Who is that who has passed here in a black suit?

34. *Nyanya munini auka niatungwa nu?*
    When aunt comes, who will welcome her?

35. *Ndinganire na mama ai nerugi ii!*
    I met my uncle walking in such a hurry!

36. *Kuria nyumite kwina njira na kuria nthiie
    gutii njira.*
    Where I am coming from there is a road,
    but where I am going there is none.

37. *Mwari mwaro wina kiuno kinini.*
    A beautiful girl with a small waist-line.

38. *Aa mavitukira ava makinaga nyimbo nia?*
    Who are those people who passed here
    singing?

39. *Maria mekirite magoti mairu mathii
    kuruithia ku?*
    Where are those people in black coats
    going for a circumcision ceremony?

40. *Mikuva ya vava ti cii.*
    My father's pins are not cii.

41. *Iceru mugundari kwa vava.*
    The white ones in my father's garden.

42. *Kairu aringa na itiki.*
    The black one has crossed on a bridge.

43. *Ndungikiria mwariwa na nguo.*
You cannot have more clothes than my daughter.

Riddles on plants

44. *Ng'ombe ciakwa iraraga na micuthe iri nja ya rwaga.*
My cattle sleep with their tails outside the shed.

45. *Nyomba ya gitugi kimwe.*
A hut with only one pillar.

46. *Mwana wakwa uthiicaga atagucoka.*
My child goes and never returns.

47. *Njiaraga ciana cii na njuiri ta cia Muthungu.*
I usually give birth to children whose hair resembles that of a European.

48. *Njugu Kirinyaga nwaidi ciaraa.*
The pigeon peas on Mount Kenya have just blossomed.

49. *Kairu itiri.*
The black one under the leaves.

50. *Nguku yakwa irekagiria matumbi miguari.*
My hen lays eggs on thorns.

51. *Mwari mutune rware.*
A brown girl on big piece of land.

52. *Nathii na muvuro ngiratia gacanga na murio.*
I have travelled along the river in search of the carrier of sweetness.

53. *Aya matetemanirite uu makarua ri?*
When will these furious ones fight?

54. *Cuguo mbou.*
Your useless grandmother.

55. *Naruithia kavici gakwa gacoka uvici ringi.*
I circumcised my boy and he became uncircumcised again.

Riddles on natural phenomena

56. *Utuku kerere gukiugwa mbu.*
Loud screams in the middle of the night.

57. *Thaani cia vava ciiri ciiganene.*
My father's two plates are identical in size.

58. *Mundu muka uturaga athiicaga na ndanogaga.*
A woman who travels all the time but does not get tired.

59. *Andu a maguru maceke manvinyuritie.*
Thin-legged man running after me.

60. *Mundu wa itura rietu athiicaga kivwai akirauka karauko.*
My neighbour leaves in the evening and comes back early in the morning.

61. *Mugunda wa vava wa kivia kimwe.*
My father's garden with only one sorghum plant.

62. *Kari iguru riaku na ndungikanyita.*
The small thing is just above you but you can't touch it.

Riddles on modern technology

63. *Keregece.*
Keregece.

64. *Imwe ciiri ithatu njeru koma.*
One two three white press.

65. *Muthigari utatigaga ngovia.*
A soldier who never takes off his helmet.

66. *Ciana ciucurite ndauri mwita.*
A boat full to the brim with children.

68. *Mundu uricaga irio cia maguta na ndanoraga*
A person who eats fatty foods but never gets fat.

67. *Kariuriu karuta mburi kirima iguru.*
A fast-moving object has removed a goat from the hill-top.

69. *Ngiriri ngiriri.*
Ngiriri ngiriri.

70. *Nathiota na ndununge.*
I have farted and there is no smell.

71. *Nyomba yakwa ina ngoma nyondu.*
My house which has a thirsty devil in it.

72. *Kaumite ruraya kegwete kiuno na njara imwe.*
The small thing arrived from overseas with one hand on its waist.

Others

73. *Thii iyo nanie nthii ino tugocanire kwa matenderu.*
Go that way and I go this way we meet at the slippery place.

74. *Muti utangitwicika.*
A tree that no one can climb.

75. *Weta?*
Can you?

76. *Athamia kanua ngurage.*
Open your mouth I kill you.

77. *Mugunda wakwa wakethwa ni nyamu itai ikinyo.*
My garden has been harvested by an animal that has no footsteps.

78. *Nyomba yakwa itari murango.*
My house has no door.

79. *Aya maturoreitie u nitumaraira ndui?*
Which food shall we give these people who are gazing at us?

80. *Nyomba yakwa ya murango umwe na ndirica nyingi.*
My house has one door and many windows.

81. *Ngamaga ng'ombe yakwa mbikarite ce.*
I milk my cow while standing still.

82. *Mwana mwari agikindana na ithe!*
A girl wrestling with her father!

83. *Vava mukuru agwithua nthi ni vava munini.*
My father has been knocked down by my younger paternal uncle.

84. *Kirima kiria kianjagua gutuwa neguru.*
The hill which is climbed from the top.

85. *Cucu muraca utanginduira ndare.*
My tall grandmother who can't pick berries for me.

86. *Nyama yakwa itunivite taki na gutii ngi ingimigwira.*
My chunk of meat is extremely red but no fly would dare touch it.

87. *Nina ng'ombe ciakwa ithatu na imwe itai vo icio ciingi itingindutira wira.*
I have three servants and if one is missing the others cannot work for me.

88. *Ciaumwari giko.*
The dirty girl.

89. *Mukwa wakwa muraca utanginyovera ngu.*
A long rope of mine which cannot tie
firewood.

90. *Nyomba yakwa itathiraga nduma.*
My house which is ever dark.

91. *Mwacera na munyanya utakwira vuruka.*
You move around with a friend who will
never tell you to rest.

92. *Mwongia wakwa ecunjumaga akiruga.*
My wife squats while cooking.

93. *Ciathii uu ciathii uu.*
They go this way and that way.

94. *Muthungu acuthiririritie na ndirica.*
A white man peeping through the window.

95. *Cietetenga wenyu akagurua ri?*
When will your obese sister get married?

96. *Kari ava kari Ikamba.*
It is here and it is also in Ukambani.

97. *Mwari wa nyukwe nuutigire kurira?*
Has your sister stopped crying?

98. *Bugu bugu nda ya njogu.*
Bugu bugu an elephant's stomach.

99. *Gwata ugwatiririe.*
Hold and hold firmly.

100. *Varia nathinjira gaceru vatithiraga uceru.*
Where I slaughtered the white goat never
misses white colour.

101. *Kathenge mwania.*
A shouting he-goat.

102. *Kenya ni njeru mwena umwe.*
Kenya is white on one side.

Solutions to Riddles

The human body

1. *Ritho.*
The eyes.

2. *Njuiri cia metho.*
Eyebrows.

3. *Nyondo cia mundu muka.*
A woman's breasts.

4. *Rurimi.*
The tongue.

5. *Kiongo na ngingo.*
The head and the neck.

6. *Mata.*
Saliva.

7. *Kivara kia muthuri.*
An old man's bald head.

8. *Iniuru.*
The nose.

9. *Nyondo cia muciere.*
The breasts of a newly-delivered
woman.

10. *Magego.*
Teeth.

11. *Njuiri.*
Hair.

12. *Kaana gakionga.*
A baby suckling.

13. *Nyondo cia ari.*
Breasts of young women.

14. *Ngobii cia metho.*
Eyelids.

15. *Mukori ivu.*
A pregnant woman.

16. *Murithi utari nguo.*
A naked herdsboy.

17. *Nyondo.*
Breasts.

18. *Kiria.*
A shaven head.

19. *Kanua na iniuru.*
The mouth and the nose.

Animals

20. *Turi twa mathatha.*
Twin kids.

21. *Kithungu kia ntheru.*
The English language of monkeys.

22. *Nthinwa.*
A monkey.

23. *Ng'ondu ikirua.*
Sheep fighting.

24. *Mithita ya ng'ombe.*
Tails of cattle.

25. *Guikia kaara irinari ria njoka.*
To put your finger on a snake's hole.

26. *Nguru mathendu.*
Tortoise.

27. *Ndacaga naca nguru ngiugaga ni nthio.*
I was about to carve a tortoise thinking it
was a grinding stone.

28. *Nvia cia ng'ombe.*
A cow's horns.

29. *Iguku ria ng'ombe.*
A bull's hump.

30. *Nduru na gicuthe kiayo.*
A squirrel and its tail.

Insects and small creatures

31. *Njuki.*
Bee.

32. *Ndaa.*
Louse.

33. *Ndong'o.*
Beetle.

34. *Ngi.*
Fly.

35. *Kigunyu.*
Caterpillar.

36. *Irumbo.*
Snail.

37. *Igu.*
Wasp.

38. *Njuki.*
Bees.

39. *Ngurukuthi.*
Black ants.

40. *Muthorwe.*
Earthworms.

41. *Ciinvurutia.*
Butterflies.

42. *Mwongoro.*
Millipede.

43. *Muriu.*
Chameleon.

Plants

44. *Mirico ya ngwaci.*
Sweet potato vines.

45. *Ikunu.*
Mushroom.

46. *Ithangu ria muti.*
A leaf from a tree.

47. *Mucakwe wa mbembe.*
A young maize cob.

48. *Marao ma mukuu.*
The blossom of a fig tree.

49. *Mburu.*
Fruit of an oak tree.

50. *Inanasi.*
A pineapple.

51. *Mori ndigu.*
A young banana plant.

52. *Nyanyi cia thano.*
Green vegetables in dry season.

53. *Thaara.*
Nappier grass.

54. *Magoko ma nduma.*
Outer cover of an arrowroot.

55. *Kigwa.*
Sugarcane.

Natural phenomena

56. *Ngwa.*
Thunder.

57. *Itu na nthi.*
The sky and the earth.

58. *Runji.*
River.

59. *Mbura.*
Rain.

60. *Riua.*
The sun.

61. *Mweri.*
The moon.

62. *Njata.*
A star.

Modern technology

63. *Ing'otore.*
Ten cent coins.

64. *Namba cia ndege.*
Numbers on aeroplane.

65. *Muti wa kiviriti.*
A matchstick.

66. *Migui ya kiviriti kiviritiri.*
Matchsticks in a matchbox.

67. *Makathi.*
Scissors.

68. *Curia.*
Sufuria.

69. *Mucikiri.*
Bicycle.

70. *Mubikibiki.*
Motorcycle.

71. *Taa.*
A kerosene lamp.

72. *Gikombe.*
Cup.

Others

73. *Rùvirigo rwa nyomba.*
The wall of a hut.

74. *Ndogo.*
Smoke.

75. *Weta gwikia njara mborori ya muthuri?*
Can you dare put your hand into an old man's bag?

76. *Njura.*
Sheath.

77. *Kiondo.*
A basket.

78. *Itumbi.*
Egg.

79. *Meni cia nyomba.*
House ventilations.

80. *Ngunia.*
A sack.

81. *Mwatu.*
A beehive.

82. *Nthio na ithiga.*
The small grinding stone and the big grinding stone.

83. *Ithanwa na muti.*
The axe and a tree.

84. *Ngima.*
Ugali (maize meal).

85. *Njira.*
Path.

86. *Mwaki.*
Fire.

87. *Mathiga ma riko.*
The three cooking stones.

88. *Kivati.*
A broom.

89. *Njira.*
Road.

90. *Mbirira.*
Grave.

91. *Kiruru.*
Shadow.

92. *Nyungu.*
Pot.

93. *Njira cia aguimi.*
Hunter's routes.

94. *Mamira.*
Mucus.

95. *Mururu.*
Grain store.

96. *Gacira.*
Path.

97. *Ngimi.*
Mortar.

98. *Njugu imwe nyunguri.*
One pea in a pot.

99. *Nguo cii mwiri waku.*
The clothes on your body.

100. *Muu.*
Ashes.

101. *Coro.*
Horn.

102. *Mai ma nguku.*
A chicken's faeces.

PUZZLES

Traditional puzzles

1. *Mundu umwe ai na mburi yake, mirico ya ngwaci na gitang'a. Indo ino ithatu areda airingie runji kimwe gwa kimwe. Undu uria wa vinya niati atiga gitang'a na mburi niguo aringie mirico, mburi niikuriwa. Atiga mburi na mirico niguo aringie gitang'a, nako kaburi nigakwirira mirico. Indo icio nwangiya airingie; nieka atia?*

A man has his goat, some sweet potato vines and a leopard. Now, the man wants to help these three things cross the river one by one. His problem is that if he leaves the leopard with the goat, the goat will be eaten. If he leaves the goat with the sweet potato vines, the goat will eat the sweet potato vines. He must help these things cross the river safely. What can he do?

2. *Kuri andu ana mendaga kuringa muvuro. Riria maringire muvuro, andu airi tu nwao makinyire manji. Andu acio maringire atia?*

There were four people who wanted to cross a river. Now when they crossed the river, only two people stepped into the water. How did they cross the river?

3. *Rimwe tene kwai na njamba mutiri iguru. Rungu rwa muti mwena umwe kwai na iria inenene muno. Mwena ucio wingi kwai na mwaki munene muno. Riu kuu iguru ria muti gutiai na kiomba na njamba niyendaga kurekia. Njamba iyo i, ingiarekerie ku?*

Once, long ago, there was a cock on top of a tree. Under the tree on one side, there was a big lake. On the other side was a big fire. Now up that tree there was no nest and the cock wanted to lay an egg. Where would the cock have laid its egg?

4. *Kwai mundu muka wai na kaana kanini. Riu mundu muka ucio niwathiire kurima mugunda wa kuraca akuite kaana gake. Akinya niwamamirie kaana rungu rwa muti. Akamwamia vau akiambiria kurima. Wa indi arimanga, auka kwongia mwana, ethire nthinwa niyocire mwana, na yatwa muti nake. Riu mundu muka ucio angiekire atia niguo nthinwa imunengere mwana? Mugunda ucio wai na irio ta ngwaci, mbembe wana marenge.*

There was once a woman who had a small baby. One day, she took the baby with her to a garden far from home to cultivate. When she arrived, she put the baby to sleep under a tree and started cultivating. After sometime, she went to suckle her baby, but found that a baboon had taken up the tree with him. Now what would the woman have done to get her baby back from the monkey? (Note that at the garden there were crops such as sweet potatoes, maize and even pumpkins.)

5. *Mucii uria nyukwe aciarirwe kwari eritu athatu na onthe niagure. Umwe wa eritu acio ndugimwita nyanya munini kana nyanya mukuru. Ungimwita atia?*

At the home where your mother was born there were three girls and all of them are married. There is one woman among these whom you cannot call aunt. What would you call her?

6. *Wi gwaku mucii na niurenda kuringa muvuro ukavande mugunda waku muringo uria wingi. Nati mundu ndaretikirua aringe na mbeu cia mbembe. Ungika atia niguo uringe na mbeu ciaku?*

You are at your home and you wish to cross the river and plant in your garden on the other side of the river. However, people are not allowed to cross carrying maize seeds. What can you do to cross with your seeds.

7. *Mutiri kwai tuconi tuthathu. Mundu aikia ithiga akiuraga kamwe twatigarire twigana mutiri?*

There were three birds on a tree. If a person threw a stone and killed one, how many birds were left on the tree?

8. *Kwai kavici kendaga kugurana na kaurua ni ithe muviki wako kaugire kendaga kugura ucuwe. Kaurua ni ithe gitumi gia kwenda kugura ucuwe gacokirie atia?*

There was a boy who wanted to get married and when he was asked by his father who his bride was he said he wanted to marry his grandmother. When he was asked why he wanted to marry his grandmother, what was his reply?

Modern puzzles

9. *Kwai ngari ya mwaki ya thitima mwena umwe yerekere mwena uria wingi. Riu wethiite nikwagire na rukungi runene muno. Ndogo iyo yaumaga ngari iyo yagendaga mwena u?*

There was an electric train travelling from one end to the other. Now, as it was on its way, there was a very strong wind. To which side was the smoke from this train being blown?

10. *Kwai mundu umwe wendaga kuthii mocari muno. Mundu ucio angiekire atia niguo akinye mocari wana gwakua ndui?*

There was a man who desperately wanted to go to the mortuary. What could he have done so as to get to the mortuary whatever happened.

11. *Kwai ndegwa yaricagira muvakari wa Kenya na Uganda. Ng'ombe ino yakamagirwa Kenya kana Uganda.*

There was a bull which used to graze at the border of Kenya and Uganda. Where was this bull being milked, in Kenya or Uganda.

12. *Kuri itiki riringagwa na ndagika ikumi. Riu kwi mundu ucokithagia andu wa ndagika ithano ciathira. Ungika atia niguo uringe itiki riu nokinye mwera uria wingi? Mundu ucio aroragia andu wa ndagika ithano ciathira.*

There is a bridge which a person crosses in ten minutes. Now there is a man who tells people to go back after five minutes on the bridge What would you do to cross and get to the other side? That man only looks at people when five minutes are over.

13. *Kwai ngari igiri ciaringanire muvakari wa Kenya na Tanzania. Andu aria matigarire mathikirwe ku?*

There were two vehicles which collided on the Kenya-Tanzania border. Where were the survivors buried?

14. *Vari mundu urenda gukua ni kuruara na angivorua nwa manji ma macungwa. Riu kwi mundu ugutigaritie macungwa matano nake ni mwaganu na muthunu muno. Atigire akwira agicoka nienda ethire macungwa make monthe mai magima matai mateme ni mundu. Ungika atia uvonokie mundu ucio ugere gukua?*

There is a person who is about to die and he can only be cured from his sickness through drinking orange juice. Now, there is a person who left you keeping five oranges for him but he is very mean and cruel. Before he left he told you he wanted to find all his five oranges whole without having been sliced by anybody. What would you do to save the life of the dying man?

Solutions

Traditional setting

1. *Mundu uico niekoguo: oce mburi atige gitang'a na mirico. Icio itingiricana ciatigwa muringo uyu. Riu akinyia mburi muringo uuria, auke oce gitang'a. Nwati aringia gitang'a acoke na mburi ndagatige ikiricagwa. Auke atige mburi muringo uyu. Oce mirico amiringie amitige mwena uria na gitang'a. Riu wagioca kaburi wa agikaringia.*

The man should take the goat and cross with it leaving the leopard with the sweet potato vines. Those two cannot eat each other if they are left together on one side of the river. Next, he should come and take the leopard across, and bring the goat back so that he does not leave it with leopard. He should then leave it on this side as he takes the sweet potato vines to the other side leaving them with the leopard. He should then leave it on this side as he takes the sweet potato vines to the other side

leaving them with the leopard. Lastly, he should come and help the goat across.

2. *Andu acio maari mwongia wari ivu akuite kaana kamwe na kariakengi agakagwata njara. Andu aria makinyire manji ni mwongia na kaana kau anyitite njara. Aria matakinya manji ni kaana kau kai ivuri na kau gakuitwe.*

Those people were a pregnant woman carrying one child and holding another child's hand. The people who stepped on the water were the woman and the child whose hand she was holding. Those who did not step on the water were the child in the womb and the child who was carried.

3. *Njamba ndirekagia.*

A cock does not lay eggs.

4. *Mundu muka ucio angiocire irenge arimamie varia mwana amamii. Eka uguo nthinwa nayo yuke yoce irenge itige mwana.*

The woman would have taken a pumpkin and put it where the baby had been sleeping. After doing that the monkey would have come and taken the pumpkin leaving the baby there.

5. *Ungimwita nyanya niundu niwe nyukwe muguciari.*

You would call her mummy because she is the one who gave birth to you.

6. *Ningiva nguku mbembe njoke ninge nacio. Nakinya muringo uria nthinje nguku nginaruta mbeu ciakwa nginavanda.*

I would give chickens my maize seeds then cross carrying these chickens. On getting to the other side, I would then slaughter the chickens, get out my maize seeds and plant them.

7. *Gutiri; kamwe kauragwa tuu twingi twiri nitwagurukire.*

None; when one was killed the other two flew away.

8. *Ningura nyukwe tondu wanawe niwagurire nyanya.*

I am going to marry your mother because you married my mother.

Modern setting

9. *Ngari ya mwaki ya thitima ndirutaga ndogo.*

An electric train does not emit smoke.

10. *Mundu ucio angiekarire niirari gatagati akinywe ni ngari akue niguo avirwe mocari.*

That man should have sat in the middle of the road to be hit by a vehicle and so that he could die and be taken to the mortuary.

11. *Ndegwa ndikamagwa.*

A bull cannot be milked.

12. *Ningiambiriria gukira na kinvuvati thiite mwena ucio nirenda gukinya. Nerwa njoke wa ngiraruruka ngithii na mbere na kuu nirenda gukinya.*

I would start crossing backwards towards the side I want to get to. Then when I am told to go back I would turn and continue walking towards where I want to go.

13. *Andu metai akuu matithikagwa*

Survivors are never buried.

14. *Ungioca cindano iria igucagia manji ukigucia manji macungwari ukigania manji ma macungwa ma murwaru na ugitigaria macungwa ma mwene.*

You should take a syringe and use it to suck juice from the oranges. This way, you would have juice for the patient and still have oranges to return to the owner.